THE PROGRESSIVE EDUCATOR
AND THE DEPRESSION

Random House Studies in Education
Consulting Editor, PAUL NASH, *Boston University*

THE PROGRESSIVE EDUCATOR AND THE DEPRESSION

The Radical Years

C. A. BOWERS
University of Oregon

RANDOM HOUSE — New York

PERMISSIONS
ACKNOWLEDGMENTS

The publisher and author acknowledge with thanks the permission of the following publishers and organizations to quote passages from the works listed.

Appleton-Century-Crofts, Publisher, for passages from *The Educational Frontier*, edited by Wm. H. Kilpatrick, copyright 1933 by Appleton-Century-Crofts.

The Christian Century, for passages from Reinhold Niebuhr, "Our Romantic Radicals," copyright 1935 Christian Century Foundation. Reprinted by permission from the April 10, 1935 issue of *The Christian Century*.

Crown Publishers, Inc., for passages from *Whose Revolution?* edited by I. D. Talmadge, Howell-Soskins Publishers, 1941. Reprinted by permission of Crown Publishers, Inc.

The Educational Forum, for passages from C. A. Bowers, "The Messianic Tradition in American Education," *The Educational Forum*, vol. XXXI (January 1967). Reprinted by permission of Kappa Delta Pi, An Honor Society in Education, owners of the copyright.

Harper & Row, Publishers, Incorporated, for passages from Isaac B. Berkson, *The Ideal and the Community*, copyright © 1958 by I. B. Berkson.

Holt, Rinehart and Winston, Inc., for passages from Theodore Brameld, *Toward a Reconstructed Philosophy of Education*, copyright 1956 by Holt, Rinehart and Winston, Inc.

The John Day Company, Inc., Publisher, and the author, for the use of the title of Chapter I, "Dare the School Build a New Social

Order?" from George S. Counts, *Dare the School Build a New Social Order?* copyright 1932 by The John Day Company, Inc.

The Macmillan Company and the author, for passages from Norman Thomas, *The Choice Before Us,* copyright 1934 by The Macmillan Company.

McGraw-Hill, Inc., for passages from volume I of *Report of the President's Research Committee on Recent Social Trends in the United States,* copyright 1933 by McGraw-Hill, Inc.

National Education Association, for passages from the following: "Report of the Committee on Social-Economic Objectives," by Fred J. Kelly, *Proceedings of the Seventieth Annual Meeting of the National Education Association,* 1932; The Educational Duties of the Hour," by Samuel S. Greene, *Proceedings of the National Education Association,* 1864; *The Unique Function of Education in American Democracy,* by the Educational Policies Commission, 1937; *American Education and the War in Europe,* by the Educational Policies Commission, 1939; *Suggestions for Teaching American History in the Present Emergency,* by the Educational Policies Commission, 1941.

World Book Company and the author, for passages from Theodore Brameld, *Patterns of Educational Philosophy,* copyright 1950 by the World Book Company.

For

MARY

PREFACE

The decade of the nineteen-thirties was a turbulent period in the development of the American society. When the depression shattered the illusions of many Americans about the invincibility of the capitalistic system, values and beliefs that had been accepted in the past no longer seemed appropriate. Enforced idleness caused many people not only to examine the immediate causes of the depression but also to search out the underlying flaws in the nation's social values. Among the numerous individuals and groups whose criticizing, questioning, and social planning gave this period its intellectual vigor was a group of reform-minded educators. Unlike the popular image of the educator as a supine and socially weak if not indifferent figure, these educators—led by George Counts, John L. Childs, William H. Kilpatrick and Harold Rugg—were social radicals who had a deep commitment to social planning and public ownership of the means of production. This commitment made them part of the liberal movement that veered sharply to the Left during the early years of the depression. Unlike many liberals who avoided embracing the class struggle as a means for achieving their desired social goals, these educators actually yielded temporarily to its seductive appeal. They deviated in yet another important way from the liberal position; they claimed that educators had a legitimate right to direct the course of social change. Their efforts to galvanize teachers into becoming a new and incorruptible political force in American life, as well as the general relationship of their ideology to the reform thought of this period, is part of the story to be told in this book. Until now studies dealing with this remarkable period in United States history have not focused directly on the role of these radical educators; yet a complete picture of the depression years requires that their ideas and activities be taken into account.

The influence that these educators exerted on the course of the progressive education movement is the other major theme explored in this volume. For over twenty years, beginning in 1932 when the radical educators first responded to the social crisis with a series of highly polemical articles and books and ending in 1955 when the Progressive Education Association finally disappeared from the educational scene, these educators constituted one of the most important and vital factions within the movement. To them fell the task of theorizing about the methodology and goals of progressive education, and in the process they gained recognition in many quarters as the chief spokesmen for the movement. During this period they labored to give progressive education a definite social and political orientation. Only by combining political ideology with education, they claimed, would it be possible for the movement to become truly progressive and to be in harmony with both the needs of the student and the needs of society. That in the end they could claim only a partial victory is incidental to the twenty-year struggle to reconcile the conflict between political indoctrination and Dewey's experimentalism, which was one of the chief problems that prevented the unity the educators sought. Furthermore, not only were the advocates of social reconstructionism forced to battle the remnants of the once strong child-centered group for leadership of the progressive education movement, but they also found it necessary to overcome internal dissension within their own ranks and to arouse support for their educational ideas among classroom teachers who were largely indifferent to the ideological dispute then raging between the two wings of the movement.

This study does not directly examine the extent to which the principles of progressive education that filtered down from teacher-training institutions actually effected changes in the nation's elementary and secondary classrooms. A study of this particular issue would be highly desirable, for it would help settle the problem of how much influence the theoreticians actually had on the practitioners in the classroom. Most of the sources that deal with progressive education are books and articles written by professors of education. Unfortunately, they provide little help in determining how widely their contents were accepted among classroom teachers. Because this study primarily focuses on the development of educational and social ideas among the leaders of the progressive education movement, it will be left to some well-endowed research team to conduct the kind of survey necessary for settling this issue.

Another warning is also in order here. In dealing with the growth of social reconstructionism, which I have treated as an incipient movement within the larger progressive education movement, I have not limited my observations to the activities of either the Progressive Education Association or the National Education Association. Although both furthered the cause of progressive education, the contribution of the NEA has been obscured both by the popular tendency to identify progressive education too closely with the organization that bore the name of the movement and by the analyses of educational historians who have largely ignored the role played by the NEA. As long as this oversight continues it will be impossible to understand the real nature of the progressive education movement. Both organizations figure prominently in this study, but it must be kept in mind that I have not attempted to provide a complete history or analysis of either organization.

I wish to thank Paul Nash for suggesting that I send the manuscript to Random House. Thanks are also due Robert I. Weiss, editor, and Jeannine Ciliotta, manuscript editor, for recommending changes that improved the manuscript and for seeing it through the various stages of production.

C.A.B.

CONTENTS

THE PROGRESSIVE EDUCATOR
AND THE DEPRESSION

CHAPTER

1

Dare the School
Build a New
Social Order?

In 1932, George Counts, a professor of education at Teachers College (Columbia), challenged American educators to reach for political power and lead the nation to socialism. Many of the nation's leading educational theorists who accepted his challenge and spoke out about the purpose of education during the depression years possessed a sense of mission that had been a characteristic of American educators since the nineteenth century. Only their ideas about the social function of education had changed. In the nineteenth century, educators also saw themselves standing "in the foreground of all genuine improvement." As one delegate to the National Education Association Convention in 1865 boldly proclaimed: "American educators hold in their hands the destinies of this nation." [1] To them "improvement" meant uplifting the individual morally and spiritually through the inculcation of the proper patriotic and religious values. Progressive educators in the nineteen-thirties had the same Promethean attitude; yet they were divided by conflicting views on the best way to rescue the nation from the ravages of the depression.

One faction argued that the social and moral condition of man could not be improved until his social environment had been radically overhauled. Motivated by the same feeling of mission that characterized their socially conservative predecessors, members of this group believed that it was to directly reform economic and social institutions. By promoting such involvement, they were raising the fundamental theoretical problem of the progressive education movement. This group believed that the educator should identify the prevailing social ills and then deliberately use the schools to correct them, and their opponents felt that the educator should leave the task of social reform to others and concentrate on giving the student the necessary noetic skills for functioning later as an intelligent and socially effective adult. The opposing faction, although they were equally interested in creating a better society, thought social improvement could be achieved through indirect means only. Their first concern was to release the creative energies of the child. If the child were freed from the domination of an unsympathetic adult world and if his creative powers were nourished, they thought, he would be better equipped as an adult to identify for himself those areas in society that required reform. Although the two factions of the progressive education movement held opposing points of view on the school's responsibility for social reform, they both claimed to be the true custodians of the principles of progressive education that John Dewey had promulgated in *Democracy and Education*. The depression brought these underlying doctrinal differences to the surface and intensified the ensuing conflict that left the progressive education movement deeply divided from the early nineteen-thirties until 1947. In that year, those who advocated that the educator should make social reform a direct responsibility of the schools finally won control of the moribund movement.

The Setting: Progressive Education
Before the Depression

In 1931, as the depression deepened, the educators who had made a cult of the child were in firm control of the progressive education movement. They were for the most part men and women of action, not careful thinkers concerned with the exposition of educational and philosophic issues or with the exploration of the limitations and dangers of the ideas they were applying in their classrooms with such great energy. Harold Rugg has referred to them as "zealous reformers, hard working and sincere evangelists of a better childhood." One has only to examine their pronouncements in *Progressive Education,* the official journal of the movement, to see a modicum of truth in this characterization.

Their educational principles—many of which had been first expressed in Rousseau's *Emile* and later were given a form of scientific respectability by G. Stanley Hall and systematized into a philosophy by John Dewey—had become over a twenty-year period a creed for the faithful. The principles themselves were straightforward and, on the surface, easily understood, if one did not attempt a careful examination of their philosophic foundations. When he introduced Dewey as the keynote speaker at the 1928 convention of the Progressive Education Association, Stanwood Cobb, the president of the association, recalled how Dewey himself had expressed the movement's cardinal principle: "The child is the starting point, the center and the end." [2] The other principles were corollaries to the fundamental axiom that the child is the center of all educational activity. A number of these principles were formalized and appeared regularly on the cover of *Progressive Education* from 1924 until 1930: I. Freedom to Develop Naturally; II. Interest the Motive of All Work; III. The Teacher a Guide,

Not a Task-Master; IV. Scientific Study of Child Development; V. Greater Attention to All That Affects the Child's Physical Development; VI. Co-operation Between School and Home to Meet the Needs of Child-Life; VII. The Progressive School a Leader in Educational Movements.

There was nothing incomprehensible in these principles; the educator's task was to provide a natural environment and an abundance of resource materials that would be conducive to the free expression of the child's felt needs and interests. Because he had no need to worry about teaching the student to master fixed bodies of subject matter, the educator could enter into the child's learning experiences as a friendly and nonauthoritarian guide. Both could share the joyousness of learning—another principle of the child-centered progressivist. Watching the child's natural curiosity serve as a guide to the learning process was, according to all accounts presented in *Progressive Education,* an exhilarating experience for the educator. An added reward was the knowledge that the newly formulated principles of education represented a "great undertaking"; they heralded, as one progressivist put it, the dawn of a "new age" for mankind.

The general application of these principles in the classroom had been largely worked out by 1931. The next step, according to the spokesmen of the movement, was the promotion of greater proficiency in the use of the new methods of teaching and wider acceptance among teachers—especially in the secondary schools—of the basic principles of progressive education. Although experimentation was the byword of the movement, an unusual uniformity of objectives and methods developed in the child-centered classrooms. This uniformity was no doubt a result of the generally accepted idea that the initiative of the child should supplant teacher domination in the classroom.

With zeal and dedication, the progressive educators brought about fundamental changes in their classroom methods. Textbooks had for some time been considered a symbol of arbitrary teaching methods and a barrier to the development of the student's ability to learn new truths from his own experience. As a result, learning from first-hand experiences quickly replaced the use of textbooks in child-centered classrooms. Important innovations like those in reading instruction were revolutionizing many traditional school subjects, and these innovations ultimately had a lasting impact on American education. At the 1928 convention of the PEA, the conference group, chaired by Miss Caroline Pratt, the founder of the Greenwich Village Play School and a long-time leader in progressive education, reported back to the assembled delegates that the "question of the advisability of teaching young children to read was fully discussed and the generally prevailing point of view was for deferring it in favor of worth-while first-hand experiences." [3] The remarks of another progressivist also undoubtedly failed to reassure those who may have harbored doubts about the wisdom of subordinating such a fundamental skill to the whimsical interests of the child. He told the convention that a four-year grammar course had been mastered in six months by a group of thirteen-year-olds "because of the pupils' recognition of their need." The progressivist did not speculate, however, on what would have happened if the students had not recognized their own need.

The traditional curriculum of separate subjects had simply disappeared from the child-centered classroom. To replace conventional school subjects like history and geography, progressive educators built a curriculum on the new guiding principle of integration: the interests of the child. The curriculum was thus divided into "units of work" or "projects," and the nature of each project depended upon what the child wanted to learn and the nature of the problem that had aroused his interest. Learning about the "milk supply of a city" required the child to learn a few facts about the city's history, economics, and geography. The language arts necessary for writing up his findings would be introduced; art could be worked in by having students draw pictures of the milk being delivered; and if a suitable song could be found or written about the activities of milkmen, music could also be taught.

Although the progressive educators displayed an ingenious ability for devising new teaching methods, many of which have since become lasting and beneficial contributions to public education through their wide adoption, they were far less successful in clearly articulating their educational objectives. On the important issue of what the social responsibilities of the school should be, they were almost totally silent. Officials of the PEA were candid about the lack of a guiding philosophy; their statements even suggest they regarded their lack of specific objectives as a virtue. J. Milnor Dorey, executive secretary, stated that although the PEA was "interested in expounding an idea and making believers," it was not committed to "any whole system which embraces it." The PEA, he continued, "lives or dies by the common breath of all who share its spirit and glimpse its vision." [4] Like so many followers of the movement, Dorey failed to see the contradiction in calling upon educators to have a vision, but one empty of any content of the good life. A year later, in 1930, Burton P. Fowler expressed the prevailing attitude of many progressivists in his president's message, when he said:

> Although our association has never promulgated or approved anything like a program . . . we do endorse, by common consent, the obvious hypothesis that the child rather than what he studies should be the centre of all educational effort and that a scientific attitude toward new educational ideas is the best guarantee of progress.[5]

Prior to 1931, there were several minor efforts to describe the type of individual and society that the child-centered school would help create. A committee appointed at a PEA convention defined the modern man as one who possessed a scientific attitude, an ability to cope with change, and "sympathetic social-mindedness," which presumably meant the ability to cooperate with others. The writings of this period succeeded in inspiring the classroom teachers with a sense of idealism but provided them with only vague suggestions as to the nature of the goals that might be sought through education. In language that was both romantic and idealistic and clearly intended to inspire devotion to a cause, Harry A. Overstreet promised that progressive education would build "men and women emotionally equipped to take their part in life with a spirit of fine togetherness." He anticipated later developments in educational thinking when he said that educating for the new age would include "no conceits and pathetic inferiorities. Always there will be a life in and with the group, a commonness of enterprise, a togetherness of triumphs as well as of failures." Overstreet suggested that "finely humanized individuals" was a worthy goal and asked the child-centered progressivists who wished to measure their effectiveness to consider the following question: "Have they (as a result of being in your classroom) that which will go singing through their lives, making impossible the intrusion of pettiness, cowardice and meanness?" [6] For all the fine sentiment, these efforts failed to spell out in concrete terms a guiding social philosophy.

Overstreet's style of rhetoric was not an isolated example. The leading interpreters of the child-centered movement had succeeded by 1931 in giving the classroom teacher a new idiom, which it was absolutely necessary for her to master if she were to understand and be understood by other progressive educators. They also succeeded in having this idiom identified in the public mind with progressive education. The new idiom was not suited to clarity of expression and did not help its user to examine the nuances of the philosophical ideas that underlay these educational programs. It did, however, to use its proponents' own parlance, contribute to a feeling of "togetherness" in a special undertaking, and it enabled them to communicate with each other about educational programs without ever specifying the nature of their educational goals. They coined such terms as "the whole child," "learning by doing," and "meeting individual needs" to discuss methodology. When they referred to the activities and purposes of the progressive education movement, the phrases "great undertaking," "great message," "its mission," and "its vision" were often used to inspire confidence in the correctness of the educational programs. The evangelical overtones of this rhetoric were unmistakable and clearly at odds with the progressivist commitment to experimentalism.

The membership of the PEA did not include all the supporters of the progressive movement in education, but by 1931 it had achieved recognition as the leader in the field. The movement itself had roots that extended back nearly to the midpoint of the previous century. Francis Wayland Parker, G. Stanley Hall, and a number of other pioneers had outlined, fifty years earlier, in the 1870s and 1880s, the educational principles that the PEA later popularized and built upon in its child-centered classrooms. The National Education Association, whose membership in 1931 dwarfed that of the PEA by 216,188 to 6,386, had also pioneered in the development of progressive educational principles since its beginning in 1857. In 1894, the NEA organized a Department of Child Study, and in the next twelve years a total of 135 speeches, papers, and reports were given at its yearly sessions. Because it was only one of eleven departments that covered the entire educational field from industrial education to art education, however, the Department of Child Study failed to dominate the NEA.

On the other hand, the energies of the PEA were devoted exclusively to reforming the elementary classrooms, and it was this singleness of purpose that catapulted the association into the leadership of the progressive movement in twelve short years. Furthermore, many educators were members of both organizations. Many of the PEA's influential members like William H. Kilpatrick, Harold Rugg, Jesse Newlon, and George D. Strayer were also prominent in NEA circles; in fact, the latter two were permanent members of the NEA's Board of Directors. The overlapping membership and the fact that only a few of the NEA departments had members who were committed to the new pedagogy meant that the influence of the progressive education movement was restricted to only a fraction of the nation's 1 million teachers. The influence of the movement was also limited in a more important respect. Its followers were drawn almost exclusively from the ranks of elementary school teachers, of whom approximately 30 percent were in the public schools and 70 percent in private schools.

The importance of the PEA cannot be measured accurately by its numerical strength alone, however. Many leaders of the PEA were also prominent figures in the field of teacher training. From Teachers College (Columbia) and Ohio State University, as well as from numerous other centers of teacher training, neophyte teachers entered their classrooms inspired by and, in some cases, indoctrinated with the cardinal principles of the progressive school. By teaching classes that often exceeded 650 students, Kilpatrick alone taught an estimated 35,000 students between 1909 and his retirement from Teachers College in 1938.

The Confrontation:
The Schools and the Depression

The narrowness of the child-centered approach was creating a growing disparity between the tenets of Dewey's philosophy of education and their application in the child-centered classrooms. The economic depression that, in the fall of 1931, was entering its third year made this incongruity even more apparent. At the 1928 convention of the PEA, Dewey had sharply criticized his followers for conducting their classrooms as though they regarded the "orderly organization of subject-matter [as] hostile to the needs of students . . ." [7] Dewey advised the teachers to give direction and continuity to the learning process, but the child-centered classrooms remained for the most part unchanged; the child continued to initiate and conduct his own learning experience. This practice was clearly at odds with Dewey's fundamental tenet that the experience of the community should be the subject matter of education. Although Dewey regarded the school as an "embryonic community," "active with types of occupations that reflect the life of the society," [8] the child-centered schools, by giving the child's interests free reign, were isolated from social developments. Furthermore, their isolation was increasing daily as the economic crisis deepened.

If the progressive schools had incorporated Dewey's total philosophy, students would have had an enormously wide selection of social problems to deal with in the classroom. For in the 1930s the nation was in the grip of an economic and social crisis. Following the collapse of the stock market in 1929, which brought immediate financial ruin to thousands and exposed the structural weaknesses of the economy, business activity and social services fell off radically. There were an estimated 4 million Americans unemployed in 1930; by the fall of 1931 the ranks of the unemployed had increased to 8 million. Those who were fortunate enough to retain jobs found their hours cut and their wages reduced. This sudden constriction of business activity resulted in a drop in the level of national income, from $87.4 billion in 1929 to $41.7 billion in 1932. Even those who had savings in the bank were not immune to the misery that engulfed millions of lives; a total of 3,643 banks failed between 1930 and 1931,[9] rendering penniless hundreds of thousands who thought they had some security against the economic storm. Diminishing revenues and rising unemployment figures made it increasingly difficult for communities to provide adequate relief facilities. Men without money and fast losing their self-respect found that the soup line was their only source of food. Sherwood Anderson saw 700 men being fed in a soup kitchen in a southern industrial town and observed how broken and distraught they appeared. "They are like hurt creatures standing there," he wrote in *The New Republic*.[10]

When teachers returned to their classrooms in the fall of 1931, the national mood had become one of despair and apathy. Few men knew where to turn for a solution. They could not look to the White House for leadership—in numerous statements President Hoover had stressed his belief that relief was a local responsibility and that "prosperity cannot be restored by raids upon the public treasury." The businessman could not be expected to provide guidance; he was equally committed to the philosophy of self-help and his unsound business practices had helped bring on the depression in the first place. Most people simply waited and hoped that prosperity would return before their plight became too desperate.

There were some Americans, however, who were searching for the causes of the depression and for a workable solution to the crisis. Writers went into the coal fields, participated in labor strikes, and observed the anomaly of starvation and want within sight of full grain elevators. It should not be surprising that they and many other intellectuals and social reformers should have begun questioning the very principles underlying the economic system. It was becoming increasingly difficult for the thoughtful observer to understand why full employment could not be maintained when there was no lack of natural resources or technological know-how. Like the journalist and social critic Lincoln Steffens, who thought the solution to the depression had already been worked out and advised American reformers that "all roads in our day lead to Moscow," intellectuals and social reformers began turning to socialism for their blueprints of a workable and just society.

When writers, intellectuals, and churchmen shifted to the Left, in the winter of 1932, they were joined by a group of educators who represented the emerging social reconstructionist faction of the progressive education movement. These educators were deeply committed to Dewey's idea that the school must deliberately improve society by eliminating undesirable social values from the classroom, and they possessed the sense of mission that comes from a feeling of guardianship for the present and future well-being of their students. During the next fifteen years they attempted to make explicit Dewey's admonition that classroom teachers must be social reformers and to shape them into an effective political pressure group. Because many of these educators were well-known professors of education at Teachers College, it was inevitable that their efforts to give progressive education a political as well as a social purpose should result in a direct challenge to the entrenched child-centered progressivists for leadership of the movement.

The Challenge: The Teachers and Social Reconstruction

The challenge came in February 1932 when George S. Counts, a professor of education at Teachers College, appeared before the annual PEA convention in Baltimore. He began his speech, "Dare Progressive Education Be Progressive?" by expressing his optimism about the future of the PEA and by outlining its achievements: focusing attention squarely on the child, recognizing the fundamental importance of the interest of the learner, and championing the rights of the child as a free personality. Turning critic, Counts went on to castigate the PEA for having too narrow a conception of education. "If an educational movement . . . calls itself progressive," he said, "it must have orientation, it must possess direction." Others, notably John Dewey and Boyd Bode, an influential interpreter of progressive education at Ohio State University, had made the same criticism earlier, but Counts went far beyond them in the range of his reproach. He charged that the main weakness of the PEA was its failure to articulate a theory of social welfare, "unless it be that of anarchy or extreme individualism." He attributed this weakness to the close connection between progressive schools and the middle class, which Counts regarded as a group of "romantic sentimentalists" incapable of dealing with the economic and social crisis.

Counts challenged the PEA to become truly progressive—to emancipate itself from the influence of the middle class, to "face squarely and courageously every social issue . . . establish an organic relation with the community, develop a realistic and comprehensive theory of welfare, fashion a compelling and challenging vision of human destiny, and become somewhat less frightened than it is today of the bogeys of *imposition* and *indoctrination*. [11]

The vision of human destiny that he outlined was a society in which poverty and want would be banished forever through the use of science. He stressed, however, that this goal could not be achieved until the economic system was radically overhauled. "In its present form capitalism is not only cruel and inhuman; it is also wasteful and inefficient . . . it has made technology serve the interests of the profit motive." Competition and "rugged individualism" had been outmoded by science and technology, he told his audience. The new society, built on the foundation of a socialized economic system, would release people from pecuniary worries and thus allow them to grapple with higher intellectual, moral, and esthetic problems. To achieve this goal he suggested that it would be necessary to indoctrinate students about the evils of capitalism and the social values upon which it depended. Indoctrination, he maintained, will take place regardless of what the teacher does; why not, therefore, use it as a means to "check and challenge the power of less enlightened or more selfish purposes." [12]

The delegates greeted Counts' address with silence. It was a silence, recalls Frederick Redefer, then executive secretary of the association, "that speaks far more eloquently than applause." [13] The address had stirred them deeply. Most had arrived at Baltimore with a feeling of impotence against the depressed conditions that threatened the children's health, school budgets and even their own jobs. When they were told that they, the classroom teachers whose hard work was often not sufficiently appreciated, had the power to bring into existence the "American dream," they must have felt exhilarated and transformed. Dare the schools build a new social order? Dare the teachers take the lead? The challenge stirred the minds and aroused the emotions of the delegates.

Following Counts' speech, small groups gathered in lobbies and private rooms to discuss far into the night the issues raised in his address. The discussions were marked by a general willingness to accept the idea that the schools had a responsibility for effecting social change, although there was less agreement on just how the schools should go about reconstructing society. Many were also doubtful about the use of indoctrination. Prepared speeches were put aside the next day as the delegates continued their discussion of Counts' challenge. At open forums led by Harry Overstreet, a professor of philosophy at The City College of New York, and Eduard C. Lindeman, a professor of social philosophy at the New York School for Social Work, they heard the leaders of progressive education express their thoughts about the teacher's new responsibility. The discussions culminated in a resolution presented at the annual business meeting (Saturday, February 20, 1932) by Nellie Seeds, director of the Manumit School in Pawling, New York, "That we authorize and instruct the Chairman of the Board of Directors to provide for an Economics and Sociology Section or Committee within the organization, which shall promote within the schools and their affiliated bodies, thoughtful and systematic study of the economic and industrial problems confronting the world today." The delegates adopted the resolution and for a time it appeared that the PEA was preparing to give up its position of noncommitment to a particular social philosophy. The editor of *Progressive Education,* commenting on the results of the convention, noted that the "Progressive Education Association has accepted the responsibility for some share in social reconstruction." [14]

In compliance with the resolution passed by the convention, the Board of Directors and members of the executive and advisory boards, as well as special participants George Counts,

William H. Kilpatrick, and Boyd Bode (Dewey was invited but was unable to attend), met at Vassar College for a three-day session, from April 29 to May 1, 1932, to plan the association's next move. Kilpatrick set the tone at the outset by asking, "How shall we see the social function of education and the direction of social progress?" The discussion that followed revealed there was general agreement that the new type of school would have to be more than child-centered; it would also have to develop in the students "an adequate social outlook." It quickly became evident, however, that the educators could not agree on how the school could most effectively develop social attitudes. One group, fearing that it would be impossible for the educator to avoid influencing the students' social attitudes, claimed nevertheless that social reform should not be the direct business of the schools. They proposed that any attempt to reform society should be done indirectly by setting the school up "along rigidly non-competitive lines." This view was challenged by the social reconstructionist members of the committee who claimed that "we have gone too much on the assumption that if we make people good we can solve the problems of society." They advocated that teachers take an active part in community affairs so that "we can build a collective resistance against these tremendous pressures from the outside." Jesse Newlon, director of the Lincoln School at Teachers College, spoke for this group by saying: "as teachers, it is necessary that we adopt a clear system of values by which we can determine what to stand for and what to work for." The extent of their radicalism became more evident when they contended that "one of the functions of an organization like this is to effect change by the strength of collective action. . . . Propaganda can be highly educational if it brings about a clash. We should make some of this clash." [15]

The official hierarchy of the PEA was thus seriously divided: One faction argued that indoctrination should be used and that teachers should collectively take sides on social issues, whereas the other faction rejected direct teacher involvement in partisan politics. The latter held that the "American dream" could best be realized by changing the "hearts" of the students and making them more critically minded. But just how the "hearts" of the students were to be changed they could not say. In spite of internal division the board appointed a committee that included Merle E. Curti, a professor of history at Smith College, Sidney Hook, an associate professor of philosophy at New York University, Jesse Newlon, Rexford Tugwell, a professor of economics at Columbia University, and Goodwin Watson, an assistant professor of education at Teachers College. George Counts agreed to chair the committee after Dewey declined the offer. The committee was instructed to outline ways in which "thoughtful and systematic study of the economic and industrial problems confronting us today" could be promoted in the schools. It was clear the radical social reconstructionist faction had won a victory, for their group—led by Counts, Newlon, and Watson—clearly dominated the committee. The nonprofessional educators on the committee—Curti, Hook, and Tugwell—were sympathetic to their point of view.

In February 1932, Counts had journeyed to Washington, D.C., where he addressed a division of the NEA's Department of Superintendence and later appeared before the National Council of Education. His addresses received such enthusiastic responses that the John Day Company offered to print in pamphlet form a combined version of all three papers in order to satisfy, as they said in the foreword, "the many requests for the papers which have come in from the most diverse quarters." The pamphlet version appeared in April 1932 and is one of the most remarkable educational documents of the depression period. In addition to Counts' plea that the PEA align itself with socially progressive forces, it contained a lengthy ten-point defense of the use of indoctrination and it had a militant tone that was not evident in his earlier address to the PEA. In brief, Counts thought that it was impossible for the schools to remain impartial. If this premise were accepted, the issue became quite simple. Either the teacher could allow the student to absorb the socially conservative values of the community (these would undoubtedly be, according to Counts, the values of business and socially conservative groups) or the teacher could consciously indoctrinate the students with progressive social values and ideas. Counts felt that the latter choice was the only course of action open to teachers that could be morally defended.

To choose this alternative meant, of course, that the teacher would have to adopt a new role that would combine educational with political statesmanship. "I am not over sanguine," he wrote, "but a society lacking leadership as ours does, might even accept the guidance of teachers." Accepting society's lack of leaders as self-evident, he exhorted teachers to "deliberately reach for power and then make the most of their conquest." The last ten pages of his manifesto contained a Marxian analysis of the causes of the depression. "If democracy is to survive, it must seek a new economic foundation . . . natural resources and all important forms of capital will have to be collectively owned." "Powerful classes," he warned, "must be persuaded to surrender their privileges." Counts had little faith, however, in the remedial abilities of the courts or the churches: "When property is threatened, constitutional guarantees are but scraps of paper and even the courts and the churches, with occasional exceptions, rush to the support of the privilege and vested interest." Instead, he turned to the teachers as the only group who could avert disaster and restore social justice; "if a bold and realistic program of education is not forthcoming," he warned, "we can only anticipate a struggle of increasing bitterness terminating in revolution and disaster." By seeking power and then using it "in the interests of the great masses of people," teachers would be grasping "the opportunity which the fates have placed in their hands." [16] Never before had teachers been given greater responsibility and never before had they been made to feel so important.

Counts was not alone in sounding the tocsin. With astonishing rapidity other prominent educators declared their support for the idea of a political role for teachers. William H. Kilpatrick's *Education and the Social Crisis* was published in September 1932, and Jesse Newlon and Harold Rugg authored articles appearing in *Progressive Education* (the October and November issues, respectively). It is not surprising, considering the gravity of the depression, that educators finally began to emphasize Dewey's idea that the school had a primary role to play in social rejuvenation. On the other hand, one cannot help being surprised that they were not more critical in their acceptance, especially of Counts' radical extension of Dewey's original idea. Dewey had also emphasized the use of intelligence in achieving consistency, in tracing relationships, and in anticipating the consequences of ideas. Yet this emphasis was largely ignored by Dewey's followers until Dewey himself was forced to rebuke them for their extremism in 1936 and again in 1938, and even then a few continued to ignore his warnings. In the prevailing atmosphere of impending social disaster, they accepted without criticism the idea that teachers possessed the training, inclination, and right to use the classroom for partisan purposes. Dewey himself had made social reform an obligation of the teacher, and his followers dutifully set out to reorient classroom teachers to accept the new role "fate" had thrust upon them. Even more surprising, increasing numbers of intellectuals and social radicals began to look upon the teacher in the same light.

Hendrik Van Loon, historian and prominent geographer, told a dinner meeting of the PEA's regional conference in New York: "The only possible method of education—I repeat —is by means of exposing the pupil to those ideas which he *should* eventually absorb. If he is not predisposed to catch our own germs of enthusiasm and devotion, he is immune to the better life and if he hasn't got the brains to follow us, what God has put asunder, let no teacher try to put together." Bruce Bliven, who was then editor of *The New Republic,* was a speaker at the same meeting. He embraced the idea that teachers should direct social change with equal enthusiasm. "The problem which you confront as teachers," he told the gathering, "is the terribly difficult one of leading the army and yet not getting so far in front that they can shoot you; of staying within touch of the common mass of humanity, which moves with such pitiful slowness, and at the same time seeing to it that you do stay in front and that you do go in the right direction." [17] Bliven believed that the problem was not one of principle, but one of using the correct tactics.

Kilpatrick's *Education and the Social Crisis* was not particularly important for its content; it was largely a reiteration of Counts' challenge to the teacher, though in a more moderate tone. The book's significance lay in the fact that in writing it Kilpatrick had lent his tremendous prestige, which in progressive education was second only to Dewey himself, to the social reconstructionist faction that was emerging to challenge the child-centered educators for leadership of the progressive education movement. His prestigious support undoubtedly made it easier for other educators to embrace the new educational nostrum. Like Counts, Kilpatrick believed that the economic system, based as it was on the profit motive, was largely anachronistic and that it should be replaced by a system that emphasized social planning and control. To Kilpatrick, "rugged individualism" was also an anathema; he proposed that the classrooms foster cooperative attitudes instead. Counts had stated unequivocally that teachers should "reach for power and then make the most of their conquest," but Kilpatrick emphasized that teachers should not expect to reform society by themselves. They would have to cooperate with other social reform groups, but nevertheless stay in the forefront of social change.

Kilpatrick also took a more moderate position than Counts on the problem of indoctrination, and this apparently was the only issue that became a major source of dispute among the social reconstructionists themselves. "The schools," he wrote, "must educate for intelligently directed social change rather than assume to inculcate the details of a specific program." [18] Kilpatrick's unwillingness to have the schools embark on any program of deliberate indoctrination was somewhat inconsistent with his explanation of what he believed to be the proper function of the schools. He wanted the schools to imbue students with the idea that social change is normal and to be expected. He also expected the classroom to teach students to "wish for the common good," to want to reform institutions so that they conformed more closely to the interests of all segments of society, and to think in terms of social programs that would benefit all. In short, Kilpatrick was actually advocating indoctrination. He only differed from Counts in the degree that he wanted the schools to indoctrinate students with the values of cooperation and collective responsibility instead of with the older values of individualism that he associated with laissez-faire economics and selfishness in general.

Support for social reconstruction was also forthcoming from the Board of Directors of the National Education Association, though there is no evidence that the rank-and-file members ever expressed themselves on the issue. Almost a year before the PEA's Committee on Social and Economic Problems was established, the NEA's Board of Directors passed a resolution at its Los Angeles meeting (June 27 to July 3, 1931) authorizing the appointment of a Committee on Social-Economic Goals for America. The committee was supposed to provide the association with a list of desirable social and economic goals and indicate the materials and methods that the schools should use to achieve them. The Board of Directors placed $10,000 at the disposal of the committee and named as its chairman Fred J. Kelly, then chief of the Division of Colleges and Professional Schools of the U.S. Office of Education. The other members included Willard E. Givens, superintendent of public schools in Oakland, California; George D. Strayer, a member of the faculty of Teachers College; and Katherine

McHale, executive secretary of the American Association of University Women.

At the 1932 annual meeting of the NEA, which was held in Atlantic City, New Jersey, Kelly presented the first report of the committee. He began his report with a reference to the importance of Counts' pamphlet, *Dare the School Build a New Social Order?* and then went on to raise the question: "What agency shall take the lead in creating a new social order?" The NEA, he indicated, was the obvious choice; it should "assume the leadership and point the way to a new social order." "The NEA," he continued, "is saying, and I hope saying more or less militantly, that a social order can be built in which a social collapse such as the present one will be impossible. They are saying further that the educators of America propose to assume major responsibility for building such a social order." [19] Kelly recommended that the association continue the life of the committee another year so that it could take advantage of reports being prepared by a committee of the American Historical Association and the President's Committee on Social Trends before making its final report.

Kelly's interim report was received by NEA President Florence Hale and a delegate from the floor moved that it be adopted. Interestingly enough, without further comment or discussion the report that recommended a revolutionary new role for teachers was passed on to the Board of Directors for approval. The delegates at the convention then heard William Trufant Foster—an economic heretic of the twenties and now an advocate of federal deficit financing and compulsory unemployment compensation and health insurance—read a paper entitled "Managed Money and Unmanaged Men." The Board of Directors, for its part, immediately approved the report and then named John Dewey as the honorary life president of the NEA and as an associate chairman of the Committee on Social-Economic Objectives. The leaders of the NEA, who appeared to be more concerned with the technicalities of conferring an honorary title on John Dewey than with analyzing the association's commitment to social reconstructionism, thus joined the growing number of voices clamoring for the teachers to save society from ruin.

One might have expected that the NEA's Department of Rural Education would have been forced to make some connection between education and social reform by the unrest on the farms, for rural net income in 1932 was less than one-fifth of its 1929 level. Instead it was the superintendents, a group that was usually regarded as warmly sympathetic to the interests of business, who first flirted with the idea of social reconstruction. To clarify what superintendents could do to alleviate social unrest, the executive committee of the Department of Superintendence voted in April 1932 to authorize a yearbook that would deal with social and economic issues. In November 1932, the president of NEA, Milton C. Potter, appointed John W. Studebaker, United States Commissioner of Education, to serve as chairman of the Commission on Education for New Social and Economic Relationships. The commission also included, among others, Fred J. Kelly; John Childs and Jesse Newlon, both from Teachers College; Frederick Deibler, an economics professor from Northwestern University; and J. B. Edmonson, dean of the University of Michigan School of Education. The commission's recommendations were published in the form of a yearbook, *Education and Social Change,* in 1935, but its 1932 membership represents further evidence that social radicalism in educational circles was not confined to a small group of professors of education at Teachers College. In 1932, it appeared that the leaders in education had indeed forgotten about the child, the idol of predepression days, and all that the child-centered classroom entailed, in their rush to associate themselves with the new movement.

In a study of the educator's response to the depression it is necessary to keep in mind the deepening social crisis of 1932 and the reactions of other social groups. Although it cannot be used to vindicate American educators for making such radical proposals, a short examination of the social and intellectual turmoil of the period can place their activities in clearer perspective. The same month that Counts challenged the PEA to become an instrument of social reform, Herbert Hoover and his supporters in Congress defeated a bill, sponsored jointly by Senators Robert M. La Follette, Jr., of Wisconsin and Edward P. Costigan of Colorado, that called for a $375 million federal grant to the states for relief purposes. With unemployment near the 10 million mark (nearly 20 percent of total work force) and the national income less than half its 1929 level, the Hoover administration could not bring itself to violate its principles by enlarging the role of the federal government or increasing the national debt. Even if the physical health of the people was being undermined, Hoover was determined that his administration would preserve their moral health by keeping the principle of individual responsibility intact.

Social unrest was becoming so great in some areas that Counts' prediction of "increasing bitterness terminating in revolution and disaster" seemed on the verge of coming true. Men who were hungry and desperate were beginning to protest in greater numbers outside government offices and factories. With increasing frequency their protests ended in violence. On March 7, 1932, approximately 3,000 unemployed demonstrators marched with police permission from Detroit to the Ford River Rouge plant in nearby Dearborn in order to present a petition. They were met by Dearborn police and firemen who used firehoses, tear-gas bombs, revolvers, and a machine gun to turn them back. As Russian technicians looked on from their vantage point in the Ford plant, the demonstrators broke ranks and fled, leaving behind four dead and many wounded. The *Detroit Times* later reported that close to 30,000 people gathered at Grand Circus Park to honor the dead, whose bodies lay in state under a huge red banner bearing a picture of Lenin.

Chicago was also experiencing widespread unrest. There,

500 school children, most with haggard faces and in tattered clothes, paraded through the downtown section to the offices of the Chicago Board of Education to demand that the school system provide them with food. The Associated Press reported that the police were maintaining an uneasy calm in Detroit where a clash between 1,000 demonstrators and 300 policemen resulted in injuries to 10 persons. Numerous clashes between demonstrators and police erupted across the land; San José, California, was practically under martial law as a result of disorders connected with a cannery strike (August 5, 1932); 1,500 unemployed stormed the Fruit Growers Express Company in Indiana Harbor, Indiana, to demand jobs (August 15); and Communists incited mobs to march on city halls in Cleveland and New York City.

"I went to New York," wrote Lincoln Steffens in his autobiography, "to hear the semi-scientific captains of industry say in words and facial expressions that they did not know what had happened or what was to be done about it." If the captains of industry did not know what had gone wrong or what was to be done to bring a return of prosperity, who did? For many who asked this question, Steffens provided the answer. "Nobody in the world proposes anything basic and real except the communists," he told them.[20] Many American intellectuals agreed with Steffens' analysis and rushed headlong to discover what communism was all about. Recalling his discovery of communism, Granville Hicks wrote: ". . . we had to ask ourselves whether communism might be [the answer to our problems]. So—a little furtively, a little frightened of what we were letting ourselves in for—we snooped around the edges of the Communist Party and talked with each other about Marx and Lenin and whether violent revolution was or was not justified . . . the party still seemed a little gruesome, and when Edmond Wilson suggested taking communism away from the communists, we approved." [21] While educators were meeting in committees and discussing how the schools could be used to save society, the intellectuals were placing their faith in the working class, the proletariat of America.

In September 1932, fifty-two writers and intellectuals signed a manifesto entitled *Culture and the Crisis,* which proclaimed their support for William Z. Foster and James W. Ford, the Communist candidates running in the Presidential election. The manifesto was sponsored by the League of Professional Groups for Foster and Ford that had been organized that year by the John Reed Clubs. Among those willing to renounce their affiliation with the middle class in order to work on the side of the proletariat were such well-known writers and intellectuals as Sherwood Anderson, Erskine Caldwell, Lewis Corey, Malcolm Cowley, John Dos Passos, Waldo Frank, Granville Hicks, Sidney Hook, Lincoln Steffens, and Edmund Wilson. In fact, several had already taken this step in the late 1920s. The manifesto declared that capitalism was bringing "cultural dissolution" to the United States and that Roosevelt's election would only prolong the crisis—thus oppressing the laboring classes even more. It ended with a ringing declaration: "Very well, we strike hands with our true comrades. We claim our own and reject the disorder, the lunacy spawned by grabbers, advertisers, traders, speculators, salesmen, the much-adulated, immensely stupid and irresponsible 'businessmen.' . . . As responsible intellectual workers we have aligned ourselves with the frankly revolutionary Communist Party, the party of the workers." [22] Some of the signatories were about to take out membership in the party whereas others, with varying degrees of loyalty as Daniel Aaron has shown in *Writers on the Left,* went along with the party line.

Were educators inadvertently preparing students to live by values and institutions that would no longer exist by the time they reached adulthood? For those educators who were pondering this question, leading literary figures left little doubt about the kind of society that they believed would emerge from the crisis. In the summer issue of the *The Modern Quarterly,* V. F. Calverton asked seventeen prominent American writers to give their answer to the question: "Do you believe that American capitalism is doomed to inevitable failure and collapse?" Although conservative as well as liberal writers were included, only two—Henry Hazlitt and Percy H. Boynton—thought capitalism would survive. The others—among them John Dos Passos, Sherwood Anderson, Floyd Dell, John Chamberlain, Malcolm Cowley, Granville Hicks and Clifton Fadiman—expressed no doubt about its ultimate, if not immediate, collapse. In writing about this period, Daniel Bell observed that the intellectuals' genuflection before the altar of revolution was so deep, their dedication to the "historical mission of the proletariat" so complete, "that in the course of the next decade a whole generation of intellectuals found themselves castrated—and gladly accepted their eunuch roles." [23] With so many well-known intellectuals jumping aboard the train destined for the Finland Station, the thinking of the educators must surely have been influenced by their frenzied activity.

John Dos Passos expressed the feeling of many intellectuals toward the Socialists when he said, "I should think that becoming a socialist right now would have just about the same effect on anybody as drinking a bottle of near-beer." [24] Nevertheless, in the early 1930s, Socialists like Norman Thomas were also advocating a radical rebuilding of the economic system. During the election campaign of 1932, they called for "public ownership and democratic control" of the basic means of production and for a complete change in the role of government. Health insurance, unemployment and accident insurance, old-age pensions, reforestation programs, and an immediate appropriation of $5 billion each for a state relief program and for public works were all high on their list of governmental responsibilities. Although in 1932 party membership stood at only 15,000, the Socialists could claim the support of influential men who were not members of the party, like John Dewey, Oswald Garrison Villard, editor of *The Nation,* Paul

H. Douglas, a professor of economics at The University of Chicago, and W. E. B. DuBois, one of the founders of the NAACP.

Even the churches joined the movement to the Left, which had already been swollen by the inclusion of writers, intellectuals and professors of education. The spirit of Christ, it seemed, could no longer be found in the capitalist system. Church journals that had found nothing morally wrong with the economic basis of society prior to 1929 began in 1932 to denounce the "moneychangers." The Episcopal *Churchman* now found the economic system "rotten to the core," and the *Baptist* editorialized: "We can be . . . sure that in any fair conflict between the rich and poor, Jesus could be found on the side of the poor." [25] The Federal Council of Churches adopted a new social creed of the churches that declared the council's commitment to "Social planning and control of the credit and monetary systems and economic processes for the common good." Church radicalism, however, reached its height at the 1932 convention of Northern Baptists. At this convention, the denomination's Social Services Commission offered a lengthy recommendation that essentially promoted the Marxian idea of "from each according to his ability, to each according to his needs." Although the commission's report was not unanimous, the Baptists adopted it.

There can be no doubt that the educators were influenced by the thinking of these radical groups. The Teachers College group—George S. Counts, William H. Kilpatrick, Harold Rugg, Jesse Newlon, and John L. Childs—often had personal contact with John Dewey, Sidney Hook, and other radicals who were vocal critics of capitalism. They also shared the Veblen-Beard-Dewey tradition of social criticism with many of those who signed their names to *Culture and the Crisis*. Furthermore, they read the liberal journals of the day, notably *The New Republic*. The close connection that the NEA had with the socially conscious religious fundamentalists, as well as the impact of the economic depression and social unrest on the individual members, undoubtedly contributed to social radicalism within the organization. Joseph Rosier, president of the NEA, and J. W. Crabtree, secretary of the NEA, were both Methodists. Many observers believed that these officers were responsible for the religious element, "almost to the point of revivalism" (an observation of W. Carson Ryan, Jr.), that was present at many NEA conventions. The similarities between the positive attitudes of the churches and the NEA toward big business during the twenties and their subsequent moves toward socialism in the thirties may thus be more than coincidental.

On March 4, 1933, Franklin D. Roosevelt was inaugurated President of the United States. However, neither his election nor the famous Hundred Days of feverish governmental experimentation with industrial, agricultural, commercial and monetary policy that followed it restored confidence or prosperity to the American people. Roosevelt's election represented more the people's repudiation of the Hoover administration than it did their endorsement of the New Deal "for the forgotten man at the bottom of the economic pyramid." Because Roosevelt had spoken in generalities during the campaign, few, if any, people understood clearly what his policies were going to be. Consequently, while the man on the street was reaching desperately in the dark, social radicals continued to debate the imminence of the economic collapse and the nature of a more humane social order.

Events in Washington made no apparent impact on the thinking of the social reconstructionist educators; if anything, their efforts to alert the classroom teacher to the inevitability of a collectivist society were intensified and became in the process even more doctrinaire. Support for their position, which was daily becoming more radical, came from two important sources: the American Historical Association and the President's Committee on Social Trends, which had been set up in 1929 by Herbert Hoover for the purpose of examining the changing trends in American life and reporting their findings to the President.

A summary of the findings of the President's Committee was published in two large volumes under the direction of Wesley C. Mitchell and Charles E. Merriam, chairman and vice-chairman of the committee, respectively. Both were highly reputable scholars. A follower of Veblen, Mitchell pioneered in the field of economics with his study of business cycles. Merriam's fame derived from his achievements in the field of political science. Mitchell and Merriam had guided the committee in a massive effort to plot the trends in all aspects of American life and by the use of graphs and statistical charts succeeded in providing an authoritative picture. It took twelve pages alone to acknowledge all the departments and individuals that provided assistance in the compilation. In the introduction to the report, *Recent Social Trends,* the committee stated some of its conclusions and made guarded recommendations that had an immediate influence on the thinking of the socially minded educators. The introduction was intended to provide a brief overview of the committee's findings, yet its authors returned again and again to a central theme: the need for economic and social planning. There was, the committee thought, some precedent for government control over the economy during the crisis of World War I. Is it beyond man's capacity, they asked their readers, "to take the enhancement of social welfare as seriously as our generation took the winning of a war?" [26]

The committee's analysis of the depression itself was in part Marxist. The report stated that the primary cause of the depression was the social imbalance that had been the result of uneven development. Advanced cultural values and institutions had not been developed fast enough to match the progress in scientific technology. The committee also recognized that vested interest groups would resist changes in social values and institutions and thus further restrict the full exploitation of technology, and it felt that social planning was the only way out of the impasse. Before social planning could be accepted as normal practice, however, society's value system first had to be reconstructed.

The clarification of human values and their reformation in order to give expression to them in terms of today's life and opportunities is a major task of social thinking. The progressive confusion created in men's minds by the bewildering sweep of events revealed in our recent social trends must find its counterpart in the progressive clarification of men's thinking and feeling, in the reorientation to the meaning of the new trends.[27]

Although there is no evidence to suggest that the President's Committee had the social reconstructionist educators in mind when the report was written, its publication nevertheless had the effect of being a direct invitation to action to them. For here was an impartial committee, representing the President of the United States, attempting a clarification and "reorientation" of social values. Who was to clarify these values? How could vested interest groups be expected to reorient their own thinking? The committee had called for "new and emergent values" and the "construction of new symbols to thrill men's souls." Educators, who believed that they were already in the most favorable position because they helped directly formulate the values of the young, were ready to rise to the challenge.

The American Historical Association also helped reinforce the position of the social reconstructionist faction within the progressive education movement. Out of a concern for the quality of history teaching in secondary schools, the association appointed a committee as early as 1926 to investigate and to make recommendations for improvement. This committee became the Commission on the Social Studies in the Schools in 1929 and was headed by A. C. Krey, professor of history at the University of Minnesota. The work of the commission was financed by a $500,000 grant from the Carnegie Corporation. A total of sixteen reports were published by the commission,

but two reports—one dealing with the philosophy and objectives of social studies and the other with the final recommendations of the commission—had special significance for
the advocates of social reform. In the former report, *A Charter
for the Social Sciences* (published by the commission in 1932),
Charles Beard rejected the idea that the schools could lead in
social reform. "The schools have no access to super-wisdom.
If they do," he wrote sarcastically, "then, educators might well
take over the government of the country." Somewhat inconsistently, Beard then suggested that teachers, because they
could not present all the facts or viewpoints, would have to
emphasize certain issues. He admitted that the teachers' mental
pictures of the ideal social order to be preserved or realized
would necessarily be the criteria they used in selecting the facts
to be presented.

Beard confused the issue even more when he stated in
Deweyan language that "any social science worthy of the
name must objectify itself in the development and improvement of individuals, institutions, human relations, and material
arrangements already in the course of unfoldment in the United
States." [28] Although Beard did not realize it, he actually agreed
with the social reconstructionists on several points and this
bias colored the whole report. Despite Beard's praise for
freedom of opinion and the liberation of intelligence, he had, in
the eyes of many readers, committed the commission to a policy
that condoned the use of indoctrination in the classroom.

The final report of the commission contained a clearer statement of its position than Beard's report had. The commission—
minus Frank W. Ballou, Edmund E. Day, Ernest Horn and
Charles E. Merriam, who refused to sign the report when it was
published early in 1934—declared that "the age of individualism and *laissez faire* in economy and government is closing and
that a new age of collectivism is emerging." The report stated
that the commission viewed education as a means to "a form
of action on the part of some particular social group" and as
". . . one of the highest forms of statesmanship: a positive and

creative attack" on social problems. The commission recommended that the public schools be used to ease the birth of a socialized society by giving the American people the proper understanding and new values. "If education continues to emphasize the philosophy of individualism in economy, it will increase the accompanying social tensions." The commission concluded, however, that if educators were to organize "a program in terms of a philosophy which harmonized with the facts of a closely integrated society, [they] will ease the stress of the transition taking place in actuality." The commission believed that educators could not remain neutral; "The making of choices cannot be evaded, for inaction in education is a form of action." [29] This meant, according to the commission, that if the teacher failed to actively support social reform, he would aid or be used by the forces of social reaction.

There is no evidence that the American Historical Association ever tried to disassociate itself from the conclusions contained in the report of its commission. On the contrary, numerous references that appeared in the association's *Proceedings* lauded the work of the commission as the most important activity of the association. The association's secretary, Conyers Read, thanked the members of the commission in his 1936 annual report: "But that this report will exercise a widespread and stimulating influence on the important problem with which it deals is our confident expectation. . . . The thanks of the Association are due to Professor Krey and his colleagues, who have worked with such devotion and industry during the last five years." [30] The American Historical Association thus unwittingly contributed its prestigious support to one of the most bizarre social reform proposals to come out of the depression. Furthermore, its failure to challenge the use of indoctrination, a proposal that was implicit in the report, made it appear to many educators that the association was actually advocating this method; their own positive convictions about indoctrination were thus strengthened. If the association had made an unequivocal stand against indoctrination, the growing strength of the social reconstructionists might have been dealt a serious blow.

The PEA convened its annual conference in Chicago two days before Roosevelt was inaugurated President in 1933 and at the same time as many states across the country were declaring bank holidays in order to avert financial disaster. As the delegates gathered in unprecedented numbers during this time of extreme social crisis, it was apparent that the social reconstructionist faction had begun to exert a powerful influence on the association's policies. The convention's theme, "Educational Implications of the Changing Social Order," indicated a growing determination to hammer out a policy that would define the educator's responsibility for reforming society. At the first session there was a round table discussion of the report of President Hoover's Commission on Social Trends; Ernest Horn, professor of education at the University of Iowa, outlined its implications for educators. This was followed by a panel discussion of the social issues teachers would have to face in the future. On the following evening, George Counts, H. P. Chandler of the Union League Club, and Horace M. Kallen of the New School for Social Research (New York) exchanged views on the methods teachers should use to handle controversial issues in the classroom. The issue that concerned the delegates most, however, was whether or not the PEA would accept the forthcoming report of the Committee on Social and Economic Problems. This report was widely rumored to be radical, and if the PEA accepted it, it would be committing itself to the policy of social reconstruction and, more specifically, to the creation of a socialistic society.

Since its organization in late April 1932 the Committee on Social and Economic Problems had held several meetings in the Columbia University Faculty Club and adopted a plan to present a statement at the forthcoming PEA convention that would be a "statement of leadership" for the nation's educators. The composition of the committee, especially the inclusion of George Counts and Sidney Hook who had already renounced his bourgeois allegiance by joining fifty-two other intellectuals to support the Communist candidate for the Presidency, caused several board members to fear that the committee's report would irreparably damage the future of the PEA. The several progress reports made by a member of the committee only gave substance to their fears. In order to prevent any direct association of the PEA with social radicalism, conservative board members, led by Carleton Washburne, superintendent of schools in Winnetka, Illinois, tried to block the committee's report by disassociating the PEA's official position from the reports and recommendations of its committees.

As the assembled delegates eagerly waited to hear the much-publicized report, the Board of Directors, meeting in the nearby Palmer House, argued the relationship of committees to the parent organization. The Washburne faction finally triumphed, and the board passed a resolution that stated in part: "That neither the Board of Directors nor the Association is committed officially to or as a whole to any philosophy, program or policy embodied in the report of any national committee." George Counts then submitted to the board a tentative report of the Committee on Social and Economic Problems. Miss Elsie Clapp, associated with the Rogers Clark Ballard Memorial School in Louisville, Kentucky, and an advocate of the school as a community center, immediately denounced the report as too negative. Washburne then stated that the report would, as far as the general public was concerned, definitely commit the association to a social philosophy, that this social philosophy was socialistic, and that it might result in a loss of membership. He reminded the board that teachers and administrators were working under pressure from school boards concerned with cutting back educational services in order to economize. If the PEA had any association with socialism, he thought, the pressure would be increased. Another board member countered this charge by suggesting that the association should not fear that it would be considered socialistic. He assured them that "equally strong recommendations and reports have been made by the churches and were in circulation in the better magazines." [31] V. T. Thayer then moved that the report be made available to the members of the association. The report, which had been criticized because it might cause loss of membership and not because it advocated quite inconsistently both indoctrination and the experimentalist approach to problem-solving, was thus sent to the PEA delegates for consideration.

On the floor of the convention delegates charged the board with trying to bury the report. After a flurry of debate in which Washburne reiterated his position and President Burton P. Fowler said that he would rather see the report sent out in its present form than have anyone think it was being suppressed, the report was referred to the Publications Committee and this committee was given the power to authorize publication. As the conference came to a close, it was clear that the association had not overcome the internal division over a guiding philosophy. Several months later the report of the Committee on Social and Economic Problems appeared as a pamphlet entitled *A Call to the Teachers of the Nation.* The Introduction to this pamphlet contained a careful statement that disavowed any relationship between the findings of the committee and the association's official position. Social reform was still the nemesis of the PEA.

The child-centered faction within the PEA could only claim a pyrrhic victory over the social reconstructionists. Although they had prevented the association from officially endorsing a philosophy of social reconstruction, the success of the child-centered faction had been the result of stalling tactics that had eventually discouraged the social reconstructionists. The child-centered group had been unable to take a definite stand and challenge the soundness of their opponents' ideas. Although the PEA remained under the control of the proponents of child-centered education, it continued to vacillate throughout the rest of 1933. For instance, Willard W. Beatty, vice-president of the PEA, later came out in support of the position that the association rejected eight months earlier. "Increasingly must fall upon us responsibility for leadership in the actual remaking of education, so that it may contribute directly to the building of a new and better social order," he wrote.[32] The "better social order" he envisaged would substitute social planning and control for "rugged individualism." Because it could not demonstrate either the ability to lead teachers in the fight for social reform or the capacity to criticize social reconstructionist proposals effectively, the PEA began to drift helplessly in the latter part of 1933. Almost by default the social reconstructionist educators became the only group in the higher circles of public school education to offer concrete proposals for adapting the principles of progressive education to the conditions of times.

The social reconstructionists began to receive critical attention. Surprisingly, only a few of the critics were educators of national importance: Henry Holmes, dean of the School of Education of Harvard University; George A. Coe, a professor of education at Teachers College; Horace Kallen, a professor of philosophy and psychology at the New School of Social Research in New York. In a series of articles that appeared in *Progressive Education,* all three criticized the use of indoctrination. They thought, as Horace Kallen put it, that "the method of the schools should be the method of open, free discussion, aiming at consensus—the method of science applied to social issues." [33] Two noneducators, however, made the most effective and direct criticisms of the social reconstructionists. Journalist Agnes de Lima, in an article in *The New Republic,* observed that although Counts' call to reconstruct society was stirring, "to expect teachers to lead us out of our morass is fantastic indeed. . . . A class long trained to social docility and economically protected by life tenure of office—on good behavior—is unlikely to challenge unduly the status quo." [34] De Lima also noted that there was little evidence that teachers, even "scientists and scholars of the highest rank," could use power wisely even if they were capable of seizing it. This observation struck at one of the idealistic, but wholly un-examined, assumptions underlying social reconstructionist thinking.

James Truslow Adams, historian and author of *The Epic of America,* questioned several assumptions that the social reconstructionists had stated in their writings as truisms or accepted facts. The claim that the American people possessed sufficient control over nature and productive capacity to usher in an age of plenty for all was, in his opinion, as questionable as the idea that "the individual can be guaranteed freedom for cultural and spiritual growth only by abandonment of economic individualism." He also took exception to the idea that the "privileged" were always "malevolent"; and he was staggered by the social reconstructionists' assumption that society could be rebuilt with relative ease.[35] Adams believed that the real job of the teacher was to train the individual to have an open and well-informed mind and to teach him how to use intellectual skills, reference books, and accumulated knowledge. The development of the powers necessary for self-direction con-sequently precluded any consideration of the teacher's right or preparation to reorganize society through the schools.

No matter how judicious the criticism is, when it is directed at would-be social reformers during a time of crisis, those will-ing to listen are apparently few indeed. There was literally no response to the criticism of these educators, journalists, and scholars. One might have expected many educators and mem-bers of the academic community to carefully examine the proposals of the leaders of progressive education. The silence of the majority of the educators and scholars, however, left the social reconstructionists free to ignore the few who were critical of their efforts to redeem society.

Following the PEA convention in Chicago two documents appeared that made an impassioned plea for classroom teachers to take a stand against the inhumane economic system, and both attempted to arm the teacher with a philosophic justification for their newly assigned role. The first, and by far the most strident, was the pamphlet, *A Call to the Teachers of the Nation,* which had been disavowed earlier by the PEA. The other was a book, *The Educational Frontier,* which was edited by William Kilpatrick and represented a more careful interpretation and application of Dewey's educational ideas to the depression. Together they indicated that there was a broad base of support for the social reconstructionist position: The supporters ranged all the way from Sidney Hook, who came closest to actually embracing the Communist party's position, to John Dewey, whose reliance on free intellectual inquiry and the democratic process led him to support a Norman Thomas brand of socialism. Between these two ideological extremes were George S. Counts, Harold Rugg, Jesse Newlon, Goodwin Watson, John L. Childs, William H. Kilpatrick, R. Bruce Raup, and Boyd Bode—in approximately that order on a continuum moving from a radical to moderate position.

A Call to the Teachers of the Nation was written during the interregnum when the Hoover administration appeared unable to check the rapid deterioration of the financial system, but it was not published until after Roosevelt's New Deal had begun to experiment with the principle of governmental control and planning in the industrial and agricultural sectors of the economy. It is therefore surprising that, with the apparent willingness of the new administration to embark on national economic planning, Counts, Hook, and the rest of the committee did not modify the pamphlet's extreme language in the hope that in time the government would prove the effectiveness of planning. One can only conclude that the educators were fully convinced at this time that the capitalist system was not worth saving. Besides, Roosevelt, with his talk of balanced budgets, may have appeared to them to be more willing to tinker with the system in order to preserve it than to replace it with something radically new.

The pamphlet combined the apocalyptic fervor of a fundamentalist preacher, the Marxist theme of a class struggle and the evangelical promise of salvation. It proclaimed that in the face of the social crisis "teachers, the guardians of childhood, the bearers of culture, the avowed servants of the people, cannot remain silent. To do so would be to violate every trust reposed in them by society." The depression, the pamphlet continued, was symptomatic of a conflict caused by the fortunes of history and the struggle of classes. Using language that was often more shrill than any used in the 1934 Manifesto of the Communist Party of the U.S.A., the committee described the protagonists in the struggle: "At the one extreme is a small privileged minority, firmly entrenched behind the barriers of law and custom, holding title to the social means of production, and pursuing a life of luxury, extravagance, and even ostentation; at the other are the handicapped and unfortunate who after battling in vain against impossible odds sooner or later give up the struggle and enter the ranks of pauperism." In order for the benefits of production to be distributed with social justice, teachers would have to enter the conflict on the side of the workers, because teachers were "at the same time the loyal servants and the spiritual leaders of the masses of the people."

The pamphlet of the PEA's Committee on Social and Economic Problems then called upon the nation's 1 million public school teachers to recognize that "they owe nothing to the present economic system, except to improve it; they owe nothing to any privileged caste, except to strip it of its privileges." [36] The committee concluded that the progressive-minded teacher could only succeed in this mission by uniting "in a powerful organization, militantly devoted to the building of a better social order and to the fulfillment . . . of the democratic aspirations of the American people." Although this call to action failed to stir the classroom teacher to mount the barricade, the pamphlet's analysis of the causes of the depression, the attitudes of the workers and unemployed, and the social consciousness of teachers was one of the most extreme and utopian statements to be made by any group during the depression. It even eclipsed the radicalism of the Communist party, which labored under the Marxian idea that no help could be anticipated from the schools because of their subservience to the dominant class. At the same time, of course, the social gospel movement was also trying to prove that Marx was wrong about the churches.

Whereas *A Call to the Teachers of the Nation* was meant to incite teachers to act, *The Educational Frontier* was intended to provide a philosophic basis for combining politics with education. It also gave the social reconstructionist movement greater respectability, as its contributors—Boyd H. Bode, John Dewey, John L. Childs, William H. Kilpatrick, R. Bruce Raup, H. Gordon Hullfish and V. T. Thayer—were leading progressivists, but more politically moderate than the authors of the pamphlet. The book stressed that the school must not be regarded only as a place where students acquire knowledge but rather as an ideal community in which students practice cooperation, self-government, and the application of intelligence to social problems. This meant the school would have to intervene actively in the community at large to nullify outworn values by making the problems of the community the central focus of the curriculum. Educational programs would thus be developed with "definite reference to the needs and issues which mark and divide our domestic, economic, and political life. . . ." Although each author, in his respective chapter, emphasized the "method of intelligence"—which for the progressive educator is the scientific method—and questioned the use of indoctrination, none were able to state clearly how the teacher could provide leadership in remaking society according to his idealized conception of man and, at the same time, avoid indoctrination.

The problem is inherent in Dewey's statement in *The Educational Frontier*: "The philosophy of education must discover and ally itself with the social forces which promote educational aims, as well as uncover and oppose the vested interests which nullify and reduce them to mere flourishes or to phrases on paper." Isn't Dewey here saying essentially the same thing as Counts said in *A Call to the Teachers of the Nation,* though in less extreme language? The connection between Dewey's thinking and the idea that teachers should join in a class struggle is easily suggested by his further comment: "Admit that education is concerned with the development of individual potentialities and you are committed to the conclusion that education cannot be neutral and indifferent as to the kind of social organization which exists. . . . The conditions of their association with one another, of their participation and communication, of their cooperation and competition, are set by legal, political and economic arrangements . . . education must operate in view of a deliberately preferred social order." [37] In Dewey's view, therefore, those social values that are in conflict with the goals of the school were to be overturned by the teacher.

Although *The Educational Frontier* dealt at length with the application of progressive education principles under depression conditions, it left the classroom teacher with many unresolved problems. Vague statements that suggested that teachers organize themselves into a new political force were no substitute for concrete proposals, and repeated calls for a better social order were not adequate in themselves. The authors did not explain how a class struggle would lead to a more democratic society or how indoctrination could be used by teachers who called themselves experimentalists. Even though the contributors to *The Educational Frontier* gave the movement added prestige, they did little to resolve the glaring inconsistencies that prevented grass roots support among teachers from growing. Furthermore, they failed to outline in any greater detail the specific steps teachers would have to take if they should decide to join the social reconstructionist movement.

By late fall of 1933 it was obvious to many social reconstructionists that the PEA officialdom was too weak and divided for that organization to provide effective leadership in the coming struggle. Social reconstructionist writers were also beginning to find it more difficult to get their articles published in the association's journal, *Progressive Education*. Beginning with the printing of Counts' challenge to the 1932 conference, articles dealing with ideological issues appeared regularly. Titles like "Nurturing Sincerity in Dramatics" and "Making Stage Scenery," which were typical prior to 1932, gave way to more militant sounding titles like "Must Teachers Sink Without a Struggle?" and "Russia Can Teach Us." Now that the officials of the PEA feared the taint of political radicalism, the directors of the journal wanted to devote its pages entirely to informing teachers about classroom techniques and materials. When the social reconstructionists realized that the PEA was no longer receptive to their ideas and that the editors of *Progressive Education* were no longer willing to print their articles, they began to seek other means of gaining the support of the classroom teacher.

When Norman Woelfel and Mordecai Grossman, who were graduate students at Teachers College, suggested the establishment of a magazine dedicated to social criticism and educational reconstruction, Kilpatrick was understandably receptive to the idea. He in turn discusssed the possibilities of such a magazine with John L. Childs, Jesse Newlon, Harold Rugg, and other social reconstructionists. At a luncheon meeting held in New York late in 1933, the decision was made to go ahead with the project if Counts could be persuaded to serve as editor. Counts demurred for a time because of heavy obligations elsewhere, but when Grossman and Woelfel agreed to serve as associate editors and carry the main burden of promotion, writing and solicitation of articles, he consented. Names for a board of directors were then suggested and letters of invitation sent to them. Financial support for the journal was obtained without delay from the members of the newly established board; one board member pledged $100, whereas the rest contributed $25 or less. The journal was to be called *The Social Frontier*, indicating that the frontier had moved from the realm of geography to that of social affairs, and it was decided that the first issue would appear in October of the following year, 1934.

As the social reconstructionists prepared to take their ideas directly to the classroom teacher, they were optimistic that a further clarification of progressive principles—especially those that dealt with social change—would stimulate teachers to action. Teachers would seek greater control over administration, curriculum, and the formulation of the school's objectives and thus gather the power to alter the direction of social change. There was no doubt in the minds of the social reconstructionists, however, about the direction that society would take. It was axiomatic for them that the aims of progressive education—the free play of intelligence, cooperation, and equal opportunity for all to seek their own place in society—could only be realized in a socialistic society. For only socialism held out to them, as well as to other social dissidents, the promise of a society based on cooperation and a more equitable distribution of both wealth and responsibility.

NOTES

1. James P. Wickersham, "Education as an Element in Reconstruction," *Proceedings of the National Education Association,* vol. VII (1865), p. 549.
2. Stanwood Cobb, "The 1928 Conference," *Progressive Education,* V (July–August–September 1928), 196.
3. "Group Conference," *Progressive Education,* V (July–August–September 1928), 281.
4. J. Milnor Dorey, "The Present and Future of the Organization," *Progressive Education,* VI, 1 (January–February–March 1929), 73.

5. Burton P. Fowler, "President's Message," *Progressive Education,* VII (May 1930), 159.
6. Harry A. Overstreet, "Educating for the New Age," *Progressive Education,* VI, 1 (January–February–March 1929), 63, 62.
7. John Dewey, "Progressive Education and the Science of Education," *Progressive Education,* V (July–August–September 1928), 201.
8. John Dewey, *The School and Society* (Chicago: Phoenix Books, The University of Chicago Press, 1962), p. 29.
9. The President's Research Committee on Social Trends, *Recent Social Trends in the United States* (New York: McGraw-Hill, 1933), vol. I, p. 262. Hereafter cited as *Recent Social Trends.*
10. Sherwood Anderson, "Factory Town," *The New Republic,* LXII, 779 (March 29, 1930), 143–44.
11. George S. Counts, "Dare the School Build a New Social Order?" *Progressive Education,* IX, 4 (April 1932), 257, 258.
12. *Ibid.,* 259, 261, 263.
13. Frederick L. Redefer, "Resolutions, Reactions and Reminiscences," *Progressive Education,* XXVI, 6 (April 1949), 188.
14. "Notes on the Convention," *Progressive Education,* IX, 4 (April 1932), 288, 289, 290.
15. *Minutes of the Meeting of the Board of Directors and Advisory Board of the Progressive Education Association* (April 29–May 1, 1932), pp. 2, 3.
16. George S. Counts, *Dare the School Build a New Social Order?* (New York: John Day, 1932), pp. 28, 45–46, 52, 54.
17. Henrik Van Loon and Bruce Bliven, "Must Teachers Sink Without a Struggle?" *Progressive Education,* X, 1 (December 1932–January 1933), 6, 7. The italics are mine.
18. William H. Kilpatrick, *Education and the Social Crisis* (New York: Liveright, 1932), pp. 3–4, 8–9, 13, 60.
19. Fred J. Kelly, "Report of the Committee on Social-Economic Objectives," *Addresses and Proceedings* (1932), pp. 208–9.
20. Quoted by Granville Hicks, "Communism and the American Intellectual," in I. D. Talmadge (ed.), *Whose Revolution?* (New York: Howell-Soskins, 1941), pp. 81–82.
21. *Ibid.,* pp. 80–81.
22. League of Professional Groups for Foster and Ford, *Culture and the Crisis* (1932), p. 3.
23. Daniel Bell, "The Background and Development of Marxian Socialism in the United States," in Donald D. Egbert and Stow Persons (eds.), *Socialism and American Life* (Princeton, N.J.: Princeton University Press, 1952), vol. II, p. 350.

24. "Whither the American Writer?" *The Modern Quarterly* (Summer 1932), p. 11.
25. Paul A. Carter, *The Decline and Revival of the Social Gospel* (Ithaca, N.Y.: Cornell University Press, 1956), p. 145.
26. *Recent Social Trends, op. cit.,* vol. I, p. xxxii.
27. *Ibid.,* p. lxxv.
28. Charles A. Beard, *A Charter for the Social Sciences* (New York: Scribner, 1932), pp. 44, 56.
29. The American Historical Association's Commission on the Social Studies in the Schools, *Conclusions and Recommendations* (New York: Scribner, 1934), pp. 16, 30, 37. The report was signed by Charles A. Beard, Ada Comstock, George S. Counts, Avery O. Craven, Guy Stanton Ford, Carlton J. H. Hayes, Henry Johnson, A. C. Krey, Leon C. Marshall, Jesse H. Newlon, and Jesse F. Steiner. Isaiah Bowman signed only after his reservations were printed along with the report.
30. *Annual Report of the American Historical Association: Proceedings, 1933, 1934, 1935* (Washington, D.C.: U.S. Government Printing Office, 1936), pp. 19, 24–25, 92.
31. *Official Minutes of the Board of Directors of the Progressive Education Association* (March 4, 1933), pp. 2–3, 3–4.
32. Willard W. Beatty, "Editorial," *Progressive Education,* X, 6 (October 1933) 304.
33. Horace Kallen, "Controversial Social Issues: What Shall We Do About Them?" *Progressive Education,* X, 4 (April 1933), 188.
34. Agnes de Lima, "Education for What?" *The New Republic,* LXXI, 922 (August 3, 1932), 317.
35. James Truslow Adams, "Can Teachers Bring About the New Society?" *Progressive Education,* X, 6 (October 1933), 310–13.
36. Progressive Education Association's Committee on Social and Economic Problems, *A Call to the Teachers of the Nation* (New York: John Day, 1933), pp. 6, 9, 19, 20.
37. William H. Kilpatrick (ed.), *The Educational Frontier* (New York: Appleton-Century-Crofts, 1933), pp. 36, 38, 291.

CHAPTER

2

The Road to
Social Radicalism

An analysis of social reconstructionist thinking reveals a number of disquieting characteristics that have deep roots in American educational history. Most important, and perhaps most striking, is the ubiquitous sense of mission that has been referred to earlier. Psychologically, it was both a source of motivation and an emotional release. Educators expressed their undoubtedly sincere desire to contribute to the improvement of society in terms of this sense of mission. It was this somewhat naïve belief that education alone could create a more ideal social order that caused educators to expect so much both from themselves and from their calling. Unfortunately, this sense of mission has also obscured the need for vigorous intellectual analysis; and thus many of their proposals were not subjected to any criteria except that of emotional appeal.

Another characteristic of social reconstructionist thinking, which continually appears in their writings, especially during the nineteen-thirties, is utopianism. This tone is obvious in the social reconstructionist promise to remake society along lines that would provide everybody with happiness and social justice and in the expectation that this could be brought about through the education of a single generation. The belief that teachers possessed the educational background, the will power, and the necessary confidence of society to effect the social transformation they envisioned was also an example of utopian thinking. These beliefs also represented a romantic attitude toward the power of education to eradicate the evil in the world, an attitude that has been held by a great many other social reformers. This attitude, more than any other, reveals that the social reconstructionists were captives of the Western tradition that has maintained since the time of Socrates that all men desire to be good and fail only out of ignorance. Once this premise is accepted, then education seems the most obvious way to release man's propensity for doing good. The fact that some men want neither to be educated nor to subscribe to prevailing middle-class standards of goodness and morality has rarely been questioned by reform-minded educators. Consequently, both their assumptions about the essential goodness of human nature and their own motives for wanting to dispel the forces of evil have generally gone unexamined.

It is surprising that the social reconstructionists were such poor social analysts. Although these social educators thought of themselves as students of social change, none was able to view realistically facts that were obvious to most laymen. These educators apparently lacked an understanding of the teacher's actual position in society. Even though teachers had no real protection from being dismissed arbitrarily by school boards— and they thus possessed neither economic security nor the ability to formulate significant policy—the social reconstructionists viewed them as a force capable of directing social change. Not only did these educators fail to realize that teachers make few decisions that are socially significant, but they also failed to comprehend that in a time of severe crisis it was impossible for society to wait for the teachers to organize and educate themselves for their new role. Events in the early thirties simply would not stand still while educators argued about their social responsibilities—government leaders knew this, the unemployed walking the streets were poignantly aware of it, but many educational leaders were apparently oblivious to this fundamental fact.

Although the social reconstructionists thought of themselves as experimentalists and therefore would have denied any intellectual kinship with the educators of the nineteenth century, they were nevertheless heirs to many of the attitudes prevalent among their predecessors of the previous century. Their desire to reform society, their utopianism, and their evangelistic approach to education were also characteristic of nineteenth-century educators. Although both groups of educators thought of themselves as social reformers, there was a fundamental difference between the two. Whereas the educator in the nineteenth century was basically religious and viewed his social role as one of instituting reform within the established framework of moral and social absolutes, the social reconstructionist of the twentieth century was conditioned to think in terms of changing values. To him change was an inescapable, even dominant, reality. Stated somewhat differently, the nineteenth-century educator wanted to reform certain elements in society within a framework of an established system of values, whereas the twentieth-century social reconstructionist wished to reform the social system itself.

In the nineteenth century, educators generally believed that dominant social values were beyond criticism. Consequently, they turned their attention to disciplining those individuals whose behavior deviated from the accepted standards. On the other hand, individual behavior was not one of the major concerns of the social reconstructionists, because their attention was focused primarily on the shortcomings of social institutions. Although both groups believed that the school should be an instrument of reform, the nineteenth-century educators thus performed the essentially conservative role of correcting social deviance, whereas the activity of the social reconstructionists was aimed at socially radical changes in the community itself. For the student, however, education in both periods was not a liberalizing experience, for it did not provide him with the noetic skills necessary for independent thinking. It was rather a molding process intended to prepare him to live in accordance with the teacher's conception of the good society. In order to understand why the American educator took the road to social radicalism, it is necessary to examine the historical forces that first shaped the self-image of the teacher and of his perception of his professional responsibilities toward society, as well as the forces that contributed to his transformation in the 1930s.

The Historical Roots

Prior to the Civil War, the American educator was influenced by an interplay of cultural forces, of which the Christian religion was the most dominant. Religion dictated the customs of early New England society, making property a virtue of the godly, power an expression of God's will, and education a necessity for those who desired to meet their temporal needs in accordance with the Scriptures. From its earliest beginnings when the Puritans of Massachusetts Bay Colony enacted a 1642 law to ensure that their children developed the "ability to read and understand the principles of religion and the capitall lawes of this country," [1] formal education in America evolved as an adjunct to religious thought and need.

It was clear that the colonists believed it was impossible to separate formal education from religious training. As early as 1692, Massachusetts adopted the practice of having teachers licensed by the clergy as a way of ensuring the orthodoxy of the teachers' religious tenets. The New Netherlands required teachers to be members of the Dutch Reformed Church; the practice of requiring teachers to be members of the official church was prevalent in other colonies as well, notably New

Jersey and Maryland.[2] The procedure of drawing into the classrooms teachers who were both conservative and not inclined to differ with those members of the community who articulated the purpose of education was thus established early. Individuals who entertained unorthodox ideas were simply not invited to take charge of a classroom.

The close relationship between the schools and the churches was also manifest in the kinds of duties teachers were called upon to perform and in the curriculum and textbooks that were frequently religious in character. The duties of Johannes van Eckkelen, schoolmaster and chorister of Flatbush, New York in 1682, are typical of the religious tasks a teacher was expected to perform. Van Eckkelen's contract stipulated that in addition to the normal routine of teaching basic subjects, he was responsible for instructing the children in the common prayers, catechizing them, cleaning the church, assisting the minister with the services by reading before the congregation when the minister was away, providing the water for the baptismal basin and the bread and wine for the celebration of the Holy Supper, giving out the funeral invitations, digging the graves, and tolling the bell.[3] The expectation, which has only recently disappeared in many areas, that the teacher would instruct the Sunday school class or the church choir can be traced back to this early practice of regarding the teacher as a handyman who carried out the minor religious chores of the community.

Because he was charged with the responsibility of overseeing the moral development of the young, it was inevitable that the teacher's own morals would come under the closest scrutiny by the community. Though teachers were poorly paid and lacked high social status, they were nevertheless expected to be models of Christian character. Those who failed to measure up to their communities' standards of morality were promptly dismissed from their posts. Because over a long period the communities rewarded teachers for religious commitment and social orthodoxy with continued employment and punished any deviance by dismissal, the teacher in pre-Civil War America developed a self-concept that was socially and morally conservative, obedient to the will of the community, and deeply religious. Although the schools were generally secularized in the 1830s, neither the teacher's self-image nor his sense of social responsibility changed substantially.

When leaders of the educational revival in the 1830s like Horace Mann and Henry Barnard argued for the support of secular public schools, they frequently promised that public education would reform the immoral elements in society, making them both more industrious and more Christian. Mann claimed on several occasions that if all the children could be exposed to the "elevating influence of good schools, the dark host of private vices and public crimes which now embitter domestic peace, and strain the civilization of the age, might in ninety-nine cases in every hundred, be banished from the world." [4] Another educator, a veteran of twenty-four years in the classroom, expressed a belief commonly held among nineteenth-century teachers when he said: "If a well-conducted education produces benevolence, justice, truth, patriotism, love to God and love to man, in one case, the same education, in the same circumstances, will produce the same results in all cases." [5] The teacher had been subservient to the religious element that dominated colonial and frontier America for so long that his own thinking and rhetoric had become completely colored by it. The supposedly secular schoolhouse and the church thus reinforced each other because they were both dedicated to the same ends—elevating the level of morality in society and enabling the people to live a more Christian life. Because educators believed that education necessarily included the inculcation of Christian values, they were incapable of questioning the social system. Nineteenth-century American society was sanctioned by the Protestant ethic, and teachers could not examine it objectively to determine if it might not be in part responsible for creating the crime and pauperism they wished to eradicate. Any such examination would have inevitably meant questioning the morality of the Protestant ethic itself, an endeavor that was unthinkable to most people.

The growth of the democratic-humanist movement that emerged at the turn of the nineteenth century also shaped the educators' thinking. In particular, it contributed a new sense of optimism about the perfectibility of human nature and the efficacy of education. Prior to the dissemination of eighteenth-century French liberalism by the Jeffersonians in the South and West and by the Unitarians in New England, the Puritan view of human nature had dominated American thought. The Puritans had an extremely pessimistic view of man, and maintained that human nature was afflicted with a hereditary taint so pervasive that it contaminated every natural impulse. Man could escape his depraved condition only by throwing himself upon God's mercy—which for the Calvinist was indicated by early economic success. Those who did not experience material success could only hope that their faith and obedience were sufficient to win them salvation in the next life. This view of human nature slowly gave way to a more positive view of both man and God as American intellectuals began to be influenced by the ideas of John Locke, Thomas Paine, and the French exponents of the Enlightenment.

Between 1790 and 1815, Jeffersonian social and political ideas spread westward from Virginia. By emphasizing natural rights, freedom of the individual, and the right to restrict the coercive powers of the state, the Jeffersonians upheld a view of human nature that was clearly at odds with Protestant theology but ideally suited to the demands of frontier life. At approximately the same time, Unitarianism was undermining the Calvinist dogma of election and reprobation in New England. The Unitarians challenged the Calvinist idea of a wrathful God and gave the individual the worth and dignity that Calvinists had denied him. Unitarianism thus contributed to an intensification of individualism and a theory of progress upon which democratic institutions must rest. Both intellectual forces, transformed en route, merged in the West. The new synthesis was a coonskin form of self-reliant individualism that was intensely optimistic about the inner virtues, the innate wisdom, and the future of the common man. By 1830 the new ideas had been shaped by the preacher, the New England businessman, and the frontier farmer into a cult of the self-made man that stressed the inner qualities and the character of the individual as the key to success.

For educators who had struggled for decades with individuals whose souls had been damned at the outset, the new image of man was electrifying. If it were possible to perfect man, the teachers quite naturally believed that education was the logical means to this end. Although the teachers adapted to the changing intellectual climate, they did not, however, think to question such virtues as competitiveness, self-reliance, and frugality that were generally held to be requisite for success, and they never questioned the source of the optimism with which they had become so deeply imbued. Instead, they proceeded to instill and reinforce the values that society expected and rewarded.

Nowhere was the optimism about the character-building potential of education more concretely expressed or more influential than in the McGuffey readers (122 million copies were used between 1836 and 1920). Although America was experiencing a period of intellectual and social unrest, the McGuffey books gave their young readers nothing that would incline them to doubt the established values and institutions. The ideas presented in the readers were conservative and highly moralistic, although they never suggested that virtue was its own reward. The characters in the stories always received something tangible as a reward for their virtuous acts. Morals were clearly and forcefully drawn and the young reader was continually reminded that God, omnipotent and omnipresent, would punish the transgressor. The students of *McGuffey's Newly Revised Second Reader* (1844) were told that "God made the poor man, as well as the rich" and that "the poor if they are but good, may be very happy." *McGuffey's Newly*

Revised Rhetorical Guide (1853) suggests a great deal about the educator's role in pre-Civil War America, as well as the attitudes he wished to foster in his students:

> If you can induce a community to doubt the genuineness and authenticity of the scriptures; to question the reality and obligations of religion; to hesitate, undeciding, whether there be any such thing as virtue and vice, whether there be any external state of retribution beyond the grave; or whether there exists any such being as God, you have broken down the barriers of moral virtues and hoisted the floodgates of immorality and crime.[6]

Educators could help shut the "floodgates of immorality and crime" by teaching the proper virtues, and they could thus build characters that would in turn build a powerful nation. Their writings, which extolled the advantages of education, revealed their unflagging optimism. There was no criminal tendency and no taint of character that could not be corrected through public education. Horace Mann, secretary of the Massachusetts State Board of Education, promised to prove that "the great body of vices and crimes which now sodden and torment the community may be dislodged, and driven out from amongst us, by such improvements in our present common-school system as we are abundantly able immediately to make." [7] Governor George Wolf of Pennsylvania also believed that education had strong restorative powers; he told the legislature of Pennsylvania in 1833 that "universal education would operate as a powerful check upon vice, and would do more to diminish the black catalogue of crime . . . than any other measure." [8] The secretary of the Connecticut Board of Commissioners of the Common Schools, Henry Barnard, had an equally optimistic view of the character-building potential of education.[9] The reformist tendencies of the nineteenth-century educators were limited, however, by the belief that only the individual needed perfecting; they remained staunchly conservative as far as social institutions and values were concerned.

Educators had long been treated as public servants who were hired and fired at the discretion of the community. Since the earliest experiments with public education in colonial Massachusetts, they had known no other form of existence. Consequently the attitudes that the nineteenth-century educators had toward their profession and themselves were formed in accordance with the prevailing image of a public servant. Because many were barely literate and none had experienced a tradition of professional and intellectual independence, early colonial educators were incapable of combatting, intellectually or otherwise, the popular belief that because the community pays for public education, it has the right to control what goes on in the classroom. In the eighteenth and nineteenth centuries, educators thus tended to view the purpose of education in conservative terms that were acceptable to the most influential elements in the community. In the sense that they usually taught only what the dominant pressure groups in the community found acceptable and were willing to pay for, American educators were sophists. They possessed neither an independent spirit of inquiry nor a tradition of intellectual integrity. For it was tacitly understood that one of the conditions of employment was that the teachers would present truths tailored to the particular demands of the community.

The public servant mentality that American public school teachers adopted early in United States history was further reinforced by the rise of Jacksonian democracy. The spread of equalitarianism through the West did more than put Andrew Jackson in the White House and force the extension of manhood suffrage into republican strongholds where the word "democracy" was generally regarded only as a euphemism for the mob. Jacksonian democracy also, as Richard Hofstadter has clearly shown in his recent book, *Anti-Intellectualism in American Life,* gave a powerful and widespread impulse to anti-intellectualism in American life. The era of the common man encouraged intellectual leveling as much as it promoted social and political equalitarianism. In its most virulent form, it was manifested in a deep distrust, and even hatred, of the educated individual who was suspected of placing himself above others. On the other hand, a trust that frequently bordered on reverence was placed in the native and untutored intelligence of the ordinary man. The impact of this anti-intellectualism on nascent educational systems and on the attitudes of public school teachers was immediate and especially critical because teachers were just beginning to form a self-image as a profession.

Jacksonian democracy made community control of education, which had already ensured that public education would be a morally conservative force, an instrument of anti-intellectualism. The Jacksonians believed that teachers needed no special training or advanced education; the common man was considered qualified to fill any public office, and this idea was easily extended to teaching as well. Besides, the teacher who was more literate than the rest of the community was often suspected of entertaining radical and dangerous ideas. If a teacher failed to gain the trust of the community by thinking and acting in accordance with local mores, he was inevitably dismissed. Consequently, when the American teachers needed most to think of education as a liberalizing process, one that was truly in harmony with the principle of social pluralism, they were overwhelmed by the stringent requirements their communities imposed on them as public servants. Nineteenth-century public school teachers, as a result, failed to discover the necessary relationship between the teaching profession and academic freedom—which is so necessary if the educational process is going to help the student examine the assumptions underlying the values and ideas that he learns from his culture.

The anti-intellectual overtones of the equalitarian dogma also contributed to the low status of teachers and to their subservient attitude. Individuals who relied on the Bible as the only written guide to thought and action viewed education beyond minimum reading and writing skills with suspicion. In addition to being considered vaguely undemocratic, the popular mind thus also considered education an encumbrance to a man of the spirit. Because most early public education was largely limited to providing the skills needed to sign one's name and to read the Scriptures, the teacher could make no special claim on society. Anyone who was able to read, write, and make simple calculations was thought capable of teaching these skills to others. Because teachers were unable to identify themselves with any expertise recognized as valuable by the rest of society, it was inevitable that they would accept their low social status without visible protest.

By the early twentieth century, the educators' proclivity to think of public education as a panacea for every social ailment was deeply ingrained. Indeed, this unrealistic conception has dominated the numerous pronouncements about the aims of education for the past two centuries. This attitude directly links the radical social reconstructionists of the 1930s and the socially conservative educators of the previous century. In order to understand the origin of this particular phenomenon, one must realize that the educator, in part, learned from pressure groups around him to view education in an overly optimistic manner.

During the first decades of the nineteenth century both population growth and economic development began to increase more rapidly, and social groups started to assert themselves more vociferously, thus increasing social tension. Liberal elements demanded that the franchise be extended to all white males, a right which they regarded as a logical extension of the constitutional guarantees. The emerging labor movement demanded both an end to economic privileges for special classes and increased political power for themselves. Conservatives wanted to ensure that the masses did not get so far out of hand that their advances jeopardized social order and property. Nativist groups began to express concern over the corruption of cherished values by immigrants who brought with them foreign customs and the Catholic religion. Although each group frequently made social demands that conflicted with the interests of other pressure groups, they all looked to education as a means of achieving their objectives.

The early labor movement, committed to laissez-faire liberalism, believed that universal education would destroy harmful social distinctions and extend freedom to more classes of people and would thus enable the classes to compete socially and economically on more equal terms. After examining the aspirations of the labor movement, Rush Welter observed that "workingmen and radicals alike believed that universal public schooling would solve contemporary problems and secure universal justice." The early labor movement's commitment to universal education was shared by democrats who believed that the people must govern but that they first must be educated to do so. Conservatives also considered public education as a panacea for the immorality, vice and crimes against property that threatened to undermine established institutions. They thought the threat could only be averted if the people were instructed to respect the law and were inculcated with the proper moral values. The governor of New York, De Witt Clinton, clearly articulated this point of view when he told the legislature of New York in 1822 that "A general diffusion of knowledge is the precursor and protector of republican institutions; and in it we must confide as the conservative power that will watch over our liberties, and guard them against fraud, intrigue, corruption and violence." [10] Even nativist groups, finding violence ineffective, turned to education as a means of Americanizing the foreigners who were arriving in steadily increasing numbers. Whereas 23,000 immigrants came to the United States in 1830, 84,000 arrived in 1840. In effect, public education during the pre-Civil War decades was an endless source of hope for diverse and often conflicting groups.

The numerous claims made on public education, often expressed in prose heady with optimism, effectively conditioned educators to believe that the schoolhouse could indeed effect the social reforms demanded of it. An examination of their writings reveals how deeply they believed public education would lead to the fulfillment of all the demands made upon it; all, that is, except for the expectations of the labor movement. There were few educational leaders who advocated general education for the workers on the grounds that it would enable them to live fuller lives and participate more effectively as citizens. Horace Mann was a notable exception. He argued in his report of 1848 to the Massachusetts state board of education that "Education then, beyond all other devices of human origin, is the great equalizer of the conditions of men, —the balance wheel of the social machinery." Mann, perhaps more than any other educator, exemplified the unqualified faith that the nineteenth-century man placed in the redemptive powers of public education.

An examination of the educational literature of this period reveals little evidence to indicate that the educational spokesmen carefully weighed the demands made on the public school. If they had, they would have undoubtedly been struck by the fact that the implementation of many of the social objectives that education was supposed to achieve would have actually canceled each other out. For example, the conservative claim that education would provide a bulwark against the political encroachments of the masses on the political power of those who were regarded as best qualified to govern was in direct conflict with the democrat's claim that education would enable the individual to retain his freedom by giving him access to political avenues of expression. Early nineteenth-century educators, then, were not realists who were concerned with promising reasonably practical results; instead, they were idealists who were swept along by the optimism of the time. Conditioned to thinking and writing about the aims of education in a hyperbolic manner, the leaders of the common school movement left a legacy of idealism that has distracted their successors from examining seriously the limitations of using the school as an instrument of social reform. Later educators—in the second half of the nineteenth century and the first three decades of the twentieth century—simply accepted their roles as social reformers, although they interpreted them quite differently and failed to understand the inherent dangers both to society and to the idea of education as a liberalizing process, one that frees the mind of the student for critical and independent thinking.

The Civil War was a watershed in the development of public education. After they had won both conservative and liberal support for the principle of the common school during the ante-bellum period, educators began to transform the principle into a reality. After 1865, the American education system expanded rapidly at both the elementary and secondary levels, and the growth was buttressed by state compulsory attendance laws. Educational development paralleled in time the transformation of rural America into an industrial and urban society, a process marked by frenzied exploitation of human and natural resources. In a generation that extended the old idea of the individual's inalienable right to govern himself politically to the right of the individual to preempt, exploit and squander natural resources, the growing support and expansion of educational facilities stands in sharp contrast. Individualism had apparently not been as entirely simplified into the acquisitive instinct as some writers suggest.

Even if the expansion of public education appeared somewhat incongruous amid the materialistic tumult of postwar years, educators themselves were not immune to the changes in values then taking place. They quickly accepted the "gospel of wealth"—the guiding philosophy of the Gilded Age—and became staunch supporters of the society that was built upon it. No real changes in attitudes were required of educational leaders; the sense of mission, the utopianism, the language of the evangelist that were so characteristic of the previous era served them equally well under the new conditions.

The gospel of wealth that dominated both intellectual circles and the practical world of business until the beginning of the twentieth century received its theoretical support from two divergent sources, religion and science. Although on the surface the two doctrines appear incompatible, they were interpreted in such a way that they not only lost their incompatibility but were frequently used to reinforce each other. Vernon L. Parrington sardonically observed in his book *Main Currents in American Thought* that the people of the Gilded Age heeded somewhat too literally the Biblical injunction to take no thought for the morrow, so busily intent were they on squandering the resources of the continent. People used the Bible to justify acquiring wealth and power. Intellectual leaders like Presidents Noah Porter of Yale and James McCosh of Princeton declared that property rights were derived from God; they thus thought of industry and thrift as religious virtues. This doctrine had roots that ran back to the Puritanism of the seventeenth century, but in the post-Civil War period it was asserted with new force.

With the exception of the Lutherans, virtually all the leading Protestant denominations produced nationally known clergymen who popularized the theme that wealth was the primary means of achieving virtue (the Catholics generally avoided this rather un-Christian tenet). The purpose of man, they proclaimed, is the accumulation of wealth, and only the godly could expect to succeed. Russell H. Conwell, a nationally popular Baptist minister, said in his lecture, "Acres of Diamonds": "to secure wealth is an honorable ambition and is one of the great tests of a person's usefulness to others." In an article published in *Hunt's Merchants Magazine* in 1854, a Congregational clergyman, Matthew H. Smith, wrote that "Adam was created and placed in the Garden of Eden for business purposes; it would have been far better for the race if he had attended closely to the occupation for which he was made." [11] Other clergymen glorified the accumulation of wealth in numerous books bearing such suggestive titles as *How to Succeed* (written by Lynan Abbot, pastor of Plymouth Church, 1887) and *Uncrowned Kings* (written by Methodist Daniel Wise, 1875). By harmonizing competitive acquisitiveness with the fundamental moral law, Protestant churches gave their sanction to the success cult and turned their backs on the plight of those stricken with poverty.

Andrew Carnegie once said that individualism, private property, the "Law of Accumulation of Wealth," and the "Law of Competition" were the foundations of modern capitalistic society. Although the first law received the immediate blessing of Protestantism, the "Law of Competition" was the stepchild of scientific theory as interpreted by Herbert Spencer in his *Social Statics* (1850). Spencer had adopted Charles Darwin's theory of evolution to the conditions of society. Darwin's new theory of evolution had presented an explosive challenge to American theological thought until religious leaders discovered that the theory of competition could be applied to the struggle between the forces of evil and good. This discovery made it possible for them to find in Darwin's theory a divine purpose. In reference to individuals who failed to succeed, Spencer wrote: "The whole effort of nature is to get rid of such, to clear the world of them, and make room for the better. . . . If they are not sufficiently complete to live, they die, and it is best they should die." [12] Spencer's social Darwinism, in effect, lent scientific support to what nineteenth-century Protestant theologians had known all along. God had willed that the weak should perish, and now it was evident that nature had no use for them either. The belief that only the fit should survive was thus the common ground upon which both the social Darwinist and the theologian could heartily agree. This belief provided the moral and theoretical justification for "rugged individualism" and laissez-faire capitalism. Perhaps most conveniently of all, it freed the people of the Gilded Age from the need to feel compassion for those who failed in life's struggle.

In an era that regarded the merchant as a "moral educator, a church of Christ gone into business—a saint in trade . . ." and expressed the desire to "build him a shrine in Bank and Church, in the Market and the Exchange . . ." (Irwin Wyllie, *The Self-Made Man in America*), it is not surprising that the educator should identify himself with the conservative business elements in society. Educators had learned from the church that poverty springs from laziness, vice and lack of thrift. Following the lead of the church, they viewed poverty as an individual matter and not an evil rooted in the economic and social system. Their acceptance of social Darwinism, which attained its peak of popularity about 1882, further paralyzed their thinking. They remained rigidly conservative and immune to the suggestion that the social system itself might need overhauling. Besides, poverty could be viewed as a proving ground of individual mettle, a transient state for those who learned that hard work and frugality were the great lessons of life. No less a person than Andrew Carnegie testified to the beneficent effects of poverty when he said somewhat boastfully, "The millionaires who are in control started as poor boys, and were trained in that sternest but most efficient of all schools—poverty."

Although educational leaders were restricted by the prevailing social dogma, they nevertheless continued to wear the mantle of the social reformer. The social system itself appeared beyond reproach, but the educators did not stop promising that the schools would continue to be agents of social reform. They could still claim that the schools guarded the health and destiny of the nation against intemperate and lawless elements. The precedent for the expression of reform sentiment in the second half of the nineteenth century was set by a nonprofessional educator. At the first anniversary meeting of the National Teacher's Association held in Cincinnati in 1858, Daniel Read, professor of moral philosophy at the University of Wisconsin, told the assembled educators that they were "the appointed watchmen of the advance of human progress." This theme was repeated over and over in subsequent years and no doubt gave professional educators a feeling of importance that a society intent on embellishing the reputations of the titans of industry traditionally denied them. At the 1860 meeting of the NEA, the delegates were told:

"In moulding the character of the nation the teacher shapes its fortunes, and directs, almost determines its destiny. What a fearful consideration! How startling the responsibility of the American teacher!" In 1865, James P. Wickersham, who later became the state superintendent of public instruction in Pennsylvania, stated this view even more categorically when he declared: "American educators hold in their hands the destinies of this nation." Throughout this period educators continued to proclaim the regenerative powers of the schools in language that one usually associates with evangelists. The remarks of President Samuel S. Greene at one NEA convention were typical:

> Let our sessions bear testimony to the spirit of earnestness and devotion which animates the leading educators of the land. Let us gather inspiration from personal fellowship, and from this interchange of fraternal good will; and let us return to our several fields of labor, moved anew to the gigantic task which lies before us.[13]

The postwar educator's program of social reform was largely limited to teaching lawless and nonconformist groups to be obedient to the laws and morals of the established order. References to teaching obedience were especially numerous in the educational literature during this period. Because social reformism was circumscribed by the prevailing social and moral absolutes, educators conceived the nature of the ideal school in simple and straightforward terms. The school should be staffed by teachers who could be "in humble measure like Christ" and who could "lift their pupils by a divine contagion of virtue." After the paper containing these remarks was given before the 1880 NEA convention, a delegate suggested that there be no further discussion of the paper. He feared that it would spoil the effect of the paper, which he likened to that of a "beautiful rose." The ideal school should also make the training of the student's will power its primary goal, thus "making him obedient to authority, self-controlled, polite, and industrious," as William T. Harris, a leading educational spokesman, confidently expressed it at the 1887 meeting.

To apply these goals to foreign immigrants and laborers, however, was an entirely different problem. When the post-Civil War educator confronted these social groups, he revealed that he lacked the mental and emotional capacity to be an impartial social reformer. There is no evidence to indicate that any important educator during this period thought to question the popular belief that the successful businessman was the outstanding example of a moral educator. On the contrary, the evidence suggests that educators looked upon businessmen as exemplars and allies. In 1895, for example, the U.S. Commissioner of Education told a meeting of super-intendents that they would find their greatest support in "conservative businessmen." With even greater candor, in 1913 a school superintendent claimed that because schools are maintained at the expense of the business interests and because they exist for "the sole purpose of developing the businessmen and women of the future, it is evident that there should be perfect harmony between the school authorities and the business interests."

During a period of labor unrest in the 1870s and 1880s, educators were quick to take the side of business against the laboring classes. The strikes were grave reminders to these educators that the schools' tasks remained unfinished. The railroad strike of 1877 spread through more than a dozen Eastern states and was finally put down by federal troops only after more than nineteen rioters had been killed in Pittsburgh alone. NEA President M. A. Newell told the national convention later that year that it was "the good sense of an immense majority of hard working people, created, fostered, and developed by public education, that saved us from the terrors of the French Commune." "Would such an outbreak have been possible," he asked the delegates, "if the workingmen engaged in it had been men accustomed and trained to think as well as toil?" As labor disturbances continued, educational leaders concluded that the school's special task was to "detect and expose the fallacies of socialism," because they thought this philosophy had been instrumental in causing labor agitation. They proclaimed that only the schools could prevent further violence and social unrest. Their general orientation was most pronounced when they responded to the Pullman Strike of 1894 by passing a resolution at the annual NEA convention that commended the "wisdom and firmness" of President Cleveland because he had restored order with federal troops. At the same convention, the delegates also resolved that the schools would accept "the duty of preparing the rising generation for intelligent and patriotic citizenship, by inculcating those principles of public and private morality and of civil government upon which our free Republic is based, and by means of which alone it can endure."

Since the first waves of large-scale immigration in the 1840s, American educators had pursued their social reformist goals through the Americanization programs in the schools. In these programs, the children of foreigners were, with varying degrees of efficiency, inculcated with concepts that were intended to make them loyal supporters of republican institutions and enthusiastic participants in the free enterprise system. The program was both conservative and nationalistic. With the outbreak of labor strife in the early 1870s, educators began to fear that the workers were coming under the influence of foreign and radical ideas. "Riot, incendiarism and conspiracy are not native growths, but have come among us by importation. They cannot long survive the clear air of American life," declared a report of the NEA Committee on Resolutions. Social unrest moved NEA President Newell to ask: "These rioters, were they not foreigners, for whom our schools are in no way responsible?" Many educators, however, thought that the schools were indeed responsible, and a greater effort was made to make them special instruments for molding the foreign-born into the standard American image.

While school teachers were joining clergymen and businessmen as stewards of the gospel of wealth, new ideas were emerging that would ultimately corrode traditional modes of thinking and effect sweeping changes in psychology, law, philosophy, economics and education. These ideas would also eventually cause the educator to reinterpret his role as a social reformer and transform him from a conservative into a social radical who would take upon himself the responsibility for initiating social change—as the social reconstructionists attempted to do in the nineteen-thirties. The new intellectual climate would not, however, cause the educator to lose his sense of mission, nor would it alter his utopian ideas about the powers of education to elevate society to an even higher level of moral existence.

Science provided a new thought structure that undermined the traditional concept of a "block" universe, one that could be enclosed within a single rational system. Herbert Spencer had used science to justify the creation of yet another deterministic universe, one that subordinated man to the control of the environment. At the same time others were beginning to gain new insights into the meaning and application of science that would eventually have the opposite effect. Darwin's theory of evolution led them to question whether or not evidence could be found for maintaining that any part of the universe was fixed and enduring. To the great discomfort of many, including the supporters of social Darwinism and Hegelian idealism, they began to argue that ideas and values were as relative and as subject to change as the material world. Science thus interpreted became increasingly potent as a countervailing force to the social and moral certainties of the postwar years.

By applying the method of scientific investigation to a general theory of meaning, Charles S. Peirce (1839–1914), founder of the famous Metaphysical Club and a distinguished mathematician, laid the foundations for the new philosophy. His seminal idea was this: "The meaning of a concept . . . lies in the manner in which it could conceivably modify purposive action, and in this alone." This was a profoundly new idea, one that would shortly exert a great influence on the direction of American thought. It would soon no longer be possible to depend upon reason alone to determine the meaning of an idea. Henceforth, its meaning could be most accurately determined by acting on it and then observing the effects. This operational theory of meaning precluded the possibility that ideas could have universal meaning and was therefore in harmony with the experimentalism of science.

The Harvard psychologist, William James, expanded Peirce's functional approach to the meaning of ideas into the pragmatic theory that made workability the criterion of truth. His contributions in psychology also influenced the social thinking of educators. Prior to James the mind had been regarded as an entity distinct from the body and subject to different laws. James abolished this artificial distinction by treating the mind as an instrument that enabled the organism to adjust to its changing environment. Both the mind and body evolved together and in relation to each other. "Our minds are not here simply to copy a reality that is already complete," he said. "They are here to complete it, to add to its importance by their own remolding of it, to decant its contents over, so to speak, into a more significant shape. In point of fact, the *use* of most of our thinking is to help us to *change* the world." [14] Although James was not entirely successful in overcoming the problem of supernaturalism, he did bring psychology into harmony with Darwin and helped to advance philosophy a step in that direction.

At the same time Peirce and James were using the scientific method to break down the absolutes upon which many nineteenth-century institutions and values rested, a more humane attitude toward the child, which had been imported from Europe, was changing educational methods and causing educators to reassess the goals of education. After they had read the educational writings of Jean Jacques Rousseau (1712–1778), Jean Heinrich Pestalozzi (1746–1827), Johann Friedrich Herbart (1776–1834), and Friedrich Froebel (1782–1852) and after they observed the experimental schools in Europe at first hand, a few American educators began to enthusiastically support the idea that education must assist the natural development of the child. They now believed that the child's nature was inherently good. Knowledge of the child's nature was a guide to teaching methods that were most appropriate at any given stage of his development. The pioneering work of Edward A. Sheldon at the Oswego State Normal School and of Francis W. Parker, superintendent of schools in Quincy, Massachusetts, helped to popularize the new approach to education, especially the new principle that the child learns through his own physical activity.

Starting in the early 1880s, educators began with increasing frequency to present papers at NEA conventions that dealt with the needs, interest, and abilities of the child. They developed their own lexicon, romanticized the child, and demanded that he be emancipated from the discipline, authority, and regimentation of an adult world. Francis Parker succinctly expressed the feeling of this new mood when he wrote in his *Talks on Pedagogics* (1894): "We must believe that we can save *every child*." [15] The merit of the practice of deriving educational principles from the nature of the child was further supported by the work of G. Stanley Hall, the founder of the child-study movement. Hall's psychological studies lent a measure of scientific respectability to the progressive educational techniques then under development. Unfortunately, Hall weakened the value of his contribution to the emerging progressive education movement because he expressed his ideas in metaphorical language that fostered emotionalism and obscured unresolved social and psychological problems. "The guardians of youth," he told his readers in an article written in 1901, "should strive first of all to keep out of nature's way . . . they should feel profoundly that childhood, as it comes fresh from the hands of God, is not corrupt, but illustrates the survival of the most consummate thing in the world. . . .

Nothing else is so worthy of love, reverence, and service as the body and soul of the growing child." [16]

If Hall, a scientist, could state that "childhood is . . . our pillar of cloud by day and fire by night," then the intellectual climate in which the American educator found himself at the turn of the century was certainly changing. Social and moral absolutes were giving way under the pressure of scientific thought, and this attrition was beginning to free the educator from the task of inculcating the child with final truths. The child could now be allowed the freedom to find his own truth. Hall's statements also indicate how easy it was for many people, including educators, to apply the scientific method to educational problems and to couch their findings in quasi-religious terminology. It is more important to note that the acceptance of the idea that the child's nature is inherently good also caused educational theorists to view social institutions as the source of any evil in the child's behavior.

The Turning Point: John Dewey

These two movements—the philosophy based on the canons of experimental science and the more humane attitude toward the needs and worth of the child—converged in the thinking of John Dewey. Although Dewey was born the same year Darwin published *The Origin of Species* (1859), he was a follower of Hegelian idealism for a brief period before he rejected it in favor of the more concrete formulations of Darwin and James. James' *Principles of Psychology* had a large impact on Dewey's thinking, because it caused him to interpret the mind as an instrument for reconstructing experience. Whereas both James' pragmatism and his psychology focused on the individual, Dewey built on both to erect a system that made the philosopher as well as the educator a social engineer. He was no less indebted to the Darwinian idea of change, which became the underlying motif of his philosophy.

Dewey believed that the philosoper should be concerned

with the current social problems rather than with metaphysics. In the process of overturning various absolutes, he also destroyed the basis for the educator's argument that the schools should reform the individual in accordance with preexisting moral and social patterns. He suggested instead that educators interpret the social responsibilities of the school in a radically new way. Education had been one of Dewey's earliest interests. In fact, he wrote his major works on education, *The School and Society* (1899) and *Democracy and Education* (1916), long before he had developed fully his philosophical ideas in *Reconstruction in Philosophy* (1920), *Experience and Nature* (1929) and *Logic: The Theory of Inquiry* (1938). Dewey's ideas about the psychological nature of learning and the social responsibilities of the school began to solidify while he was connected with the Laboratory School at the University of Chicago (1894–1904).

Dewey decided that it was impossible to separate the purpose of philosophy from that of education. He wanted the philosopher to abandon the sterile task of analyzing concepts that were abstract and remote from daily experience and instead to concentrate on the more sanguine task of bringing about a better society. In the same sense, Dewey felt that education should cease to be an exercise in memorizing the cultural products of past ages and that the learning experiences of the student should be harmonized more closely with the needs of contemporary society. His technical definition of education as the "reconstruction of experience which adds to the meaning of experience, and which increases ability to direct the course of subsequent experiences" reflected his concern with improving the quality of individual and social experience. Philosophy, as Dewey understood it, was essentially a critical evaluation of social values and beliefs. Because these values can be tested only in the experience undergoing reconstruction, education and philosophy are inseparable. Education, with its emphasis on growth, experience, and the use of intelligence in solving social problems was therefore a natural corollary of his own philosophy. In fact, Dewey often identified philosophy as essentially an educational process.

It was not surprising that Dewey thought of education as a moral process because it involved a continuous improvement in the quality of experience undergone by the individual. He felt however, that education has no specific end other than its contribution to the individual's capacity for growth in his ability to solve problems. This criterion, coupled with Dewey's idea that growth itself is the only moral end, has broad and important social implications. Social institutions that inhibit individual growth become, in a sense, immoral and subject to change through reconstruction or even to elimination. Because the school is the social agency that fosters directed growth through a curriculum aligned closely with the problems of society, the growth the students achieve in their capacities to reconstruct experience is largely social. In other words, they become more efficient in identifying and solving social problems.

Dewey's educational writings are filled with references to the importance of the individual's own experience in the learning process. This emphasis on experience is one of the keys to both his educational and philosophical ideas. He considered experience an ongoing process, a transaction between an organism and its environment that had both antecedents in the past and consequences for the future. Dewey was fully aware that all experiences were not equally educative; he therefore believed that only those that would facilitate more growth should be cultivated. Experiences that hinder or arrest further growth were to be eliminated from the school environment. One of his recommendations for reform called for the elimination from the school environment of social values that were not in harmony with the educator's idea of "the good society." The social environment, by the same token, would be subject to reconstruction by educators when outmoded institutions or values restricted growth, for the organic relationship between the school and society gave them common interests and ideals.

If, as Dewey contended, experience was an ongoing multi-dimensional transaction between the individual and the environment, then the individual was not a passive receiver; he was a dynamic participant whose intelligence, judgment, and self-control modified the quality of experience in the same way he was modified by experience himself. The encounter was educational because it increased the student's problem-solving ability. Dewey's emphasis on intelligence and overt participation precluded the routine and mechanical activity that had characterized much of nineteenth-century education. To his social reconstructionist followers, applying his ideas meant involving students in an active process of finding solutions to the problems they experienced in the larger society outside the classroom. The social reconstructionists learned from Dewey to identify as a social problem any institution that obstructed the growth of the individual members of society.

In Dewey's educational writings the school was always pictured as the primary distributing agency for whatever values and purposes any social group cherished. Regardless of their quality, past as well as current cultural achievements would, he contended, remain valueless as long as they were not distributed throughout society. Dewey therefore maintained that the special values and purposes that characterize a democracy would have to receive the widest possible distribution, which would thus help make democratic values part of the mind and will of all the members of society. In addition to casting the school in the role of a vehicle for cultural transmission, he believed that the school had the task of balancing the various elements in the social environment so that each student had the opportunity to escape the narrowness of the social group in which he lived. Dewey was especially sensitive to the limitations on intellectual and cultural growth inherent in the experience of lower economic and ethnic groups and in the restrictions of social institutions like laissez-faire capitalism.

At one crucial point, Dewey's educational philosophy became, in a broad sense, political philosophy. Because the school provided an environment that could be conducive to learning how to solve social problems through cooperation, deliberate control of the school environment would foster the proper mental and moral attitudes in the students. Dewey thus believed that an idealized school environment could be created by deliberately screening out the unworthy features of the larger social environment. In a more concrete sense, such deliberate control would substitute cooperation and the "spirit of service" for the more competitive social values. If it were purified of undesirable social attitudes and practices, the school would perpetuate only what the educator regarded as the most desirable aspects of the culture. The school would then assume responsibility not only for transmitting the culture but also for deliberately improving it. When the educator consciously prevented unworthy values and respect for the outmoded institutions of the society from being passed on to the younger generation, he would assume the mantle of the statesman. Dewey's often-repeated argument that "Education is the fundamental method of social progress and reform" provided his followers with a theoretical justification for using the schools to bring about the social reforms that they desired. Although he cannot be held directly responsible for later distortions, Dewey must bear some responsibility for giving education a political aspect. Furthermore, the notion that education is a form of political statesmanship might not have been taken so literally by Dewey's zealous followers if the rest of his philosophy had not so thoroughly de-emphasized the formulation of aims that do not arise directly from the ongoing experience of society.

The publication of Dewey's writings marks the transitional point in the educator's interpretation of his role as a social reformer. Prior to Dewey, reform-minded educators identified with the conservative social elements; after Dewey, they felt free to align themselves with any social group that supported their programs of reform. Whereas their predecessors, lacking a theoretical justification for using the school as an engine of reform, carried on their reform activities as a direct response to conservative demands, the social reconstructionists of the twentieth century were, in effect, emancipated from class domination by Dewey's educational philosophy. Hereafter they thought of themselves as having a significant influence on the quality of social and political life.

The role of educator-statesman was further strengthened by other intellectuals who were in revolt against the abstractions of the previous century. Thorstein Veblen's probing study of economics revolutionized subsequent thinking in that field and Charles A. Beard armed a generation of liberals, including the social reconstructionist educators, with a non-Marxian economic interpretation of history. Veblen, the son of Norwegian immigrants and Dewey's colleague at the University of Chicago, turned economics into an evolutionary science when he published the *Theory of the Leisure Class* in 1899. Using the Darwinian idea of process and function, Veblen constructed a social theory that explained the evolutionary development of social customs and institutions as an expression of predatory practices and pecuniary values. He showed that business principles actually pervaded art, law, religion, education, and politics; he also believed that they constituted the most dynamic force in society. Veblen argued, however, that business was essentially antisocial because of its sabotaged production in order to keep prices high and supply limited—this argument was later to have a significant influence on individual members of the social reconstructionist group. By showing that institutions, as products of the past, were never fully in harmony with the requirements of the present, Veblen also supplied educators with an argument that they were to use to support their claim that all institutions must be continually scrutinized in the classroom.

The liberals also hailed Charles Beard as a hero for his *An Economic Interpretation of the Constitution,* which was published in 1913. Raised in the Populist Midwest, Beard later joined the faculty of Columbia University, where he became a close friend and philosophical ally of John Dewey. In Beard, the liberals found a courageous mind capable of stripping the false idealism away from the country's most sacred institutions. His examination of the Constitution revealed that its originators did not necessarily possess the high-mindedness so frequently attributed to them; instead they were men who believed that private property took precedence over government and that it should not be subject to control by popular majorities. Because he showed with scientific detachment that the Constitution was an undemocratic document designed to protect an undemocratic society, Beard unmasked for liberals the economic basis of political institutions. Beard believed that history was economically determined; "The disastrous evolutions which the world has witnessed," he wrote in *The Economic Basis of Politics*, "have been revolutions against property." [17] Beard's economic determinism, fathered by James Madison rather than by Karl Marx, gave the liberals a tool for analyzing the development and purpose of contemporary institutions. In addition, Beard complemented the influence of Dewey and Veblen on the liberal ideology of the twenties when he maintained that laissez-faire capitalism was incompatible with democracy and that the historic clash between the interests of property and democratic forces would end only after centralized social planning was adopted.

The majority of the social reconstructionists were college students during the years when Dewey, Veblen, and Beard were laying the basis of the new liberalism. During this period, reform politics underwent a philosophical transformation that pulled the students in several directions at once. The new liberal insurgency that eventually dominated the thinking of social critics in the nineteen-thirties and the doctrine subsequently adopted by the social reconstructionists differed from the progressivism of the previous decade. The progressive mind was, as Richard Hofstadter has argued, preeminently a Protestant mind. Even though the movement was strongest in the cities, it inherited the moral traditions of rural evangelical

Protestantism. Progressives spoke out with as much moral indignation against the abuses of trusts and city bosses as they did against prostitution and dishonest merchandising practices. Progressivism flourished in a prosperous era. It is noteworthy that the movement's primary objective was to curb excesses in government and business in order to maintain the success cult of the strong moral individual. At the turn of the century, the clamor for really basic changes in government and in its relationship to business did not come from progressives but from socialist and syndicalist elements that had recently immigrated to this country. In *The Age of Reform,* Hofstadter observed that the progressive was "trying to keep the benefits of the emerging organization of life and yet to retain the scheme of individualistic values that his organization was destroying." [18]

Ignoring the counterreformation ethos of progressivism, which Richard Hofstadter maintains was directed at restoring economic individualism and political democracy, the young social reconstructionists chose instead the emerging Dewey-Veblen-Beard brand of liberalism. Their social ideas reflected the scientific detachment of the new liberalism instead of the abstract idealism of the earlier progressive period. For them experience was the ultimate authority, and intelligence was their instrument for solving social problems. The social reconstructionists also inherited Dewey's idea that education is a form of social action, a conception he had formulated when he was confronted with the growing gulf between educational methods and the rapid industrialization of American society at the turn of the century. There is nothing to indicate that the social reconstructionists were, during their early development in the late 1920s, especially sympathetic to the radical wing of the liberal movement. The radicals had begun to follow the lead of Max Eastman, John Dos Passos, and Lincoln Steffens who had tired of chiding the controlling class about the miscarriages of social justice and were looking more and more to communism as an alternative to capitalistic excess.

"One by one after 1926 I had watched the new members of the group join our staff—Counts, Childs, Raup, Watson, Brunner, Newlon, Clark, Johnson, Cottrell, and others," [19] reminisced Harold Rugg. These men, who later became members of the social reconstructionist group, joined the staff of Teachers College at Columbia when their ideas had not yet been fully developed, but they all had been significantly influenced by Deweyan ideas. Three members—William H. Kilpatrick, Harold Rugg, and George Counts—had started their careers in education much earlier than the others. They all came from widely differing backgrounds, but slowly, through close association at Teachers College and under the influence of Dewey, their educational and social views converged. Others, like John L. Childs, Goodwin Watson, George Hartmann, and R. Bruce Raup, had taken their doctoral degrees after 1925 and were newly appointed members on the Teachers College faculty.

Kilpatrick had been at Teachers College the longest of the group. Born in 1871 in White Plains, Georgia, Kilpatrick attended Mercer University, an academically undistinguished Baptist institution. While he was a student there, however, Kilpatrick read Darwin's *The Origin of Species*. "The more I read of it," he later recalled, "the more I believed it and in the end I accepted it fully. This meant a complete reorganization, a complete rejection of my previous religious training and philosophy." [20] At Teachers College, which he entered in 1907 to prepare for a doctoral degree in education, Kilpatrick studied under Dewey and became an ardent disciple. In 1913 he joined the faculty and began a long career of interpreting Dewey to the students in his philosophy of education classes. His early works, *The Montessori System Examined* (1914) and *Froebel's Kindergarten Principles Critically Examined* (1916), were critical evaluations of educational theories that were then widely respected. In 1918, his essay "The Project Method" was published and promptly established his reputation as a leading progressive theorist. The project method was intended to make "purposeful activity" initiated by the child in a social environment the center of the educational process. Kilpatrick further developed the implications of the project method in his major work, *Foundations of Method* (1925).

In this book he emphasized Dewey's idea that the school should be an embryonic and idealized community. The project method was thus intended to integrate subject matter with the problems of social life and to help the student develop proficiency in planning, executing, and judging in what educational theorists have commonly called "life situations." Because the project method was supposed to teach the student *how* rather than *what* to think, the curriculum could not be determined in advance if the method was to be effectiv~. ~. should be kept in mind that during this period Kilpatrick was still vacillating between the child-centered approach mentioned in the previous chapter and Dewey's idea that the school should be used as an instrument for social action.

Harold Rugg was one of the few members of the social reconstructionist group who did not have a strong affiliation with a religious group during his formative period. Rugg's early interest was engineering, and in 1908 he graduated from Dartmouth with a degree in civil engineering. After teaching civil engineering for several years, he did graduate work in psychology, sociology, and education at the University of Illinois and received his Ph.D. in 1915. He then spent two years at the University of Chicago where, under the guidance of Charles Judd, he published *Statistical Methods Applied to Education*. During World War I he worked for the army's Committee on the Classification of Personnel. Following the war Rugg joined the staff of Teachers College as director of research for the newly established Lincoln School, which became a model progressive school. The war had jolted him into an awareness of social problems, and during his first years at Lincoln School he began to read Veblen and Beard. He also studied R. H. Tawney's *Acquisitive Society* and John R. Common's *History of Labour in the United States*.

Rugg's intensive and somewhat feverish study of the rise of industrialism convinced him that the high schools should introduce students to the study of "the great human migrations of the world . . . man's increasing control over nature, the crucial importance of trade, the increasing dominance of 'distribution' over 'production' in economic life, the tendency in economic life toward concentration in the ownership and control of wealth . . . the transportation of a self-sufficient peoples into a fragile society of interdependent peoples, the spread of economic imperialism." [21] "Aroused mentally and emotionally," as he explained in his semiautobiographical *That Men May Understand* (1941), Rugg embarked on an ambitious program to write a new series of elementary school textbooks that would provide an integrated (although they ultimately had a disproportionate stress on economics) approach to the social sciences. Rugg's study of society, which lasted over the next twenty years, was influenced by ideas he had gained from his personal association with social critics like those of *The New Republic* who had managed to keep liberalism alive during the reactionary twenties.

In addition to the social studies textbooks, Rugg collaborated with Ann Shumaker on *The Child-centered School* (1928), a summary of educational innovations across the country that gave particular attention to the problems of creative expression in a commercialized industrial society. The depression caused Rugg to turn his attention to the problems of social reform. In *Culture and Education in America* (1931), he developed the idea of a school-centered community where the frontier spirit would be kept alive and the economic abundance and artistic freedom inherent in the democratic promise would be realized. Two years later, Rugg argued in *The Great Technology* (1933) that man's creative potential could be liberated only if the scientific method were used to resolve social problems.

Like Rugg, George Counts also took an early interest in the statistical approach to education. Counts had grown up in

Kansas, a populist-oriented state that had undergone an enormous expansion in agriculture in the 1860s. "Haste to get rich has made us borrowers," wrote William Allen White about life in Kansas, "and the borrower has made booms, and booms made wild men, and Kansas became a vast insane asylum covering 80,000 square miles." [22] The boom collapsed abruptly in the winter of 1887–1888. Counts was born the following year in Baldwin, Kansas, and grew up in an atmosphere that still seethed with acrimonious hatred for the Eastern banking conspirators who were held responsible for the collapse. While Counts was studying Greek and Latin literature at Baldwin University, Populists still argued the merits of free silver and aired their grievances against the evil commercial class in the East. When Counts went to the University of Chicago to do graduate work in 1913, he was pulled intellectually in two directions. Although he received training in the science of educational tests and measurements from Charles Judd in his sociology and political science classes, he came under the influence of Veblen's writings. Counts graduated magna cum laude with a Ph.D. in education and sociology and quickly turned to educational and social criticism, abandoning completely his early interest in standard deviations, regression equations, and coefficients of correlation—which constituted a large part of scientific measurement.

Counts' first book, *The Selective Character of American Secondary Education* (1922), showed that the high schools were perpetuating social and racial inequalities. "At the present time," he wrote, "the public high school is attended quite largely by children of the more well-to-do classes. This affords us the spectacle of a privilege being extended at public expense to those very classes that already occupy the privileged positions in modern society." [23] In *The Social Compositions of Boards of Education* (1927), Counts tried to show that the schools, although they supposedly represented all segments of society, were actually controlled by the wealthy class. Counts argued in *Secondary Education and Industrialism* (1929) that the American schools had never come to terms with realities of industrialism and criticized educators for drifting without social goals in *The American Road to Culture* (1930). As the twenties came to a close, Counts had concluded that American education was class-structured and basically undemocratic and was ready to outline a program of action for democratizing American society.

Jesse Newlon came to Teachers College in 1927 as the new director of Lincoln School. Previously, he had served as superintendent of schools in Denver where he pioneered in giving teachers a greater share in decision-making and in curriculum formulation. His efforts had received national attention in administrative circles. Newlon was also active in liberal causes and served as a member of the Academic Freedom Committee of the American Civil Liberties Union. In 1934, Newlon took over as head of the division of instruction at Teachers College.

The embryo social reconstruction group also included an educational psychologist, Goodwin Watson. Before taking his Ph.D. at Columbia in 1925, Watson had been a principal in Wisconsin, a director of religious education in Denver, and an instructor at the extremely liberal Union Theological Seminary in New York. Immediately after he received his doctoral degree, Watson joined the Teachers College staff. Watson was active in the American Federation of Teachers at Teachers College and acted as director of the educational section of the New America movement.

E. Bruce Raup joined the staff of Teachers College after completing his doctorate there in 1925. His appointment marked the conclusion of a long period of uncertainty during which he had debated whether he should go into the ministry or into education. Born in Clark County, Ohio, in 1888 to Lutheran parents, Raup attended Lutheran-affiliated Wittenberg College. Like Kilpatrick, he had fully accepted Darwin's theory by the time he was graduated from college. In 1914, with his doubts about the ministry temporarily resolved, he entered and was graduated from McCormick Theological Seminary (Presbyterian) in Chicago. With the outbreak of war, Raup resigned the post he had taken as a pastor and teacher in Nebraska and became a chaplain in the army. In 1920, however, he decided against a religious career and enrolled for graduate study at Teachers College. In the summer of that year, Raup had his first introduction to Dewey's ideas when he took a philosophy of education class that was being taught by Boyd Bode while Kilpatrick was on sabbatical leave. After reading *Democracy and Education* and listening to Bode's "masterful exposition of Dewey's thought," Raup was deeply impressed. Recalling the experience many years later, Raup said: "[I] did not find Dewey a complete surprise. I was surprised that so much had been said along lines that had already vaguely occupied my mind; in other words he was talking to me." [24]

When John L. Childs went to Teachers College in 1928, he already fully believed that a class struggle was taking place in America. Unlike Counts and Rugg, both of whom had been largely influenced by both Veblen's and Beard's critique of American institutions, Childs had developed his social ideas during his undergraduate experience at the University of Wisconsin. There he learned from the teachings of Charles Van Hise and the political ideas of Robert M. La Follette that education and politics were interrelated. Childs also learned about the powerful social forces that opposed the enlightened governmental policies then being worked out by politicians in conjunction with University of Wisconsin faculty members. Because he had accepted the idea of social planning before he came to Teachers College, Childs quickly discovered that Dewey could provide him with a theoretical basis for his own social commitments.

The year 1927 was especially significant for American intellectuals. In his book, *Only Yesterday,* Frederick Lewis

Allen observed that the intellectuals of the twenties gradually became disillusioned with their own rebellion; Allen noted that the debunking and "tobogganing into mental chaos" reached its peak in 1927 and thereafter quickly began to wane. Although they had helped revolutionize the morals of the country by overturning the sentimentality and false modesty of Victorian morality, the intellectuals were largely directionless.

They had become disillusioned with Dewey because he had supported America's entry into World War I. They were appalled by the conservative reaction that set in following the armistice and by the smugness and materialism of a society that made a fetish of business in the postwar years. Jane Addams' Hull House and the Russian experiment were for most of them the only bright spots on the horizon. Many intellectuals, including John Dewey, Rexford G. Tugwell, Paul Douglas, Max Eastman, and Edmund Wilson, had journeyed to Russia and returned to write about their first-hand observations in glowing terms. Yet, more than any other, the event that awakened and polarized the intellectuals was the trial of Sacco and Vanzetti and their execution in August 1927. The episode was a deep emotional shock, and many intellectuals sympathized with Robert Morss Lovett's confession that "It forced me to accept a doctrine which I had always repudiated as partisan tactics—the class war." [25] Perhaps John Dos Passos best summed up the changed mood when he said, "All right, we are two nations."

In the same year the discussion group was formed at Teachers College. During the summer session of 1927 Raup suggested to Kilpatrick that they should form a group to discuss the influence of recent social changes on education. At first the discussion group was composed of five members who met bimonthly—Raup, Kilpatrick, who was chosen as chairman, Counts, Rugg, and Watson. Later Edmund de S. Brunner, Jesse Newlon, Harold F. Clark, F. Ernest Johnson,

Donald P. Cottrell and others joined the group. The group met regularly until 1934, only intermittently from 1934 to 1938, and again bimonthly from 1939 until several years after the beginning of World War II.

With Dewey in frequent attendance, the group discussed problems ranging from industrialization and social planning to progressive education. The relation of education to social change was a constant theme. Several members of the group had visited Russia—Dewey in 1927, Kilpatrick and Counts in 1929—and the thinking of the group was deeply influenced by their encounter with the Soviet Union. Dewey reported in *The New Republic* that in Russia he had at last seen his theories put into practice and that their value was "more than confirmed by what I saw . . . in Russian schools." Dewey anticipated future developments in social reconstructionist thinking when he wrote, "The Russian educational situation is enough to convert one to the idea that only in a society based on the cooperative principle can the ideals of educational reformers be adequately carried out." [26] Kilpatrick and Counts were equally impressed with the socially useful activities they observed being carried on in Russian schools. The fact that the Russians were using the schools to build a new society thus further stimulated the discussion group to think of the school as an instrument of social change.

That American society needed reforming was not an issue for the members of the group. There was already general agreement that the society should become more democratic and should become more experimental in its approach to problems, rather than relying on traditional formulas. Four members of the group—Counts, Dewey, Childs, and Rugg— were keenly interested in socialism. They argued that capitalism was preventing the full development of technology in behalf of all the people and this formulation seemed to be confirmed by the stock market crash in 1929. By 1932, Rugg reports, the group had achieved an extraordinary measure of intellectual cohesion—it was "taking a stand for the general conception of a welfare state and agreeing fairly closely on the constituents of the democratic principle." [27]

It is ironic that in their attempt to create a more democratic society—by no means a revolutionary idea—the social reconstructionists moved outside the mainstream of American political thought and became social radicals. Because they believed in a democratic society in the broadest sense of the term, they thought it impossible to reconcile capitalism, with its emphasis on the profit motive and competition, with their own ideal of a truly humane social order that provided for the good of all. Because they were committed to Dewey's idea that education is a form of social action, they came into a head-on conflict with the business community. Their belief in Dewey's axiom that action can never be neutral because it always involves value judgments forced the social reconstructionists to choose between social classes. They readily aligned themselves with those groups whom they identified as underprivileged. The social reconstructionists now felt that their responsibility as the leading interpreters of progressive education was to alert the classroom teacher to his role as an agent of social change. Whereas conservative social elements had once been able to channel the educator's impulse for social reform into acceptable directions, these same conservative groups now became the target of the educators' programs of social reform. The social reconstructionists were now social radicals and the partisans of the working class; they nevertheless were perpetuating a traditional characteristic of American educators—the desire to reform some element of society.

NOTES

1. "Initial Legislation on Apprenticeship in Massachusetts, 1642," in Edgar W. Knight and C. L. Hall (eds.), *Readings in American Educational History* (New York: Appleton-Century-Crofts, 1951), p. 10.
2. Howard K. Beale, *A History of Freedom of Teaching in American Schools* (New York: Scribner, 1941), p. 26.
3. Daniel J. Pratt, *Annals of Public Education in the State of New York from 1626 to 1746* (Albany, N.Y.: Argus, 1872), pp. 65–67.
4. Horace Mann, "Twelfth Report of 1848," *Life and Works of Horace Mann* (Boston: Lee and Shepard, 1891), vol. IV, p. 289.
5. *Ibid.*, p. 162. The statement was made in a letter written to Horace Mann by a Mr. S. Adams.
6. *McGuffey's Newly Revised Rhetorical Guides* (1853), p. 349.
7. Mann, "Eleventh Report of 1847," in *op. cit.*, pp. 150–51.
8. "Extracts from the Message of Governor Wolf to the Legislature of Pennsylvania, 1833," in Knight and Hall (eds.), *op. cit.*, p. 344.
9. See Henry Barnard's *Second Annual Report* as secretary of the Board of Commissioners of the Common Schools of Connecticut, 1840, especially p. 54. Published in 1940.
10. Rush Welter, *Popular Education and Democratic Thought in America* (New York: Columbia University Press, 1962), pp. 53, 30.
11. Matthew Smith, "The Elements of Business Success," *Hunt's Merchants Magazine*, XXXI (1854), 56.
12. Herbert Spencer, *Social Statics* (New York: Appleton-Century-Crofts, 1864), pp. 414–15.
13. Samuel S. Greene, "The Educational Duties of the Hour," *Proceedings of the National Education Association* (1864), p. 495.
14. *The New York Times,* November 3, 1907, pt. V, p. 8.
15. Francis W. Parker, *Talks on Pedagogics* (New York: E. L. Kellogg, 1894), pp. 3, 5–6.
16. G. Stanley Hall, "The Ideal School Based on Child Study," *Forum*, XXXII (September 1901), 24–25.

17. Charles A. Beard, *The Economic Basis of Politics* (New York: Knopf, 1923), p. 37.
18. Richard Hofstadter, *The Age of Reform* (New York: Knopf, 1961), pp. 204, 215.
19. Harold Rugg, *Foundations of American Education* (New York: World Book, 1947), p. 578.
20. Reported in Samuel Tenenbaum, *William Heard Kilpatrick: Trail Blazer in Education* (New York: Harper, 1951), p. 13.
21. Harold Rugg, *That Men May Understand* (New York: Doubleday, 1941), p. 203.
22. William Allen White, *Autobiography* (New York: Macmillan, 1946), p. 187.
23. George S. Counts, *The Selective Character of American Secondary Education* (Chicago: The University of Chicago Press, 1922), pp. 151–52.
24. Personal interview with R. Bruce Raup, 1963.
25. Robert Morss Lovett, *All Our Years* (New York: Viking, 1948), p. 190.
26. John Dewey, "New Schools for a New Era," *The New Republic*, LVII, 732 (December 12, 1928), 91.
27. Rugg, *Foundations of American Education*, pp. 578–79.

CHAPTER

3

Accepting
the Challenge:
1934–1935

When the first issue of *The Social Frontier* journal appeared in
the fall of 1934 the national mood was changing from despair
to anger. The partial success of Roosevelt's New Deal had
dispelled the earlier feeling of helplessness, but the President
had not gained the complete confidence of the American people.
The conservatives had been angered by the President's tamper-
ing with the economic system and by his disregard for the
traditional values of individual responsibility. Liberals were
equally frustrated by Roosevelt's vacillation and his failure to
scrap the capitalistic system. These dissident groups, as well
as the unemployed (11.5 million) and partially employed,
provided a receptive audience for the new political prophets
that were gaining increasing importance in American life.

Many of these charismatic figures succeeded in gaining large popular followings for their strange social panaceas and by the fall of 1934 posed a threat that Roosevelt could not ignore. Father Charles E. Coughlin, a Roman Catholic priest who broadcast his religious and social gospel from a Detroit radio station, claimed a following in the millions. Though he at first thought "the New Deal to be Christ's deal," he later attacked Roosevelt for trying to save capitalism. His weekly tirades against capitalism ("Modern capitalism as we know it is not worth saving. In fact it is a detriment to civilization.") and the National Union for Social Justice that he founded in November 1934 were supported by large numbers of people. It seems likely, however, that his skill as a demagogue rather than his social program was the source of his political strength.

Whereas Coughlin dazzled his audiences with the promise to restore prosperity and social justice through a program of nationalization, the visionary Francis E. Townsend stated that the same end could be achieved by granting everyone over sixty years of age a federal pension of two hundred dollars per month. Although the proposal of the unemployed physician from Long Beach, California, was a cruel hoax, it nevertheless attracted a large following of old folks. Townsend Clubs were started in the summer of 1934 and by December the backers of the movement claimed that there were clubs in every state and that a petition that promoted legislative enactment of their program had been signed by 20 million people. These statements were probably gross exaggerations, but there is no doubt that Townsend had captured the loyalties of a sizable number of people—his paper, the *Townsend National Weekly,* had a circulation of more than 200,000.

The most serious threat to Roosevelt and the most flamboyant of the demagogues, however, was Senator Huey Long of Louisiana. Under normal social conditions Long's personal characteristics, which were both amusing and exasperating, and his political program would have made little impact outside his own state. The depression, however, had created poverty, misery, and despair on a scale never before experienced in America. Huey Long was quick to exploit the people's plight. In the early 1930s, his program for sharing the nation's wealth had a magnetic appeal. Long claimed that the mal-distribution of wealth was the cause of all social distress and this diagnosis was readily accepted by the man on the street. By 1934, Long was proclaiming that the government should take by taxation the vast fortunes of the wealthy and use the expropriated money to provide each family with a "homestead allowance" of $5,000 and a yearly income of $2,000. His talent as a demagogue and the appeal of economic security thus produced widespread popular support for Huey Long; Roosevelt's advisers predicted in 1935 that Long would receive 3 to 4 million votes as the head of a third party. However, before the prediction could be tested against actual election returns, Long was assassinated.

Later, in the 1936 Presidential election, the threat caused by Townsend and Father Coughlin eased as they joined forces along with Gerald Smith (the man who H. L. Mencken called "the greatest rabble-rouser since Peter the Hermit") in support of the Union party of North Dakota's William Lemke. The alliance proved unworkable because Townsend, Father Coughlin, and Smith feuded among themselves and alienated pro-spective voters with anti-Semitic and pro-Fascist statements. Smith, disowned by both Townsend and Lemke, ended the campaign in a Louisiana jail, where he was put on election eve for disturbing the peace and using obscene language. Father Coughlin announced that he wanted to "close the campaign by apologizing . . . for words which ordinarily do not issue from the lips of a gentleman." In the early 1930s, however, Roose-velt had to rely on his political intuition about how the American people would respond to the political panaceas proposed by these three men. He did know, however, that the one man who could have fused the dissident followers of Townsend and Father Coughlin into a powerful political force was now dead.

Roosevelt's New Deal had started with a flurry of legislative action and Americans were momentarily hopeful that the depression would soon be over. By the fall of 1934, however, hope had given way to doubts about the adequacy of the New Deal—it was obvious that economic recovery was still a distant dream. The government had failed to restore prosperity and even those parts of its program that at first seemed successful were beginning to flounder badly. The National Industrial Recovery Act, which was intended to be the backbone of Roosevelt's recovery program, was not working out as the President and the liberals had expected. The original purpose of NRA was to facilitate cooperation between industry and labor in an effort to keep prices and wages from falling too low. Instead, large corporations were using the provisions of NRA to drive their smaller competitors out of business, and section 7a, the provision that guaranteed workers the right to organize and bargain collectively, was not consistently enforced by the administration. Labor reacted to NRA by calling it the "National Run Around" and liberals began to complain that Roosevelt was betraying their cause.

The President's prestige was further undermined in February 1934 when the Civil Works Administration had to be dismantled for reasons of economy. With over 20 percent of the labor force out of work, the liberals understandably reacted bitterly to Roosevelt's decision to end a program that was providing employment for 4 million men. Norman Thomas, the leader of the Socialist party, organized a march on Washington in protest. Many conservatives agreed with Governor Alfred M. Landon when he wrote: "This civil-works program is one of the soundest, most constructive policies . . . and I cannot urge too strongly its continuance." [1] At the same time, Roosevelt was coming under attack because he was not goading Harold Ickes, who was slowly organizing the Public Works Administration, to act more swiftly. The substance of the President's Securities Act also irritated the liberals; they wanted the government to take a stronger hand in controlling investment. The liberals felt that such a policy would be consistent with what they perceived as the philosophy of the New Deal, but instead of reconstructing the financial system along lines that would have facilitated economic planning, Roosevelt attempted to revitalize the competitiveness of the system. The editors of *The New Republic* expressed the liberals' frustration with Roosevelt when they wrote in March 1934: "Every action of his which seems to indicate a move to the Left is counterbalanced by another which moves to the Right." [2] By October the liberals were thoroughly disenchanted with the President. "Like the business cycle itself," *The New Republic* editorialized, "President Roosevelt's policy seems to pursue a rhythmic course. . . . He has never taken any real power from capitalism or threatened its prerogatives in any essential way. . . . Mr. Roosevelt can with reason assure capitalism that it will not be upset by him. What he cannot promise it is that it will not destroy itself." [3]

It was obvious that Roosevelt's political philosophy needed reappraisal. The early program of the New Deal had been built on the principles of "new nationalism," first articulated by Herbert Croly and popularized by the President's uncle, Theodore Roosevelt. New nationalism was predicated on the principle that the concentration of political power in the federal government would act as a counterbalance to the economic power of large corporations. Big business would not be atomized as the earlier progressivists had advocated, but corporations would be allowed to grow even larger—always under the watchful eye of the protective state. The NRA exemplified Roosevelt's attempt to utilize this principle in fighting the depression. His early hope had been to create a partnership between government and business so that the efficiency of large economic units could be directed toward speeding the economic recovery of the whole society. As it became more evident that businessmen were resisting such control and even manipulating the codes of the NRA to their own advantage, Roosevelt began a painful reappraisal of the partnership he had been trying to form. By the fall of 1934 he was convinced that most businessmen "can't see farther than the next dividend."

While the President was trying to make up his mind about how best to bring the business community into line with his New Deal, the nation drifted without a coherent program for recovery. The period of drift began in midyear and lasted until early 1935; it was both the nadir and a turning point of the New Deal. For liberals who had continually warned Roosevelt against the dangers of trying to cooperate with business, it was an especially exasperating period. The level of unemployment was about 21 percent of the labor force, and there were no signs that the situation would improve. The growing popular support of demagogues like Coughlin, Long, and Townsend served as a further reminder that if national recovery did not come soon, America might be the scene of the kind of political upheaval then taking place in Germany, Italy, and Austria.

The Social Frontier:
Forum for the Social Reconstructionists

It was during this period of grim uncertainty that Norman Woelfel and Mordecai Grossman had suggested to Kilpatrick that they publish a journal that would galvanize the classroom teacher into active participation in building a new society. For the reform-minded educators events moved rapidly. In the spring of 1934, the men who became members of the journal's Board of Directors quickly pledged financial support, and two small foundations donated $900. The members of the social reconstruction group met once a month during the spring and summer and hammered out the journal's organizational structure and format. Woelfel recalled later that although editorial policies were seldom discussed at these meetings, names of people who could be expected to write articles were frequently suggested. Using Woelfel's New York apartment as the journal's office, mailing announcements were sent out to selected names all over the country. Reminiscing about the more than 2,000 subscriptions that came in for the first issue, Woelfel said, "The time was ripe for the enterprise." Indeed, the response exceeded the most optimistic expectations.

When the first issue of *The Social Frontier* was mailed to subscribers in October, the journal's organizational structure included a twenty-seven-man Board of Directors and a three-man editorial staff headed by Counts. The Board of Directors, which included John Dewey and Sidney Hook, held monthly meetings during the first year to discuss the journal's business operations. Woelfel later said that he could recall no critical discussion of the journal's editorial policy by the board. Counts, Grossman and Woelfel determined the contents of the editorials at dinner meetings held two weeks before the journal went to press. The associate editors usually outlined the editorials and then presented them to Counts for approval. "I can remember," recalls Woelfel, "no single time when Dr. Counts suggested changes."

From the beginning the journal contained articles and editorials redolent with crusading zeal. The sponsors intended *The Social Frontier* to provide a rallying point for those educators who were receptive to the idea of using the school to bring about immediate social reforms. The journal attempted to alert its audience to the weaknesses of both the capitalistic system and the programs of the New Deal. The reasoned criticism of the editors indicates that they were much closer in their thinking to the large group of radical liberals who were then leaning heavily toward socialism than they were to the messiahs like Huey Long and Father Coughlin. The sponsors of the journal also set out to state the immediate goals of social reconstruction and the most effective methods the schools could use to work toward them.

In order to gain support among the uncommitted educational theorists for their social program—which required, among other measures, that capitalism be replaced by economic collectivism

—the journal's three editors and the most frequent contributors directed their criticisms at what they regarded as the three most obvious failures of the capitalistic system. Although they believed that the failure of capitalism to utilize fully and consistently the benefits of technology was very significant, the social reconstructionist writers gave this shortcoming by far the least attention. Liberals had already devoted a number of books to the exegesis of this subject (for example, *Whither Mankind* [1928] and *Toward Civilization* [1930] by Charles Beard and *Individualism Old and New* [1929] by John Dewey), and the contributors to the journal felt that further elaboration was unnecessary. Consequently, the other two failures, the immoral and miseducative effects of capitalism, received the most attention in the pages of *The Social Frontier*.

The social reconstructionists were directly concerned with the moral effect of capitalism on the individual; they believed that the profit motive had a particularly pernicious effect on individual morality. Kilpatrick was especially critical of this facet of capitalism. His interpretation of a profit motive economy differed markedly from the classical theory. Classical economists held that free competition would sufficiently reward individual effort and that both the production and distribution of wealth would thus be carried on at the most efficient level. Kilpatrick and the many other reconstructionists who shared his view thought differently. An economy predicated on the profit motive, they decided, produces and distributes goods essentially for the sake of private gain and not for the more laudable purpose of serving the needs of all the people. The capitalistic stress on individual self-interest, Kilpatrick maintained, encourages a general disregard for the public welfare, which results in political corruption and debasement of consumer taste for the sake of profit.

Laissez-faire capitalism posed a still greater threat: the loss of economic security for vast numbers of people. Without employment and adequate income the individual's freedom to pursue a full life was thwarted. Kilpatrick recognized that in previous centuries limited resources had forced man to live under an economy of want. He observed, however, that the development of technology had made possible an economy of abundance that was capable of providing an adequate standard of living for all. Kilpatrick believed that the basic problem was now to create a new system of social values that would alter the manner in which the society distributed its wealth.

There was also a general consensus among the members of the social reconstruction group in their recognition that a basic difference existed between their conception of freedom and the one held by the business community. In one of their more moderate moments, the editors of *The Social Frontier* summed up this difference:

> Freedom does not exhaust itself in the socially guaranteed right to buy and sell at a profit. It means rather a state of affairs which facilitates the optimum expression of all impulses and capacities of man. Where freedom to buy or sell seriously conflicts with the broader conceptions of freedom, the need for the elimination of the narrower meaning is clearly indicated.[4]

Although the social reconstructionists criticized capitalism for debasing the very cultural values they hoped to foster through education, they also took the schools to task for failing to develop a social philosophy that took into account the interests of the total society. Again Dewey spoke for the group when he charged that the school must assume responsibility for the negative effects of capitalism. Social drift and chaos, Dewey claimed, were being furthered by the school's emphasis upon an economic form of success that was intrinsically pecuniary and egoistic. By accommodating their activities to the wishes of conservative social elements, the schools had also assumed responsibilities in areas that possessed dubious educational value. The Daughters of the American Revolution, the members of the American Legion, and the religious fundamentalists, among others, had imposed their points of view on the schools with the result that flag saluting. singing of appropriate patriotic hymns, compulsory Bible reading, and loyalty oaths had become part of educational life in certain states. Dewey felt that such impositions on the educational process were furthering beliefs that scientific and technological progress had rendered obsolete.

In Dewey's view, the teacher occupied a pivotal position in society. The teacher could either help to perpetuate capitalism and its value system by refusing to recognize the corrupting influence it exerted on education or he could "throw himself in with the forces and conditions that [were] making for change in the direction of social control of capitalism." It was clear Dewey favored the latter course, which meant that the schools would deliberately set out to instill in the minds of the young the mental disposition to cooperatively control social change through the use of scientific techniques. Dewey was certain that when people learned to rely upon their own collective intelligence as the guide to social action instead of blindly following traditional mental and moral habits, capitalism would automatically give way to a cooperative form of social planning that would ensure that economic resources would be used for the benefit of all.

The editors and supporters of *The Social Frontier* were deeply concerned because the values nurtured in progressive classrooms were frequently in sharp contrast with the guiding values of the economic community. This discrepancy, they claimed, nullified the best efforts of teachers and confused the student at the critical time when he was unsure of which values to adopt. Kilpatrick noted that if the contemporary socioeconomic system makes material success the chief aim in life, it is extremely difficult for the teacher to broaden and deepen the student's aspirations. He thought that economic competition was especially harmful because it frustrated the teacher's efforts at character training. When achievement of material success appeared to depend on a dubious skill in obtaining wealth at the expense of others, ambitious and daring youth naturally sought out these roads of achievement. Furthermore, the educators' efforts in citizenship training programs were also hindered by an economic motive that placed individual above community interest. Kilpatrick believed that the contemporary socioeconomic system was making it increasingly difficult for the school to produce worthy members of the society. If the educator finds that the profit motive hinders and negates his efforts, then he must, concluded Kilpatrick, accept an enlarged responsibility in order to accomplish his work. The new and broader social responsibility that Kilpatrick called upon the educator to assume entailed the reconstruction of social values and institutions in order that the common good would take precedence over capricious individual gain.

The depression provided added weight to arguments in *The Social Frontier;* if the other criticisms of capitalism were not convincing, the depression's tangible effects on student health, appearance, and enrollment gave the arguments of the social reconstructionists even greater cogency. After he had ruefully observed that the fate of the schools had become too dependent upon the economy, George Beiswanger, head of the department of philosophy and social science at Monticello College, stated: "The economy, based on private profit and private ownership of the means of production, is now invoking economic sanctions against culture itself and against those institutions whose function it is to support and to raise the cultural level.[5] Sentiment among the social reconstructionists and their supporters was unanimous on this point: Education cannot thrive and help make society more humane if at the same time it compromises with the ethics of laissez-faire capitalism.

Although they subjected capitalism to intense criticism, the editors never thoroughly and systematically examined the New Deal's social philosophy as embodied in legislative enactments. Editorials were frequently directed at certain aspects of Roosevelt's program, but, for the most part, the more systematic evaluations appearing in *The Social Frontier* came from members of the journal's board of contributors and others who shared the same ideological persuasion. Dewey, unfortunately, did not use the journal to express his own opinion of the New Deal, but his views were widely circulated in other liberal journals. Dewey, however, did use the pages of *The Social Frontier* to denounce the Civilian Conservation Corps as a piecemeal action that left untouched the basic social, economic, and moral forces that had created the need for emergency measures and to support Norman Thomas, the Socialist Presidential candidate in 1932. Both these positions made it abundantly clear that he thought no "compromise with the decaying system [was] possible." Equally unfortunate was the failure of Boyd Bode, John Childs, and Bruce Raup to express their views on the New Deal's experimental efforts in the realm of social welfare. Those who did write about the New Deal evaluated its social philosophy in terms of the values of the social reconstructionists—values that were widely shared by the insurgent liberal movement in the 1930s.

In an evaluation of Roosevelt's social philosophy as represented in one and a half years of New Deal legislation, Henry Pratt Fairchild, a professor of sociology at New York University and a member of *The Social Frontier*'s board of contributors, lamented the lack of consistency in policy. Because Roosevelt was both a conservative in economics and a liberal in politics, his policies frequently demonstrated a lack of clarity about ultimate goals. Fairchild believed that the President's failure to abandon capitalism as a workable social system under modern conditions had nullified his recovery program.[6] Roosevelt had instead tried to preserve capitalism by designing his relief and recovery program to stimulate increases in profits and wages. Even though Fairchild lauded the Civilian Conservation Corps and the Public Works Administration because they indicated that the government was assuming a degree of responsibility for social welfare, he found that these agencies were in reality buttressing the old social order. The humanitarian relief programs were in the end actually profiting the wealthy. Rather than tax the rich to finance his relief program, the President had borrowed the money from those who could afford to loan it. Roosevelt had thus saddled the nation with an additional debt that would have to be paid as interest when the economy recovered.

Fairchild reserved his sharpest criticism for the New Deal's farm and labor policy. The social reconstructionists believed that the government should create new social institutions that would make maximum use of the material abundance produced by modern technology. Roosevelt, on the other hand, had deliberately created an artificial scarcity of farm products in order to facilitate the working of private capitalism in agriculture. The social reconstruction group also thought that labor-management conflicts should be replaced by the spirit of cooperation resulting from collective ownership of the means of production. This conviction led Fairchild to interpret Roosevelt's attempt to promote collective bargaining between labor and management as one of the "most disheartening features of the New Deal." Whereas the President may have thought he was adopting a liberal attitude toward labor, Fairchild contended, his conservative predilections, particularly his belief that capital and labor should be preserved as distinct and competing factors in the productive process, were actually intensifying antagonism and bitterness by promoting labor strikes. Fairchild concluded that the tragedy of the New Deal was its lack of a consistent social philosophy. The administration's humanitarian eagerness to minimize the sufferings of the victims of the old order had not been supported by an equal desire to abolish the order that made such suffering inevitable. He was certain the New Deal's failure to propose a genuine program of reform would eventually lead to the collapse of capitalism.

Broadus Mitchell, another member of the journal's board of contributors, was also scornful of the New Deal. As an associate professor of economics at Johns Hopkins University and as the Socialist candidate for governor of Maryland in 1934, Mitchell was deeply concerned with the problems confronting the federal government. Through the haze of ideological confusion, Mitchell thought it was possible to discern three characteristic features of Roosevelt's program. First, the program was the result of necessity, not of deliberate design. Second, Roosevelt's improvisations followed historical trends already established, that is, when it relaxed the antitrust act the administration was simply recognizing a "progressive" concentration of industrial and financial control. Third, the New Deal attempted to buttress the profit system, not discard it. Mitchell was reluctant, therefore, to say that there was anything worthwhile in New Deal policies. Even the Tennessee Valley Authority, an experiment that many thought a hopeful portent, did not escape Mitchell's vindictive criticism: ". . . in reality, the TVA betrays the disabilities of its more suspected companion projects . . . the TVA consumes the Muscle Shoals kilowatts in trivialities—table toasters, percolators, curling irons, window screens that electrocute mosquitos and house flies." [7] In spite of its lack of balance, Mitchell's criticism was fundamentally perceptive—for a healthy social order does not spurn the greatest effectiveness attainable in the production of goods and services by wasting its resources on relatively insignificant consumer items.

Reviewing the first two years of Roosevelt's administration, the editors observed that the nation was little better off than it had been when the President took office on March 4, 1933. Roosevelt had been unwilling to exert vigorous leadership when the time was propitious for giving the people a true "new deal"—economic socialization. Relief measures like WPA and TVA were soporifics, substitutes for an authentic New Deal. The editors thus found themselves unable to refute the Communist and Socialist charge that Roosevelt was attempting to buttress the business system by introducing "spurious benevolence." What might Roosevelt have done during these years? Did not a real new deal mean revolution, a sharp break with traditional practice and thought? To their own questions, the editors answered that Roosevelt could have initiated a social revolution consistent with American traditions. The President could have used the press and radio to educate the people to accept the transformation to a socialized economy. "What would have stopped Roosevelt with his marvelous political equipment and his ingratiating personality from exercising effective leadership in this direction at a time when great masses of people were desperately ready for almost anything?" [8] The editors of *The Social Frontier* firmly believed that nothing could have prevented Roosevelt from creating the institutions of a new America by the end of his first term in office.

Oddly enough, *The Social Frontier* never printed a statement that clearly delineated the specific goals that would be achieved through social reconstruction, although a number of the early articles and editorials give a general picture of the kind of society that the editors were urging teachers to build. There are two possible explanations for the journal's failure to give a definite policy statement on social goals. First, the journal was dedicated to arousing teachers to react to social problems, and a detailed, reasoned policy statement would have been out of place in the vitriolic and historically deterministic editorials that were designed to achieve this objective. Second, the social reconstruction group undoubtedly took for granted the social philosophies of the more prominent contributors, and they probably thought that a more complete exposition of their educational and social goals was unnecessary for most of the readers of the journal.

The social reconstruction group concluded that only a truly democratic society would have the self-reconstructing capacity necessary to provide the optimum opportunities for educational growth. Only the truly democratic society would depend on a new form of education to shape the experience of the young so that they could make their own contribution to the ongoing social process. The truly democratic society would not aim at simply passing on old habits and values but would try to ensure that new values, related only to the current experience of society, would be formed anew by each generation. The reconstructionist educators maintained that before this society could be achieved the conservative institutions that obstructed social advancement would have to be replaced. Harold Laski later expressed this common belief, though in a more specific way, when he said, "the new education can only triumph where there is a change in the productive relations of society." [9]

Another of the journal's primary goals was the extension of democratic values into the economic realm. The editors believed that as long as capitalism prevailed, only lip service could be given to democratic principles. Declared Dewey: "The tragic breakdown of democracy is due to the fact that the identification of liberty with the maximum of unrestrained individual action in the economic sphere, under institutions of capitalistic finance, is as fatal to the realization of liberty for all as it is fatal to the realization of equality. It is destructive of liberty for the many," he concluded, "precisely because it is destructive of genuine equality of opportunity." [10] The social reconstructionists believed that democracy could be restored if the socioeconomic structure were modified in such a way that technological developments would harmonize with the emerging pattern of social behavior that emphasized cooperation. At the same time habits of individual acquisitiveness would be replaced by the progressive habits of mutual interest and cooperation. It was an article of faith for the reconstructionists that a socialized economy, unlike the economy of capitalism, would be democratically used in the interests of all, rather than for the benefit of only a few.

In the new social order envisaged by these reform-minded educators, the institution of property was to be fundamentally altered by the initiation of social ownership of the means of production. Dewey observed that the goals of democratic liberalism "can be obtained only as the control of the means of production and distribution is taken out of the hands of the individuals who exercise powers created socially for narrow individual interests." [11] Purged of selfish and reactionary elements, the new classless society would provide a cornucopia of wealth for all. Most of the prominent contributors to the journal, including George Counts, William H. Kilpatrick, John Dewey, Sidney Hook, John L. Childs, and Harold Rugg, felt that this fundamental alteration in the economic structure would have to be achieved before the schools could succeed in reconstructing other social values. The primary problem that confronted them involved obtaining the cooperation of all classes—especially the privileged upper class—to construct a socialistic economy consonant with the nation's democratic ideals. Because democratic cooperation was the key to the self-repairing society, the social reconstructionists could not, without jeopardizing the very principle of democracy they wanted the school to instill, employ undemocratic methods of coercing groups that did not want to restructure society along socialistic lines. Unfortunately, they were never able to resolve this basic conflict. The methods advocated in the early years of the journal suggest that some social reconstructionists were unaware that the problem even existed.

The Social Frontier strongly advocated that educators should immediately take an active and continuing part in social reconstruction. Not only did the journal feel that the schools should be used to obtain specific social objectives, but the contributors also believed that even after the present problem had been resolved, it would be necessary for the schools to work continually on the frontier of social change. Goodwin Watson echoed this point of view when he declared that he could not separate social development from the educational process. He abolished all distinction between the two when he said, "education is society in the process of becoming." In order for education to be the "cutting edge of an advancing civilization," it must have a social philosophy relevant to the social needs of the time. The social philosophy adopted by education would then find appropriate expression in a new curriculum.

In contrast to the easy acceptance of views on capitalism and on the general goals of social reconstruction, ideas concerning the methods the school was to use to effect desired social reforms were discussed in detail in *The Social Frontier*. Capitalism had been sharply criticized and doomed to historical oblivion, but there had not been a single dissenting voice to argue its positive aspects or to hold out the possibility of its social usefulness in a modified form. There were virtually no articles in *The Social Frontier* that questioned the characterization of capitalism as a social device that was employed by reactionary elements to retain their position of affluence and power and to arrest social progress.

In a similar manner, the virtues of economic collectivism had been accepted without an analysis of the social, political or psychological problems involved. For instance, the restrictions that economic collectivism would impose on certain freedoms traditionally cherished by liberals were not considered. For the social reconstruction group, collectivism represented a progressive state of social development in which public morality and cooperation would make it possible for education to take its rightful place in the vanguard of social progress. At first it appeared that there was going to be the same uncritical agreement on the methods the school should use to rebuild society. After February 1936, however, when the editors turned to class warfare as the solution to this problem, the facade of unity was broken by factionalism within the social reconstruction group itself. As a result, the proposals for social reform were given a detailed analysis and evaluated in terms of both the educational philosophy of experimentalism and the social goals that were sought by the reconstructionists.

With an optimism characteristic of many advocates of the social progress doctrine, the editors had announced in the first issue of *The Social Frontier* (October 1934) that the age of individualism in economic activity had ended for Americans and that the age of collectivism had begun. As evidence, they pointed out that the nation had already made the transition from the rural and self-sufficient economic units characteristic of the Jacksonian era to the integrated and highly complex economy of the early 1930s. They viewed the years immediately ahead as a period in which the American people would be called upon to make historical choices entailing significant programs of social reconstruction. Although they believed that social collectivism was imminent, they thought that the American people had to choose whether or not the transition would be characterized by social strife. If such strife occurred, the social reconstructionists firmly believed, the tradition of democracy would disappear with the individualistic economy to which it had been historically linked. A peaceful transformation to the new system, on the other hand, would guarantee the survival of democracy in an age of close economic interdependence. To the extent that education dealt with the social realities involved in the transition, it would have, the journal editorialized, a responsible part in facilitating the people's choice. On the other hand, if educators ignored their responsibility to teach social issues, they would unwittingly serve the conservative cause because their lack of concern would retard the process of adjusting the democratic ideal from an individual to a social basis. Educators could not remain neutral; they would all have to make broad choices concerning which alliances should be consummated, which values should be preserved, which interests should be defended, and which social goals should be achieved.

Although they asserted that the final decisions would have to be made by the American people, the editors nevertheless committed the journal to the task of consolidating the power of those educators who were convinced of the historical inevitability of collective planning and control. To pursue this objective, the editors dedicated the journal to promoting the "broad role of education in advancing the welfare and interest of the great masses of people who do the work of society—

those who labor on the farms and ships and in mines, shops, and factories of the world." [12] The journal also declared that it would work to unite educators with other progressive groups to ensure that society was raised from insecurity to security, "from the lurid contrast of vulgar luxury and dire want to the shared abundant life made possible by technological advance." [13] The editors repeated Counts' suggestion that the social crisis gave the teachers an excellent opportunity to bid for control of the process of rebuilding society, but they questioned whether teachers would have the courage to assume this responsibility.

The editorials in the November 1934 issue of *The Social Frontier* continued in the same vein; they reaffirmed the journal's belief that the rise of collectivism was irrevocable. At the same time, the editors felt it necessary to admonish educators to face the fact that they had a moral responsibility to clarify the social issues and to align themselves with progressive social forces. The heavy emphasis on historical determinism and the dogmatic tendency to automatically associate all things progressive with good and all things conservative with evil, however, failed to shed needed light on the social realities with which President Roosevelt was trying to deal. The editors also failed to illuminate the educational issues implicit in the suggestion that educators become involved in ideological conflicts —for example, how propaganda and knowledge were to be kept separate in the classroom and whether or not educational involvement in ideological disputes would arrest the immature student's development toward self-determination.

By December, however, the editors were ready to give more specific instructions concerning the preparation of the public mind for participation in modifying economic, political, and social institutions. Educators, they claimed, could contribute to reshape the public mind by vigorously "disseminating" such ideas as these: (1) When the freedom of a small group carries as a consequence the impoverishment of life for the bulk of the population, the freedom of that group should be curtailed.

(2) The champions and carriers of freedom are industrial workers, farmers, teachers, and all other persons engaged in performing useful services. (3) The rise of technology renders individual economic freedom unworkable, and only collective ownership and democratic control of the wealth of the nation will guarantee freedom.[14] Although the editors did not use the term indoctrination, it is clearly implied, for such "dissemination" bears little resemblance to the educational functions of analysis and critical evaluation.

In January 1935, *The Social Frontier* published an article, "1,105,921," which represented a further development in the journal's position. The title referred to the total number of teachers in the country, and the editors suggested that most of these citizens belonged to an underprivileged section of the population that had been dispossessed of political power. Because this vast number of teachers possessed significant influence on the destiny of the schools and also had immense potential political power as a unified body dedicated to a definite social philosophy, the editors maintained that it was necessary to reconsider the old question of whether the school should follow or lead in the process of cultural change. They firmly declared that *The Social Frontier* would reject any simple and dogmatic answers to this question. Nevertheless, the editors promptly rejected the traditional idea that the school should limit itself to transmitting knowledge and values accumulated and tested in the past on the grounds that it did not allow the student to test ideas and values in terms of his own experience.

The editors next examined the Marxian idea that the school is a reactionary tool used by the dominant class to resist change. They found that the main difficulty was the Marxist belief that all education represents a form of indoctrination carried on by the dominant class. If this were true, education could not be used by the nondominant social elements to reconstruct society. The editors quite naturally rejected this position and instead took the stand that social and educational problems were indistinguishable. In order to resolve the problems that arose in the classrooms, therefore, educators would have to assume responsibility for improving the total society, and the school would be their special instrument in this crusade. The editors also took exception to Marx's idea that the history of man has been a history of two juxtaposed and antagonistic classes, although they did admit that the nation's growing oligarchy of wealth was creating a class society. Their primary desire, therefore, was to abolish all vestiges of class in order to allow education to perform its function in a community of freely associating individuals. At this time, the editors considered their own position to be opposite that of the Marxists.

In formulating their solution to the problem of whether the school should take active social leadership or remain a passive follower, the editors acknowledged that the historically conservative role of the school would be a factor that would have to be overcome. In 1935, they wrote: "In the state now emerging organized education must take its place alongside the other great coordinate functions of industrial society and become an integral part of government. Indeed, it is already there, unconscious and blind though it may be, actually shaping things to come." Although the editors did not specify what they meant when they stated that education was already functioning as an agency governing social policy and change, they were undoubtedly referring to Dewey's belief that one of the school's tasks was the elimination of unworthy social values from the classroom environment. The editors wanted educators to recognize that their control over the school environment was actually a policy-making function and to direct their influence toward making a democratic-socialist society.

The fact that there were so many teachers exerted a strange fascination on the editors and caused them to become even more visionary about the potential political power of educators. The editors assured their readers that "if organized and conscious of their strength, they could wield enormous power.

They might even become an influence in the political life of the country, if they should so desire." [15] The editors believed that two factors contributed to the potential political strength of the teachers. First, educators possessed a strategic and organizational advantage over other groups, because there were distinct groups of teachers in every community in the United States. Second, as representatives of the major fields of knowledge, educators were particularly well equipped to deal with social issues. The 1935 article was concluded with an admonition to reform-minded educational theorists to use their power by identifying with the masses in a common cause.

In the same 1935 issue, Dewey answered the question posed in his article, "Can Education Share in Social Reconstruction?" with a qualified "yes." He believed the schools were incapable of literally building a new social order. If the schools allied themselves with progressive social movements, however, they would have a share in the process. Dewey felt that the historical trend toward collectivism had increased the possibility that a new society could actually be created. Interference with genuine educational freedom was a sign that reactionaries were trying to reverse this trend. It was inconceivable to him that anyone would consider it possible for the schools to adjust to the prevailing social conditions. The anomaly of unemployment and lack in a country favored with great natural resources could not be eliminated by accommodating the schools to existing social conditions. Dewey believed that those who did not choose to develop the intellectual and moral bases for a new society were little better than cowards.

Although Dewey felt that educators had a definite mandate to improve society, he did not suggest that others should embrace his social philosophy without criticism. Each educator had to formulate his own social values, although he should always be conscious that whatever his predilections he would be serving either the conservative or progressive cause. Unlike Counts, the potential political strength of educators did not interest Dewey. He was more directly concerned with those educators who were unconsciously obstructing social progress by drifting along without social convictions. Dewey felt that it was essential for each educator to examine intelligently the competing social values to determine which ones would improve man's moral and physical estate. Dewey thought *The Social Frontier* could facilitate this process by clarifying both the social issues of the thirties and the role of educational institutions during the crisis. Although Dewey placed greater stress on the use of intelligence than most of the social reconstructionists, he nevertheless often used phrases that conveyed the same sense of mission that characterized so much of the editorial writing. When he referred to teachers as "active and militant participants in the creation of a new social order," Dewey left the reader in doubt about the precise measures that the teachers were supposed to apply in order to attain this goal. Even though his enthusiasm resulted from an intense belief in the value of a socialistic society and in the intelligence of educators to arrive at the same convictions he had reached, one can discern in Dewey's writing a radicalism that he perhaps did not entirely intend to show.

In the early months of the journal's publication, Charles Beard, Merle Curti, and Sidney Hook (all three were loosely associated with the social reconstruction group) provided a broad historical and cultural perspective from which to view social reconstruction. Although Beard and Curti did not concern themselves with the specific role of the school, they nevertheless tried to show a historical precedence for revolutionary action when democracy appeared threatened. Beard outlined in broad terms the effect of economic values on the realization of the broader democratic values during the country's early history. He suggested that if educators wished to retain a democratic society they should study closely the writings of the Founding Fathers. Such a study could illustrate workable methods for applying democratic principles to changing social conditions. Curti was more direct. He stated that American history was replete with public figures who unequivocally subscribed to the right to revolt. Although the conservatives controlled the schools, Curti thought that educators should tell their students that the radicals, rather than the Daughters of the American Revolution and kindred groups, were the true inheritors of the American revolutionary tradition. Because Curti failed to specify his precise understanding of the term "radical," however, his article actually gave the educator little concrete guidance.

Sidney Hook's article made a more fundamental contribution to the journal's position. Although the editors had urged educators to identify their interests with those of the working class, they were not yet ready to accept the thesis that every social philosophy has a class orientation. Hook did not share their reluctance. Like Dewey, Hook thought that the dominant values of education, like those of the cultural milieu, historically had been the values and ideals of the dominant economic class. If new educational values were to be implemented, they had to be adopted by a large interest group or class who considered them the expressions of their needs and aspirations. Hook posed the problem of what class point of view education should adopt, apparently unaware that to suggest that educators had a choice negated his premise that educational values were the expression of the dominant class. Hook promptly dismissed both the conservative upper class and liberal middle class philosophies as possible sources of appropriate educational values because he believed they were incompatible with the new goals of education. Hook felt that only the working class was working for the realization of a classless society in which educational and social processes would be inseparable. He therefore urged the educator to adopt the working class philosophy, because it promised to extend the fullest educational opportunities for all. Hook had earlier described himself as an unaffiliated Communist "without dogmas," and at the time he wrote his article he still retained his belief in a communistic form of society.

Hook's article strongly implies the necessity for a class

struggle. If the ideal social philosophy for educators is identical with that of the laboring class, the inevitable opposition of other classes to such a philosophy would give the choice of methods to achieve educational aims crucial importance. Hook thought an educational policy of social experimentation was an unrealistic solution. It seemed unlikely that the privileged class would be willing to experiment with the hypothesis that its destruction would benefit the society as a whole. The only way for educators to aid social reconstruction, Hook suggested, was to promote the value of critical intelligence. In this way, the implications of the various class views could be evaluated, and the common values of both classes could be discovered. Even if Hook were correct in his analysis of a class society, it still is difficult to believe that the potentially threatened class would allow an intelligent examination of its views. Hook had argued in an article that appeared in *The Modern Quarterly* ("Why I am a Communist," April 1934), that it was possible to subscribe to a nondogmatic form of communism that allowed the free play of intelligence,[16] and there is little reason to doubt that he was sincere in this belief, but his faith in the efficacy of critical intelligence to persuade the entrenched classes to accept the communistic position seemed unrealistic. If the capitalist class remained recalcitrant, the Communist's only alternative would be a class struggle, and it is questionable that even Hook would accept a means that would destroy so many humanistic values.

The problem of indoctrination had been raised by Counts as early as 1932, and it continued to be a controversial issue for the social reconstructionists. To clarify the issue, *The Social Frontier* solicited articles on the educational implications of indoctrination from representatives of various political and educational philosophies. The journal's willingness to present more than one point of view contributed to a clearer understanding of the differences between indoctrination and education and provided significant insights concerning the value that was placed on the use of indoctrination by certain social philosophies. The editorial that prefaced the January 1935 issue of the journal stated that the articles would use the issue of indoctrination as a point of departure to clarify the primary task confronting the schools. Indoctrination, the editors observed, could not be distinguished from the historical inculcation of patriotic and religious beliefs by special interest groups. The editors commented that the objections they had raised in the past were not directed against indoctrination itself, but rather against particular forms of indoctrination. During the late twenties, the editors noted somewhat cautiously, advocates of educational experimentalism, John Dewey and Boyd Bode, for example, had dismissed all forms of indoctrination as harmful. These critics had felt that values and meanings should be derived from the individual's own ongoing experience. Although they considered this position laudable, the editors felt that this view conflicted with the proposal that the schools be used to disseminate a new social ideal.

Articles were submitted by F. J. Sheed, a Roman Catholic writer; Harry D. Gideonse, a University of Chicago economics professor; Earl Browder, general secretary of the Communist party of the U.S.A.; Lawrence Dennis, the associate editor of *The Awakener* and an advocate of fascism; George A. Coe, a former professor of religious education at Union Theological Seminary; and Boyd H. Bode, a progressive educator at Ohio State University and a long-time critic of progressive educators who tried to derive the aims of education from the needs and interests of the child. Of these six contributors, only Bode and Gideonse were opposed to all forms of indoctrination. F. J. Sheed asserted that it was foolish to depend upon human intelligence to discover man's purpose when it can only be revealed by God. He stated that one of the primary functions of the school is to preserve the Catholic faith by conscious imposition of God's will.

In another article, George A. Coe reasoned that indoctrination cannot be separated from the general process of education. Therefore the educator should consciously use it in the service of the whole community by promoting social and humanitarian values that would benefit everybody. Coe believed this conclusion implied that the students should be taught to see that capitalism stands in the way of a cooperative and equalitarian society. Lawrence Dennis bluntly stated the fascist belief that a humane civilization can be achieved only when the dominant elite gives direction to the rest of the people. "Whatever the elite impose on the people, they should use good educational technique to make the people like it." [17] Earl Browder made a distinction between progressive and reactionary indoctrination. The Communists were compelled to use indoctrination by the schools as one method of counteracting the influence of reactionary groups. Browder concluded that indoctrination in the schools was incidental to the party's larger task of guiding the class struggle. Changing the methodology of schools would therefore remain a secondary priority until the revolution succeeded.

For those educators who were vacillating between promoting the social reforms advocated by the social reconstruction group and relying on the efficacy of individual intelligence, Bode's article was more helpful than the others. He thought the schools could not remain indifferent to economic and social problems, but he was unwilling to accept the solutions offered by *The Social Frontier* and its followers. Bode thought the editors had been blinded to the broader issues by their indignation over the inequity of the distribution of wealth. The values of capitalism were clearly undesirable, but the major task for educators was to estimate the comparative value of different kinds of "liberties" and "opportunities." Bode felt that the editors had failed to provide a criterion for assessing the worth of such values as initiative and resourcefulness, which had been successfully nurtured in the past by capitalistic competition. In Bode's opinion, these values were as worthy of preservation as any values that would derive from a more equitable distribution of wealth. Bode was the first of the reconstructionists to recognize that if social reform were limited to a simple reshaping of the economic values of society, the result would be a hollow victory.

Like Dewey, Bode thought all values have their origin in individual experience and therefore are relative. Each individual thus becomes responsible for formulating his own values. The final success of any program of social reconstruction, Bode believed, should therefore be measured in terms of how much it contributed to individual self-discovery of values. Given this emphasis on individual judgment, it is not surprising that Bode unequivocally rejected the proposition that the schools be used as an agency to promote a previously determined social program. Bode was firmly convinced that education could only be carried on in an atmosphere that included no fixed or final ends; he felt that education becomes a sham if conclusions of the educational process are decided in advance. Bode wanted to emphasize the process of education, or to put it another way, learning how to think. This emphasis implied, in Bode's view, that the teacher fulfills his responsibility when he provides conditions conducive for learning without trying to achieve a predetermined outcome. Direct participation in social action, he maintained, should be left to the discretion of the individual.

The issue on indoctrination was concluded with an editorial statement. It rejected on behalf of *The Social Frontier* the view that the schools should dogmatically inculcate a fixed body of social doctrine. Nevertheless, the editors also stated that objectivity in the schools' approach to controversial issues was equally unacceptable. The teacher could only avoid the dangers of either approach by consciously formulating his own social philosophy. Reference to this philosophy would then determine which social values were to be introduced to the student. The editors maintained that the ideals of individualism and collectivism were diametrically opposed and thus found themselves in fundamental disagreement with Bode on yet another issue. After dealing with these theoretical considerations, the editors exhorted teachers to substitute human rights for property rights and security for social anarchy. In addition to expounding the vague generalizations that succeeded in glossing over the important issues raised by Bode, the editors thus introduced a new element of radicalism.

The editors anticipated the objection that teachers were not qualified to participate in the task of social reconstruction, but in doing so they demonstrated an increasing intellectual irresponsibility by asserting: ". . . the teachers of the country should accept the responsibilities of their calling and proceed to battle for the faith that is in them. They will receive their education in the course of the battle." [18] Although the editorial was motivated by a desire to mitigate the social abuses caused by a selfish form of individualism, it was becoming clear that the means the editors now proposed to use in reforming society would not lead to an enduring and viable social life. The editorial staff refused to acknowledge the inevitable dilemma. If most individuals were not capable of critically formulating their own social values, educators or perhaps some other less benign group would continually have to come to the aid of a faltering society by imposing their own social philosophies on the educational process. Such a condition would be contrary to the social reconstruction group's original intent.

In the February 1935 issue, Dewey responded somewhat indecisively to the challenge of indoctrination. He agreed with the editors' assessment of the social conflict and with their suggestion that educators needed to make a choice between opposing social orientations. Dewey believed that the educators should not need to debate the social ends they wished to attain but instead should discuss the various methods of achieving them. In an obvious reference to Bode's position, Dewey said: "I cannot agree with those who think that making intelligence central in education signifies a neutral, aloof, and 'purely intellectual,' not to say mechanical, attitude toward social conflict." [19] Dewey cited his own case as an example of how the intelligent study of the way in which the advance of science and technology was creating new social patterns that would lead students to the same conclusions he had reached.

At the same time, however, Dewey refused to place as much faith in individual intelligence as Bode had done. There may have been a faint doubt in his mind that the student might not reach the same conclusions as the teacher without direct guidance. Dewey thus was torn between his admiration for the social ideal of collectivism and his repugnance for the use of indoctrination. Until the method of implementing the new orientation has been found, the whole subject of indoctrination would remain ambiguous.

Why did Dewey fail to acknowledge unconditionally the importance of the free play of the student's intellect? Although his interest in socialism suggests a partial explanation, the answer to this question relates more directly to a significant defect in his educational philosophy, that is, his penchant for identifying learning with problem-solving in a social milieu. Dewey correctly recognized that the social milieu conditions and directs the learner. He did not, however, conceive of education as a process that reinforces the critical intelligence of the immature student against the natural impositions of the social environment. Dewey's problem-solving approach to learning instead emphasized shared experience (his term was "conjoint activity") as the most effective way of thinking. This approach had the unfortunate effect of transferring the determination of solutions from individual to group control. Dewey's position was thus necessarily prejudicial against the critical and self-reliant individual who could be expected to exercise a large degree of intelligent control over the direction that his social philosophy takes.

In a polemical article that appeared in March 1935, John L. Childs questioned Bode's thesis that inculcation of a definite social outlook would retard the growth of the individual and the liberation of his intelligence. Childs wondered if Bode's respect for the right of the individual to choose his own beliefs was not a correlative of the historic policy of laissez faire and economic individualism. The shift to a collective society, Childs reasoned, made the cultivation of a common outlook an imperative. Childs declared unequivocally that deliberate inculcation would actually produce individuals superior to those whose development had been left to unguided childhood experience. "Hence, the right of the individual to choose his own beliefs is not and should not be made an absolute." [20] Childs proposed to use social conditions as criteria for determining the kind of individual that education should create. The unfortunate effect of this proposal was to make the development of the individual dependent upon the educator's interpretation of the social realities.

The Social Frontier presented few new ideas during the rest of the publication year. Nevertheless it was not a period of quiescence for the journal—attention had merely been diverted to other less controversial topics. The editors observed at the close of the first year that although the journal had not brought about the new social order, it had at least challenged educational complacency and conservatism. For the most part the journal's challenge to reconstruct society had been repeated *ad nauseam* in an oversimplified form. Educators had merely been asked to declare themselves as either being for or against the new social order. After the arguments were presented there had been little development and almost no critical evaluation of the educational implications of the political strategy. If Bode's had not clearly rejected indoctrination, the reader would have been left with the impression that a unanimous agreement prevailed about the school's role in reforming society.

Other Groups and Other Forums

Social reformism in educational circles was not, however, limited to *The Social Frontier,* which had six thousand subscribers its first year. The Department of Superintendence of the NEA published *Social Change and Education* in 1935, after its Commission on Education for New Social and Economic Relationships had worked on the project since May

1933. Originally the department had hoped to place in the hands of local superintendents a handbook that would provide a "blueprint" for using the classroom as a laboratory where students could experiment with different ways to solve social problems. After it became apparent that the members of the commission could not agree among themselves on how to apply the Deweyan method of problem-solving to social issues, the department decided to present the nation's school superintendents with an analysis of recent social changes and suggestions for making the social studies curriculum more relevant to the social crisis.

There was general agreement among the members of the commission that the schools should foster a more intensive study of economic and social problems and should nurture the spirit of cooperation in the classroom. Unfortunately, the members could not achieve consensus on the degree of direct political involvement the school should assume. Three points of view were presented in the yearbook. The conservative faction held that the school should not actively work for the redistribution of wealth and income. The school's responsibility for social reconstruction, conservative members maintained, was limited to giving the people the facts needed for an intelligent understanding of social problems. The radical members of the commission declared, "To the extent that [the school] takes its social democratic ideals seriously, it will be obliged to join with those forces which are striving to build a cooperative worker's society." [21] Although the Department of Superintendence did not support the latter position, it was clearly sympathetic to a less radical form of social reconstructionism.

Nearly 210,000 teachers also read the NEA's report, *Social-Economic Goals for America*. This report was the work of a committee the NEA had created in 1932 to define the social goals that teachers should try to achieve. The report outlined the ideal society in broad generalities—it would guarantee physical and mental security, equality of opportunity, cooperation, freedom—but the authors did not describe the methods such a society should use to ensure that these goals would be achieved. The discussion of teacher responsibilities was more specific: Every teacher was to "make himself a student of these social-economic goals and interpret them to the people." Teachers were to act as catalysts, stimulating a vigorous discussion of social issues among the adults of the community as well as the children. The schoolhouse was to become, as Dewey had envisaged it, the center of the self-repairing community. Although the report avoided references to a class struggle and was silent on the issue of indoctrination, the authors did adhere strongly to the social reconstructionist's position that teachers should become leaders of social change.

Another NEA committee prepared a report, which was published in 1935, on how progressive school districts were conducting "social-economic education." Throughout 1934 and 1935 the NEA devoted an enormous amount of energy to the task of encouraging the classroom teacher to take a greater interest in social issues and to provide leadership in his community. At one time during this period ten subcommittees composed of leading educators from across the country, in addition to the NEA's research division, were hard at work preparing a more complete statement of the social ideals of America. The social reconstructionist group at Teachers College was obviously not alone in advocating that educators should become statesmen. Many superintendents and professors of education at other schools also held this belief, judging from the NEA's activities during this period.

Social reform was also the ideal of a group headed by Paul R. Hanna of Stanford University. This group prepared a pictorial magazine for use in social studies classes. The editors stated that the magazine's purpose was "to promote a realistic understanding of the basic activities and problems of American life, economic, political, social"; they also proclaimed that different sides of controversial issues would be presented, but they asserted that the magazine would leave "the reader free to formulate his own conclusions." [22] Sponsored by the NEA's

Society for Curriculum Study and supported financially by Lincoln School and Teachers College, the magazine, *Building America,* was sent out to high schools in the fall of 1935. Each issue was devoted to a particular social problem—for example, housing, food, men, or machines—and contained pictures, statistics, and descriptive accounts of the particular topic under examination. Generally the treatment of each topic was notably free from bias. It seems unlikely, however, that the editors could have failed to predict the student's attitudes after he was exposed to the magazine's issue on food (scenes of the destruction of foodstuff on the farm and pictures of hungry people in the city were juxtaposed). In the first year 7,000 subscriptions and 75,000 single copies were sold; 5,556 copies of *Building America* were used in California schools, 5,032 in Michigan and 4,816 in New York. The *Building America* series was on the fringe of the social reconstruction movement. Yet although it lacked the militant tone of *The Social Frontier* and the sense of mission that the social reconstructionists invoked in an effort to rally the teachers to action, it nevertheless yielded the most concrete results by involving a great many students in an analysis of the social crisis.

How radical were the social reconstructionist educators and how far to the Left were they in relation to other insurgent groups? For educational theorists to claim that "the rise of a collectivist order is irrevocable," that the national economy should be put on a production-for-use basis, and that Roosevelt had failed to fulfill his mandate to make revolutionary changes in American life, seemed both unduly radical and alarmist. Yet when the social views of educators are compared with those held by other dissident groups during the latter part of 1934, they appear to fall largely within the mainstream of liberal thought.

"Failure is a hard word. . . . Yet we believe," editorialized Alfred Bingham and Selden Rodman of the liberal journal, *Common Sense,* "the record indicates that nothing but failure can be expected from the New Deal." [23] This gloomy prognosis was made in September 1934, a month before the social reconstructionists launched *The Social Frontier,* and it was representative of liberals' attitudes toward President Roosevelt. Bingham and Rodman stated succinctly the source of the liberals' opposition to Roosevelt's program: "*Our* job is to take over the industries of this country so that a planned economy of abundance may be possible. *His* [Roosevelt's] job is to perpetuate a system of dead, frozen, stagnant capitalism, with a low standard of living for all, maintained by increasing dictatorship." [24] Heir to the Dewey-Beard-Veblen tradition of intellectual progressivism (the progressivism of national economic planning), *Common Sense* articulated the liberals' impatience with Roosevelt and conveyed their sense of urgency about getting on with the task of building a truly democratic society.

Most liberals agreed that socialism in some form was inevitable, but they could not agree on how to achieve it. A questionnaire sent out by *The New Republic* in April 1935 to ninety leading liberals—among them Lewis Mumford, Roger Baldwin, Henry Elmer Barnes, John Dewey, Louis Hacker, Horace M. Kallen, George Soule and Senator Robert F. Wagner—reveals how much disagreement existed in their ranks on the issue of method. Fifty of the liberals believed that socialism could be approached gradually through constitutional means, while the remaining number thought that the establishment of a socialist order would provoke forcible resistance by the reactionaries and that this could not be suppressed without violence.

Many of the liberals' proposals for wresting power from the reactionary classes and establishing a new society were similar to those sanctioned by *The Social Frontier*. In January 1935 the editors of *Common Sense* outlined a program for obtaining power. Progressive forces, they claimed, would have to adopt three weapons in order to shape a better world: (1) independent political action as a third party, (2) inner guidance from a disciplined corps, trained to secrecy and offensive tactics, (3) concentration upon the most advanced section of the country to both gain a foothold and to demonstrate a proposition.[25] Although there is no evidence to indicate that anyone ever acted on these proposals, they were significant for what they revealed about the current state of liberal thinking.

There was an obvious sense of urgency and of growing impatience with democratic methods, indicating that the strains of the depression were beginning to break many liberals away from their traditional commitment to reason as the best means of bringing about social change. Militant phrases like "alignment of forces" and "the battle for collectivism" began to appear with increasing frequency in the liberal journals, as well as in *The Social Frontier*. Even Dewey, the liberals' chief ideologue, adopted a militant tone in denouncing trial and error social experimentation; in warning liberals against settling for a "controlled and humanized capitalism," he declared that "no such compromise with a decaying system is possible."

The Dewey-Beard brand of liberalism had failed to provide a compelling plan for achieving socialism, and scores of intellectuals began to abandon the democratic methods that this philosophy had advocated. In communism they found the certainty that democracy could not guarantee them. However, the number lost to communism was small compared with the number of liberals who diluted their effectiveness by aligning themselves with such leftist political organizations as the Farmer-Labor Political Federation and the nascent political movement of the social reconstructionists. Throughout 1934 and early 1935, the social reconstructionists remained part of this larger radical liberal group. Although they were able to resist the appeal of the Communist solution, they frequently found that they, like many other liberals, were unable to muster arguments to refute the Communist claim that America was engaged in a class struggle.

The social reconstructionists received direct personal encouragement from leading liberals in their attempt to combine ideology with progressive educational theory. Dewey, of course, had long ago given a certain respectability to the practice of politicizing educational theory. Charles Beard had also supported the thesis that the schools could be used as an instrument of social reform; his position had been clearly stated in *A Charter for the Social Sciences* (1932). Many other liberals lent their names if not their direct support to *The Social Frontier* enterprise. In addition to Beard and Dewey, Merle Curti, Lewis Mumford, Henry P. Fairchild, and Broadus Mitchell were members of the journal's original board of contributors; Sidney Hook, Eduard C. Lindeman, and Harry A. Overstreet were on the Board of Directors.

Furthermore, during the first year of publication, the liberal and radical intellectuals who published articles in *The Social Frontier* were also leading contributors to *The Nation, The New Republic* and *Common Sense,* and they participated in public meetings held under the auspices of *The Social Frontier*. At one such meeting, Charles Beard, Heywood Broun, Louis Hacker, and George Counts gathered in the Rose Room of the Traymore Hotel in Atlantic City, New Jersey, to discuss "Steps Forward in Education." When, in an era of radicalism, the social reconstructionists proposed that teachers should organize and join other progressive groups who were working for a collectivist democracy, they were neither ridiculed nor dismissed by other liberals. Although the liberals promptly criticized the Townsend Plan and Father Coughlin's National Union for Social Justice, they were apparently willing to support the somewhat utopian proposals of the social reconstructionists. Indeed, there was even praise for the high quality of *The Social Frontier,* and the editors of *Common Sense* suggested on one occasion that "organized teachers" be included in a new third party that was to be made up of a coalition of leftist groups.

The loose alliance between the radical liberal and professional educator represented a new departure from the latter's traditional support of conservative causes. Though the liberals welcomed the change as a manifestation of the educator's growing social enlightenment, there is no indication that they fully understood the Promethean role the educators had assigned to themselves. Not satisfied to merely echo the liberals' positions, the educators came to advocate a more extreme course than the one they had already outlined for the schools and, in the process of doing so, demonstrated their independence of the liberal ideologues.

NOTES

1. Quoted in Arthur M. Schlesinger, Jr., *The Age of Roosevelt: The Coming of the New Deal* (Boston: Houghton Mifflin, 1959), p. 277.
2. "Mr. Roosevelt's First Year," *The New Republic,* LXXVIII (March 4, 1934), 117.
3. "Roosevelt Calms Capitalism," *The New Republic,* LXX (October 1934), 297–98.
4. "Champions of Freedom," *The Social Frontier,* I, 3 (December 1934), 9.
5. George Beiswanger, "The Atrophy of Education," *The Social Frontier,* II, 8 (May 1936), 246.
6. Henry Pratt Fairchild, "A Sociologist Views the New Deal," *The Social Frontier,* I, 1 (October 1934), 16–18.
7. Broadus Mitchell, "The Choice Before Us," *The Social Frontier,* I, 2 (November 1934), 14–15.
8. "The Roosevelt That Might Have Been," *The Social Frontier,* I, 3 (December 1934), 7–8.
9. Harold Laski, "A New Education Needs a New World," *The Social Frontier,* II, 5 (February 1936), 147.
10. John Dewey, "Liberalism and Equality," *The Social Frontier,* II, 4 (January 1936), 105–6.
11. John Dewey, "The Meaning of Liberalism," *The Social Frontier,* II, 3 (December 1935), 75.
12. "Orientation," *The Social Frontier,* I, 1 (October 1934), 4–5.

13. "Educating for Tomorrow," *The Social Frontier,* I, 1 (October 1934), 5.

14. "Champions of Freedom," *The Social Frontier,* I, 3 (December 1934), 9.

15. "1,105,921," *The Social Frontier,* I, 4 (January 1935), 6.

16. Hook develops his arguments for an undogmatic form of communism in "Why I Am a Communist," *The Modern Quarterly,* VIII, 3 (April 1934), 143–65.

17. Lawrence Dennis, "Education—The Tool of the Dominant Elite," *The Social Frontier,* I, 4 (January 1935), 14.

18. "The Position of *The Social Frontier,*" *The Social Frontier,* I, 4 (January 1935), 33.

19. John Dewey, "The Crucial Role of Intelligence," *The Social Frontier,* I, 5 (February 1935), 9.

20. John L. Childs, "Professor Bode on the 'Faith in Intelligence,'" *The Social Frontier,* I, 6 (March 1935), 23.

21. The Department of Superintendence of the National Education Association, *Social Change and Education* (Washington, D.C., 1935), pp. 24–25.

22. Robert E. Newman, Jr., *History of a Civic Education Project Implementing the Social-Problems Technique of Instruction* (unpublished Ph.D. dissertation, Stanford University, 1960), pp. 58–59.

23. "Franklin Delano Roosevelt," *Common Sense,* III, 9 (September 1934), 2.

24. *Ibid.,* p. 3.

25. "On Obtaining Power," *Common Sense,* IV, 1 (January 1935), 3.

CHAPTER

4

Educators and
the Class Struggle

June 1935 marked the end of *The Social Frontier*'s first year of publication. The prophecies of the earlier editorials were not yet fulfilled. America was no closer to becoming a collectivist democracy, and the classroom teachers had not emerged as a viable political force. That the journal had succeeded in sustaining a mood of revolutionary fervor among its staff and small circle of contributors and had fostered a somewhat one-sided discussion of the most pressing social issues could not be denied. The journal's effectiveness was, however, seriously hampered by the inability of the social reconstruction group to acknowledge the conflict inherent in a proposal to include both indoctrination and experimentation in the same program. If the social reconstructionists had used the pages of *The Social Frontier* to clarify the issues surrounding this problem, they might have had more success in their campaign to win over the uncommitted classroom teacher. As it was, they placed themselves in the paradoxical position of advocating the application of a philosophy of education that they assumed had been clearly worked out but that in fact had not yet emerged in a definitive form.

What has come to be called the second New Deal also began in June 1935. If the policies of the first New Deal were unacceptable to the educators, those of the second New Deal would turn out to be even more disconcerting. Ideologically, the social reconstructionists had been closer to the policy makers of the first New Deal than they had been willing to admit. The early New Dealers like Rexford Tugwell, Raymond Moley, Adolf Berle, and Donald Richberg had advocated reshaping America into a planning society with an organic economy, and such a society was akin to that envisaged by the social reconstructionists. The two groups also shared a similar temperament. "The First New Dealers," writes Arthur M. Schlesinger, Jr., in *The Politics of Upheaval,* "were characteristically social evangelists, with a broad historic sweep and a touch of the visionary, seeing America at a great turning point of its history." [1] Of the policy makers of the early New Deal only Rexford Tugwell remained in Washington after 1935, but by that time his influence had been sharply curtailed. The new advisors to the President were men of a different cast of mind and they promptly redirected the thrust of the President's program toward the restoration of economic competition.

After 1935, the social reconstructionists confronted governmental leaders who held a substantially different ideological position. The new members of the inner circle—Thomas Corcoran, Benjamin Cohen and James Landis—were supporters of Supreme Court Justice Louis Brandeis' thesis that the function of government is to maximize the freedom of the individual through federal regulation. Because they therefore accepted competitive economic enterprise as the basis of a healthy society, the personnel of the second New Deal were essentially conservative even though they opposed the interests of big business.

The changes in Roosevelt's program gradually became noticeable in the spring of 1935 but, as a reading of *The Social Frontier* will reveal, they escaped the notice of the educators. The editors of the journal were too busily engaged in espousing their own social program and in opposing the New Deal in general to notice that governmental policy was moving still further away from their own position. After the Supreme Court unanimously invalidated the National Industrial Recovery Act on May 27, 1935, the President finally ended months of temporizing and vigorously pushed through Congress a legislative program that left little doubt about how he intended to fight the depression. The Roosevelt administration had served notice that big business would no longer be regarded as its ally; business would now be regulated rather than cajoled.

Before *The Social Frontier* resumed publication in the fall, Congress had passed the Social Security Act legislation, which implied that the United States was moving in the direction of the protective state that Herbert Croly had outlined in *The Promise of American Life* nearly three decades earlier. When Roosevelt signed the National Labor Relations Act into law (July 5, 1935), he stated the purpose of the new legislation in typically Brandeisian terms: "By preventing practices which tend to destroy the independence of labor, it seeks, for every worker within its scope, that freedom of choice and action which is justly his." [2] Roosevelt also moved to undermine the support of the share-the-wealth schemes of demagogues like Long, Townsend, and Coughlin by offering Congress a new tax policy that would limit the further concentration of economic power.

The tax bill at least partially resulted from the President's bitter feeling that the wealthy had shirked their social responsibilities. Roosevelt revealed his mood by remarking sardonically at a press conference that it appeared the fifty-eight thriftiest people in 1932 "were all so thrifty that, although they had a millon dollars income a year or more, they paid no tax whatever to the Federal Government on thirty-seven percent of their net income." [3] At the same press conference, the President suggested that "tax avoidance" meant hiring a tax lawyer who would change the word "evasion" into the word "avoidance" for a fee of $250,000. Roosevelt's tax proposals caused intense public furor. Nevertheless, Congress was not allowed to adjourn until it had passed a holding-company bill designed to break up the great utility empires, a banking bill that marked a shift toward centralization of the banking system and federal control of banking, and the Guffey Act that brought the coal fields under federal regulation.

Once the President began to take decisive action in the summer of 1935, his political stock began to climb. Twenty percent of the nation's work force was still unemployed, but the momentum of the second New Deal began to restore public confidence. Pollsters of the American Institute of Public Opinion, who found that public support of the President had fallen from 69 percent in February 1934 to 50.5 percent in the summer of 1935, reported that it had climbed to 53 percent by October. Even long-time critic Charles Beard was impressed. "Seldom, if ever, in the long history of Congress," he wrote, "had so many striking and vital measures been spread upon the law books in a single session." Other liberals, however, were more reluctant to applaud the President's new show of strength.

The liberals could not agree with Roosevelt's belief that a just society could be built by imposing a welfare state on a capitalistic foundation. Much of the New Deal program appealed to the liberals: the social security system, the Tennessee Valley Authority, and the rural electrification program. They were also pleased by the President's attempt to regulate the "money changers." In their opinion, however, regulation was not enough; they wanted the capitalists driven from the temple altogether as the essential first step toward true social planning. At this time it seemed that the liberals were unwilling to compromise to obtain anything less than a planned society. Expressing indifference to the importance of Roosevelt's recent legislative enactments, the editors of *The New Republic* in mid-August 1935 wrote pessimistically, "Analyses of the New Deal as a failure in genuine social-economic planning have been made so many times that it is scarcely worthwhile to repeat them." [4] A compromise with capitalism was regarded as unthinkable. Other liberal journals remained equally cynical about the future of a competitive economy. "CAPITALISM is the breeder of wars," declared the editors of *Common Sense* in an article entitled "CAPITALISM: MURDER." [5] The intransigence of many liberals on this issue made a dialogue between the President and the liberal community difficult. Consequently, while a pragmatic Roosevelt was desperately experimenting with different methods for keeping the economy alive and expanding, the liberals would not abandon their doctrinaire position to assist the President by clarifying the intellectual issues that surrounded his attempt to combine the welfare state with capitalism.

One of the greatest dangers to Roosevelt's New Deal was suddenly eliminated in early September when a Baton Rouge doctor named Carl Austin Weiss assassinated Huey Long. Democrats had feared that Long would be a real threat in the 1936 election as a leader of a third party. The Senator's support had grown considerably in the spring of 1935; his following, which had previously been confined to Louisiana and neighboring states, had rapidly come to include discontented farmers in the prairie states. Even an estimated 100,000 voters in New York supported him. His staff claimed a mailing list of over 7.5 million persons. Although Democrats doubted the accuracy of this claim, they had no illusions about Long's ability to lure discontented party members away from Roosevelt. After Long's funeral, his followers fought for the leadership of the Kingfish's political machine, but none of them emerged as a comparable threat. Although the threat from the other important Pied Pipers, Father Coughlin and Dr. Townsend, remained, the President seemed, for the time being, to be more firmly in control.

The American political scene was further tranquilized by international events over which Roosevelt had no control. The Communists, viewing the spread of fascism as a mortal danger, called for a united front of progressive forces in a common struggle. Because they defined the New Deal program as one of the progressive forces, the extreme Left began to favor Roosevelt with less and less criticism.

Fear of fascism was the one thing that otherwise warring leftist groups had in common; and the Communists skillfully capitalized on this tenuous bond. In August 1935, the seventh world congress of the Communist International met in Moscow under the chairmanship of Georgi Dimitrov. The delegates were easily won over to Stalin's new antifascist policy. The discussion in *Pravda* of the new "democratic" constitution that was being prepared further convinced the delegates that Russia was the only genuine guardian of democracy. The core of Communist strategy was to form a united front of all the laboring classes against fascism. In the United States, the specific form this strategy would take was the creation of a Farm-Labor party. The major tactical difficulty was resolved when it was decided that it would be possible to win the support of the masses by portraying such reactionary groups as the American Legion, the Republican party and the DAR as enemies of the Constitution and of democracy. With great shrewdness, the Communists stressed the linkage between the present struggle and America's earlier revolutionary tradition. Convinced that they were the heirs of the Jeffersonian tradition, the American delegates returned home to convince others that "communism is twentieth-century Americanism."

The new image affected by the Communists produced a dramatic and immediate response. For intellectuals and party-less radicals who believed that fascism "represented the last

murderous impulse of a dying capitalism," as it was stated in
New Masses, the Communist policy represented a great step
forward in combating reactionary forces. Those intellectuals
who had not previously been able to tolerate certain Communist tactics or the typically colorless party functionary began
supporting the united front by becoming members of the party
or by participating in Communist front organizations. The
Communists' willingness to cooperate with the Socialists—
whom they had earlier described as "social fascists"—and
the liberalization of their tactics convinced many that it would
be unnecessary to "take communism away from the Communists," as Edmund Wilson had put it several years earlier.
Recalling his image of the party when he joined in 1935,
Granville Hicks said, "Party propaganda lost its Russian color-
ing and took on a flamboyantly nationalistic hue." Even
Mother Bloor, a long-time Socialist organizer, was moved by
the new Communist image. At a birthday party given in her
honor, she reportedly exclaimed, "Thank God, I have lived
to see a little sentiment in the Communist party."

The American Communists were also able to disarm the
traditionally wary Socialists enough to enlist a degree of cooperation. The decision to join the Communists in a united
front was not an easy one for the Socialist leaders to make;
and their ultimate choice created further disharmony within
Socialist ranks. Norman Thomas, leader of the party and a
member of the militant faction, thought it might be possible
to go along with the Communists on specific issues, but he
made it clear that he rejected completely their emphasis upon
violence and dictatorship. Even in making this decision
Thomas was filled with misgivings about the outcome of the
marriage. As he wrote in *The Choice Before Us:*

> Short of organic unity or a general coalition, the Com-
> munist and Socialist parties might logically be expected to
> work out a united front to achieve certain immediate ends
> upon which both sides are agreed. There is nothing illogical
> about an international united front against war and Fascism.

. . . But the Socialists of all countries are right in pointing out how difficult it is to have a united front with a party which openly boasts that good faith is a "bourgeois" virtue and which has proclaimed not once but repeatedly in its declarations of its international as well as its national bodies that the purpose of united front maneuvers is to undermine the Socialist parties and destroy Socialist leadership.[6]

In spite of his forebodings, the threat of fascism both at home and abroad appeared so grave that Thomas decided, over the objections of the old-guard Socialists, to join the united front. Time proved this decision wrong, and Thomas was quick to recognize it. He later concluded that it was both unwise and impossible to have any formal working arrangements with the Communist party.

At no time in American history was the Communist party so successful. Total membership rose from 24,500 in 1934 to nearly 41,000 during the heyday of the united front.[7] The number of fellow travelers was considerably larger. In addition, the Communist party also extended its influence by infiltrating and gaining control of numerous social organizations. Why were so many intellectuals converted to communism during this period, especially when the Russian purges were being given wide publicity? For many intellectuals, the Communist party offered a concrete program of action at a time when other political groups seemed only willing to talk. Intellectuals were also impressed by the Communists' absolute devotion to a cause, and they felt they were participating in the mainstream of history by joining the cause themselves. It appears that it never occurred to most of these idealistic but naïve intellectuals that the united front might be a device for strengthening Soviet foreign policy. It is much more difficult to explain how the intellectuals were able to rationalize the purges. The danger of a fascist takeover in America blinded some to the significance of the Russian experience. Others drew their rationalizations from the same kind of examination as Granville Hicks':

"If," I asked myself, "the worst that is claimed by the Trotskyites about these trials is true, what difference will it make to me?" And this was the answer I gave: "Even if the trials are complete frame-ups, it still remains true that Russia is on our side in the struggle against Fascism. Moreover, the good work we are doing here has no connection with what is happening in Moscow." [8]

The Social Reconstructionists in a Changing Political Climate

The social reconstructionists had set aside the task of building a new social order while the teachers were on summer vacation. Returning from their long recess in the fall of 1935, they set to work in a changed political atmosphere. The Communists were busily soft-pedaling their old themes of revolutionary violence and class struggle in order to gain liberal support for their united front policies against fascism; "democracy" and "peace" were their new rallying slogans. The social reconstructionists, like many other left-of-center liberal groups who did not follow the Communist party line but sometimes adopted similar positions quite independently, began to move in a direction that was now even too radical for the Communists. At the same time the Communists were moving toward a more moderate position for tactical reasons and proclaiming themselves to be in the Jefferson-Jacksonian tradition of militant reform, the social reconstructionists began to call upon teachers to assume responsibilities that sounded more Marxian than Deweyan.

Political theory became indistinguishable from educational theory as the editors of *The Social Frontier* (still Counts, Woelfel, and Grossman) attempted to set a bold new course for teachers. In "Teachers and Labor," an article that appeared in the October issue, the editors stated categorically that "there is no hope for the significant practice of education in a social order based on property and profit." The editors modified their earlier position, however, to state that teachers by themselves could not lay the foundations of a new society—they would have to align themselves with the workers in the factories and on the farms. Whereas a year earlier the editors claimed that a collectivist democracy would be created through the "deliverance of the historical process," they now thought it necessary to outline three steps that teachers would have to take immediately in order to give direction to the energy of the oppressed working class. First, teachers should organize themselves along the lines adopted by labor instead of along the more traditional lines. Second, teachers should participate actively in the labor movement by informing workers that the profit system was the source of their insecurity and poverty and that a "collective commonwealth" could only be achieved by "an aggressive stand of the underprivileged." "And finally," the editors continued, "in the classroom teachers might attempt to give their pupils, in the degree that it is possible in different communities, a labor orientation." The editors acknowledged that their proposals implied an advocacy of the class struggle and that some would consider involvement in such conflict inconsistent with the function of the teacher. They saw no real problem here, however. "If there should be violence," the editors continued, hoping to reassure those teachers who might be seriously disturbed by these extreme proposals, "the onus will fall on the shoulders of those few who cannot gracefully surrender their privileges in the face of a popular decision." [9]

Obscured by the discussion of a class struggle was an important educational problem: How does the teacher serve the common good of society? The editors alluded to it, but they were too preoccupied with social engineering to illuminate the nuances of this problem. Dewey himself had faced the problem but had created even greater confusion with his solution. Dewey stipulated that the school should overcome class distinctions by providing everybody with a common learning experience, but at the same time he contended that the teacher should arbitrate between competing social values by allowing into the classroom only those that meet his criterion of the ideal society. By declaring that "education is the fundamental method of social progress and reform," Dewey made the teacher a social partisan. The social reconstructionists had only to incorporate into their doctrine the idea that was already implicit in Dewey's writings—in order to serve the interests of all, the school must be used as an instrument against those social classes that cling to unhealthy social values. Illogical as this was, the social reconstructionists quietly accepted it, and education remained for them a class instrument. Now, however, it was to be wielded in behalf of the underprivileged.

In the next issue of *The Social Frontier* (November 1935), the editors acknowledged that some readers had expressed disapproval of the use of a class struggle "as a tactic of social reconstruction." The editors insisted that this criticism had not surprised them because "most teachers still glory in their professional status." The editors felt that teachers as a whole still believed that they were the servants of a classless public and that this notion was a "sufficiently potent prophylactic" to keep them from perceiving the existing social cleavages. After launching into another truculent attack on the evils of the capitalistic system, the editors concluded by saying: "The need now is not for bringing class struggle [sic] to an immediate issue, but rather for teaching the masses of farmers and workers about the facts and socially reconstructive possibilities of class divisions and conflicts." [10] The battle lines were now clearly drawn in the minds of the editors; the depression, the structure of American society, in fact every social issue was reduced to a conflict between two opposing classes, "those who *own* [the capitalists] and those who *create* wealth [the workers]." This gross reductionism clearly showed that the journal of the social reconstructionists had totally abandoned Dewey's experimental method. The editors had now only to claim Marx as their new spiritual guide.

Theodore Brameld, the author of *A Philosophic Approach*

to Communism (1933), suggested that they do just that. In "Karl Marx and the American Teacher," Brameld argued that liberal educators who accept the postulates about the evils of capitalism and the need for a collectivist democracy "must face the necessity—long postponed by most—of a frank, thorough consideration of the Marxian means to their common end." A study of Marx, Brameld assured his readers, would make educators aware of the inconsistency inherent in accepting Marx's analysis of capitalism while at the same time ignoring his method for bringing about radical social change. Marx had been more tough-minded. Unlike those who still cringed before the painful facts despite their additional fifty years of experience with capitalism, Marx had recognized the need to confront the barriers of custom, law, and police courageously and actively. Faith in the efficacy of the democratic method had not clouded his understanding of the bold means that must be used to overturn the established order. In contrast, declared Brameld, "The *Social Frontier* . . . opens itself to the accusation that it reprints in rosy colors the ideal of 'collective' control but neglects a frank examination of the strategy necessary for its attainment."

In order for teachers to become effective participants in the struggle, Brameld felt they had to understand the two propositions upon which Marx based his position: (1) "The opposition of the class in control of capitalist society is so tremendous that nothing short of counter-opposition frequently bordering upon, indeed crystallizing into, illegality will suffice to defeat it." (2) "When the ruling class is once replaced, a period of oppression will continue to be necessary until gradually the citizenry honestly comes to agree that collectivism is a better solution to our troubles than capitalism." The question, as Brameld saw it, was not whether the teacher can or cannot put into practice the tactics implied in these propositions; "the question is rather *in what degree can he?*" In drawing the implication of Marxian tactics for teachers, Brameld merely restated what members of the social reconstruction group had been advocating for some time: Unless teachers follow the old "philosophy of neutrality" they must "influence their students, subtly if necessary, frankly if possible . . ." and they "need to move much farther in the direction of class consciousness." He also advised teachers to rethink the moral issues involved in opposing capitalism. "Let us never resort to [violence] indiscriminately," continued Brameld on the fine points of Marxian tactics, "meanwhile, let us achieve by the vote all the rights we can. But let us not characterize violence categorically as immoral under all circumstances." [11]

Brameld did not, as some authors have argued, introduce the subject of a class struggle into the educational discussion. He merely stated in bolder terms the same ideas implicitly contained in Counts' *Dare the School Build a New Social Order?* (1932). As many readers could attest, class conflict had also long been an editorial theme of *The Social Frontier*. In fact, the idea was fast becoming conventional by the time Brameld raised the specter of a class struggle. Although it is not clear to what extent Brameld was expressing his own point of view —he failed to make a careful distinction between his own position and that of Marx—his article was a challenge to a small group of social reconstructionists who had moved to the far Left to acknowledge that they were Marxists and to stop paying lip service to democratic principles.

The editorial proposal that teachers indoctrinate their students with a "labor orientation" failed to evoke a response from labor spokesmen. Workers also failed to register enthusiasm for the suggestion that teachers provide the intellectual leadership for the labor movement. Even the *American Teacher,* the official organ of the American Federation of Teachers and the labor journal closest to the educational scene, ignored *The Social Frontier*'s offer to engineer a redistribution of the nation's wealth and power. There are a number of reasons for the labor movement's decision to forego a potential ally strategically placed in the classroom. First, the social objectives of the social reconstructionist group were more comprehensive and farther to the Left than those sought by labor. Like the Socialists and Communists, the social reconstructionist group never really understood that the leadership of the labor movement was primarily interested in challenging managerial power and obtaining for the workers a greater share of the wealth produced by the capitalistic system. They did not wish to overturn the system itself. Second, even though labor welcomed teachers who wanted to associate with their movement for bargaining purposes, the idea of indoctrinating students with social and political ideas was contrary to a cherished principle supported by the American Federation of Teachers—academic freedom. Most significant of all, the A. F. of T. was having difficulty with Communist infiltration.

The Communists had already taken control of its largest local, New York Local 5. The A. F. of T. could not, therefore, be expected to support any educational group that advocated the use of undemocratic methods to achieve social aims, and it was even less inclined to accept a proposal to bring the class struggle into the classroom. It must also be noted that other liberal and leftist groups did not come to the support of *The Social Frontier*'s editorial position. *The Social Frontier* found itself in an unusual position; editorially it was too radical for labor, and the Communists did not think the schools could be effectively used for revolutionary purposes because Marx had rejected them as an instrument of the dominating class. Consequently, the journal's offer to guide the class struggle was generally ignored.

At this juncture, the social reconstruction group had jettisoned both democratic principles and the experimental method and had thus moved outside the mainstream of radical liberalism. The large number of liberals who had not come under the control of the Communists remained critical of Roosevelt's policies and his lack of a comprehensive social philosophy. On the other hand, they were quite definitely unwilling to abandon democratic methods to effect social change.

In February 1935, a month before the Communists were out-voted 4 to 1 by the National Socialists in Germany and six months before Stalin convened the Seventh Congress of the Communist International to proclaim the new policy of the united front, the editors of *Common Sense* had called for "unity of the Left." They had specified, however, that although the Socialist party was welcome to join the "left-wing coalition," the Communists were not. "It is an unfortunate necessity, forced on the radical movement of this country by the fanaticism and irreconcilability of the Communists themselves," wrote the editors, Alfred M. Bingham and Selden Rodman, "that they be excluded from any united front attempt in the political field." [12] The editors responded to the Communists' call for unity by declaring, "Aside from cooperation on minor incidents, there can be no basis for uniting on a wrong method, the method of sharpening the class war." [13] A dictatorship, whether fascist or communist, was equally repugnant to them. Although they continued to advocate remaking "this America of ours along cooperative lines," the editors insisted that the means must be consistent with the end envisaged, and this stipulation precluded class warfare.

The editors of *The New Republic*—Bruce Bliven, Malcolm Cowley, Robert M. Lovett, and George Soule—were equally reluctant to advocate a class struggle. Although they expressed their anger and frustration at Roosevelt's vacillation between liberal and conservative policies, they were not driven, like the extreme radicals of the social reconstruction group, to turn fatalistically to class warfare as a means of salvation. Their usual facade of pessimism occasionally betrayed a ray of hope. In response to the President's Los Angeles speech in which he appealed to liberals to unite behind his program, the editors asked: "Have they [the liberals] not the right, on the contrary, to ask that you [Roosevelt] enroll under theirs?" [14] This little exchange was between men who still believed in the efficacy of intelligence and the power of persuasion. There was no suggestion here of the Marxist determinism that one finds in the editorials of *The Social Frontier* during the fall of 1935.

Even the Social Gospel Movement, which had eagerly embraced radical solutions during the first years of the depression, began in 1935 to pursue a more moderate course. Reinhold Niebuhr's *Moral Man and Immoral Society* (1932) had challenged churchmen to consider force as a means of establishing the kingdom of God on earth. Although Niebuhr had written that "the middle class are wrong in their assumption that violence is intrinsically immoral," clergymen in general found it difficult to reconcile Christian pacifism with the Marxian principles of revolution. A small number of influential clergymen like Henry F. Ward and Jerome Davis did embrace communism. For a time the influential and tough-minded interdenominational Fellowship of Socialist Christians, headed by Roswell P. Barnes, John C. Bennett, Buell G. Gallagher, Francis A. Hanson, and Reinhold Niebuhr, gave theological respectability to the belief that Marx's analysis of the class struggle and the inevitability of coercion was correct. The majority of clergymen, however, were able to resist being drawn into the Communist orbit. For these men, the New Deal was closer to their ideal of social justice than anything that could be achieved through a class struggle.

Negative reports of activities in Soviet Russia, as well as a genuine belief that Roosevelt was altering the capitalistic system sufficiently to eradicate its worst evils, were chiefly responsible for the clergy's growing support of the New Deal. In the October 1935 issue of the *Christian Evangelist,* Walter Van Kirk, a leader in the Federal Council of Churches, reported that during his recent visit to Russia he had seen "unmistakable evidences of the liquidation of religion." Comments like this, as well as the *Christian Century*'s growing criticism of Russia's foreign policy, accelerated the clergy's disenchantment with the far Left. Suspicions that had been earlier ignored because the evils of capitalism had apparently been considered more relevant were now being borne out by the ruthlessness of Communist tactics. Even Niebuhr now found the Communists intolerable. In an article that appeared in the *Christian Century,* he blasted the Communists for being "a hopelessly sectarian movement in American radicalism." His vehement critique continued:

> Its dogmatism, involving not only politics but every question of culture, philosophy and art, would be acceptable to vast masses of our disinherited population only after decades of fascist decay and international conflict had reduced our still vital cultural traditions to complete decay. It carries too much excess baggage in terms of a complete world view, partly derived from Russia and partly from German rationalism, and this unnecessarily accentuates opposition to its politics." [15]

A poll of the members of the Fellowship of Reconciliation, a religious group organized during World War I to resist military preparations, taken before the 1932 and 1936 elections, clearly indicates the swing away from the Communist and Socialist Presidential candidates and the increasing support for Roosevelt. Before the 1932 election 75 percent of the members were for Norman Thomas, 20 percent for Herbert Hoover, 3 percent for Roosevelt, and 1.6 percent for William Z. Foster, the Communist party candidate; in 1936 a similar poll showed 30 percent for Roosevelt, 50 percent for Thomas, 18 percent for Alfred Landon, 1 percent for William Lemke, the candidate of the Union party, and .7 percent for Earl Browder, the Communist party candidate. A director of the Congregationalist's radical Council for Social Action recalled that, during this period, "Roosevelt and the New Deal were the political expression of our stand." [16]

The social reconstruction group had taken an even more radical stance than the Socialist party; they were in fact now perilously close to the mercurial Marxists. In 1934, the Socialist party had been torn by fratricidal warfare over the adoption of a new declaration of principles written by the radical Militants. Though the old guard, led by Louis Waldman of

New York, had been horrified at the idea of adopting the new principles as a guide for the party, the declaration was far less extreme than the program for social action advanced by *The Social Frontier*. In exaggerated revolutionary tones reminiscent of social reconstructionist rhetoric, the declaration stated that "only those who labor with hand and brain in their concerted might can overthrow this monstrous system and replace it with the Socialist order." Later in the declaration, Devere Allen, author of the controversial document, suggested that strikes might be used effectively, but he categorically ruled out the use of violence as a means of overthrowing capitalism: "In its struggle for a new society, the Socialist Party seeks to attain its objectives by peaceful and orderly means." [17] Jumping to his feet after the declaration was read before the Socialist convention, Louis Waldman stated that the declaration "cannot be supported by those who believe in Socialism."

Waldman was not alone in his fear that the fiery Militants were making the party too radical and revolutionary; though the party adopted the Declaration of Principles, one-third of the delegates (6,512) voted against it. In 1935, at the time when the more radical members of the social reconstruction group were nearing the abyss, Norman Thomas proclaimed the doctrine of the "all inclusive party" in an attempt to arrest the decline of party strength. The net result of this move was increased factional strife within the party. It should be noted, however, that although Thomas' united front policies eventually brought him into collaboration with the Communists, the Communists had in the meantime come out in support of democracy.

Dissension and Change Within the Group

Boyd Bode's ironical criticism of the editors of *The Social Frontier* represented the first real crack in the social reconstruction group's facade of unity. In October 1935, the editors had printed a letter written by J. Herbert Kelley, executive secretary of the Pennsylvania State Education Association. Kelley had listed the educators whom he regarded as "safe" convention speakers, and because Bode and Kilpatrick appeared on the list, the editors called upon them to explain why they had been labeled conservative. In his "self-exculpation" in the November issue Bode responded by saying that "our Editor has a better title to be rated as an educational conservative than I can claim for myself." He asked sarcastically, "How does it happen that the Editors are keeping the peace so well, say with the traditional cultural and religious values?" [18] He suggested that the editors' interest in overhauling only the economic system was too narrow and was doomed to failure unless the whole question of social values was reopened.

Not only did Bode intimate that social reconstruction could be conceived more broadly; he also believed it should be carried out without attempting to predetermine the end result. Bode's criticism exposed the Achilles' heel of the editors, who promptly replied that "the reconstruction of our economic life is *basic* rather than preliminary to the transformation as a whole" and that criticism of social institutions was not enough. "Attitudes, ideas and ideals," must be molded and social groups organized in order to create the new life.[19] As committed ideologists, the editors were unable to grasp the subtlety of Bode's argument. Bode himself had shown a certain amount of indecisiveness by failing to denounce categorically indoctrination and the espousal of a class struggle as inconsistent with the philosophy of experimentation.

In January 1936, the editors called upon liberals, radicals, Socialists, and Communists to unite in a common struggle against fascism. The collapse of the powerful German Socialist movement seemed to presage, in the minds of the editors, the course of events at home, and they were determined that the mistakes of the progressive forces in Germany should not be repeated in America. The editors believed that fascism had triumphed in Germany because the economy had not been socialized and because the liberals, showing a lack of backbone, "looked with horror at the use of the class dynamic for furthering a more equitable distribution of economic power." In a typical Marxian analysis, the editors made capitalism synonymous with fascism by announcing that the choice was now between a "cooperative democracy and fascism." The readers were also warned against putting too much faith in the American tradition of democracy. Fascism could be averted, *The Social Frontier* assured the teachers, by combining the economic realism of the Marxists with the values of the American liberal tradition. The editors demonstrated further that they did not fully understand the liberal tradition that they believed could be so easily fused with Marxism, when they declared: "Such synthesis [sic] is true to the spirit of Marx, who predicted the decline of the police state, and to the spirit of Jefferson and Webster, who recognized the dependence of democracy upon economic equality." [20] The alliance envisaged by the editors was to be more than defensive; by supporting a "Worker's Party" it would become an offensive weapon against the fascist forces in America.

R. Bruce Raup was the first to dissent from the doctrinaire editorial position of *The Social Frontier*. From October to January, while the editors were counseling teachers to overcome their bourgeois attitudes toward a class struggle, the other social reconstructionists had remained silent. Raup's article, "Shall We Use the Class Dynamic?" provided therefore the first suggestion, aside from Bode's ineffectual exchange with the editors, that the journal's editorial position was not entirely representative of the thinking of the individual members of the social reconstruction group.

In his criticism, Raup did not directly repudiate the extremism of the editors, but he made clear his own commitment to democracy and to the efficacy of intelligence. When Theodore Brameld challenged social reconstructionists to accept Marxian tactics, he had, thought Raup, made the same error as others who had interpreted the editors' use of the terms "class" and "class struggle" as orthodox Marxian use. Although the editors used Marxian terminology, Raup argued, they believed "class struggle" connoted a nonviolent and democratic process of social change. Raup was drawing a dubious distinction, one that could not be sustained by the turgid prose of the editors. Unfortunately, in trying to excuse their extreme radicalism by suggesting that they had mistakenly used the wrong terms, Raup created even greater confusion. Yet he did help to initiate a dialogue among the social reconstructionists by calling upon them to clarify the meaning of their terminology and by warning educators against abandoning democratic ideas. "Let us not jeopardize its chances," he wrote in reference to the democratic process, "by precipitating shortsighted action through an over-simplified class dynamic." [21]

Although Raup had given the editors an opportunity to climb down gracefully from the barricades, they refused to do so. The following month they stated that, first, the employment of class concepts cannot be dispensed with, and that second, the distinction between owners of the means of production and workers is perfectly valid. Furthermore, they now took the position that the middle class must be educated to understand that they too are workers. Only the capitalists, the editors claimed, were truly class conscious. "In view of the absence of a class mentality among the workers, it should be reasonable to assume," wrote the editors, giving the schools still another task, "that it is the problem of education to induce such a mentality, rather than to take an existing mentality and base a course of action upon it." [22] The journal had long ago lost contact with the social realities that Roosevelt and his New Dealers were grappling with. This latest proposal indicated that the editors' messianic zeal had led them far down the road of absurdity. Surely, in advocating that educators create a class consciousness among workers in the "interests of a genuinely classless society," Counts, Grossman, and Woelfel were approaching new extremes of dogmatic radicalism.

The editors had now become, apparently, too extreme for

other leaders of the social reconstruction faction. In a steady procession Harold Rugg, John Dewey, Boyd Bode, and William H. Kilpatrick rejected Marx's ideas and certain concepts that the editors and their followers accepted without question. In February 1936, Rugg questioned the practical social relevance of the journal's latest and perhaps most radical suggestion. Rugg criticized the editors for applying a class analysis to social conditions in the United States. Such an attempt, he contended, ignored the empirical realities of the American social structure. Although he agreed that social reconstruction was necessary, he argued that it would have to be accomplished through methods consistent with democratic principles. Rugg declared that educators can participate in rebuilding American society only by creating consent among the people. Such consent could only be achieved if education provided American citizens with enough sophistication to discover solutions to common social problems for themselves. Rugg also rejected indoctrination because, he claimed, it would destroy the citizens' competence to discharge their social obligations.

The editors ignored the criticism of both Raup and Rugg, but John L. Childs did not. Childs was especially critical of Rugg's charge that educators who adopt a class orientation lack the support of rigorous empiricism. In a lengthy article he attempted to show that social classes were deeply divided and that teachers were now faced with the essential problem of choosing sides. Siding with the editors, Childs stated that "If the schools are to be kept free to perform their important intellectual function during this period [the transition to a collectivist society], they will need the support of those groups whose interests will be advanced by the change from capitalism." [23] Although Childs did not comment on the social analysis and recommendations put forth by the editors, it was apparent that he believed teachers were being drawn into a class struggle.

In May 1936, Dewey finally broke his long silence on the issue of class warfare. As one of the original members of both the Board of Directors and the Board of Contributors and as the author of the monthly "John Dewey's Page," he had ample opportunity to observe the journal's increasingly cynical treatment of both democratic principles and rationalism. Dewey had consistently used his monthly "Page" to argue the importance of democracy, the experimental method, the free play of intelligence, and other values dear to liberals. He had, however, nevertheless failed to unequivocally reject the use of indoctrination in the classroom and the involvement of educators in a class conflict. It is possible to speculate that Dewey failed to oppose the extreme means that were advocated by the social reconstruction group because he had not resolved the issue in his own mind. Dewey's article, "The Meaning of Liberalism," attempted to define both the "ends" and "means" of liberalism. Although he was able to convey to the reader the kind of social ideal he envisaged, he was unable, however, to state specifically the steps that would have to be taken in order to achieve it. The confusion inherent in his discussion is demonstrated by this passage:

> . . . the ends which liberalism has always professed can be attained only as control of the means of production and distribution is taken out of the hands of individuals who exercise powers created socially for narrow individual interests. The ends remain valid. But the means of attaining them demand a radical change in economic institutions and the political arrangements based upon them. These changes are necessary in order that social control of forces and agencies socially created may accrue to the liberation of all individuals associated together in the great undertaking of building a life that expresses and promotes human liberty.[24]

Although Dewey had finally found it necessary to challenge *The Social Frontier*'s attempt to synthesize Marxism and experimentalism, the quality of his rebuke revealed that he was still not sufficiently clear about his own position to lead his followers to surer ground. In "Class Struggle and the Democratic Way" (May 1936), he admitted that he was confused by the conclusions drawn by class-oriented educators. Even if massive social rebuilding were actually needed, he reasoned, the conclusion that only a class struggle could bring it about was a *non sequitur*. The nature of the social problem, although it included an element of class conflict, was not identical with the means employed for its solution. Dewey warned that if educators honestly accepted Marx, experimentalism would be of no use to them because the class struggle would determine the course of future events. Although Dewey was reluctant to believe that both the editors and Childs had really abandoned experimentalism for the determinism of Marx, he found himself in serious disagreement with their ideas. Dewey centered his attack on the editors' willingness to reduce education to an exercise in inculcating a class point of view. Dewey firmly believed that indoctrination was the antithesis of experimentalism and therefore should be consciously avoided. Because this was essentially the same position he had taken in his earlier writings, *Democracy and Education,* for example, one can only wonder why he waited until *The Social Frontier* had become so radical before he felt compelled to reaffirm this fundamental tenet.

Dewey was also deeply troubled by the extreme proposals of the editors. He had strongly urged educators to forego the comforts of social neutrality, but the suggestion that educators consciously intensify class division in order to achieve social reconstruction struck him as tantamount to abandoning all faith in education. The Marxist concept of a class struggle repelled Dewey. Not only did Marxism fail to make critical intelligence the fulcrum of the educational process, but it also subordinated education to political revolution as a lever of social change. Dewey feared that if political programs were given precedence over education, the educational process would become a form of constant indoctrination.

When he attempted to outline how social reconstruction could be carried on within the experimentalist frame of reference, however, even Dewey was unable to separate political programs from educational programs. Although he explicitly denounced the evils of Marxism, Dewey failed to further the development of social reconstructionist thought. He merely made one somewhat confusing suggestion: "It is possible to be alert and active in the struggle for social reorganization and yet recognize that it is *social* reorganization that is required, and that it must be taken in the social, rather than a class interest." [25] What action does the teacher take when the "privileged class" resists an attempt to reconstruct it? Dewey seems to answer that the teacher should continue to work for the reform of the recalcitrant class, but should work in the name of democracy and for the benefit of society as a whole, and not in the name of a particular class. Thus, Dewey had succeeded in dissociating himself from the journal's advocacy of class warfare. He had, however, left his followers still hopelessly entangled in the disputed contradiction between indoctrination and experimentalism, a conflict that continued to plague the social reconstructionist philosophy of education. Dewey's major difficulty lay in his failure to resolve the internal conflict between his own idealistic desire to let people decide for themselves the kind of society they wanted and his own deep commitment to a socialist society.

The dialogue, which was beginning to grow quite sharp, was continued in the following issue of *The Social Frontier*. John Childs took issue with Dewey because he had claimed that educators could not simultaneously be experimentalists and advocates of a class struggle. Education was a moral undertaking, argued Childs, in which "the teacher always deliberately works to produce one type of personal character and social outlook in the young as opposed to other types which might be developed." The educator's choice of values must therefore be based on a well-developed "conception of social welfare," and because there were two competing "socioeconomic orientations," capitalism and socialism, the teacher had to decide whether his allegiance was to the "small class of owners" or to those who were committed to "democratic, collective, planned, controlled production." Childs recalled that Dewey had himself warned "that the school must have a social orientation." To be committed to a class orientation, Childs continued, did not mean that the educator should deliberately indoctrinate students with his point of view. On the other hand, the educator's social orientation would necessarily shape his actions, affecting his selection of which social problems would be considered in the classroom and his presentation of historical events. Although he did not acknowledge it, Childs was arguing from the same premise that George Counts had adopted several years earlier—all education is a form of indoctrination.

Teachers who accepted a class orientation had responsibilities extending beyond the classroom, declared Childs. They should wrest from the opposing class greater academic freedom and more adequate support for the schools. Furthermore, teachers should work as citizens for specific social reforms. Childs concluded his article with an outline of the specific steps a class-oriented educator could take and still remain true to the principles of both democracy and experimentalism. For example, Childs suggested that educators should avoid encouraging class hatred and violence, support the spread of information about the "changed facts of American life," and recognize that in a democracy it may become necessary for the majority to "coerce reluctant minorities entrenched in outmoded institutional arrangements." [26] As a true experimentalist, the educator should also test his ideas by participating in political activity on behalf of labor. Childs' last proposal contained the seeds of disagreement between himself and the moderate social reconstructionists. Whereas the moderates were now interpreting experimentalism to mean a process of gathering and evaluating information, Childs understood it to mean experimentation with concrete social programs, for example, direct promotion of socialism.

Although Childs had not demonstrated that a person can retain the objectivity and detachment demanded of the experimentalist when he is at the same time committed to a particular ideology, the dialogue was not continued. Fearing adverse reaction from conservative groups, William H. Kilpatrick joined the Raup-Rugg-Bode-Dewey faction of the social reconstruction group and dissociated himself from the Marxian identification the editors had accepted. In June, he announced that as chairman of the journal's Board of Directors he found it necessary to warn the journal that it was deviating from its avowed purpose of stimulating critical thought on educational and social issues. Kilpatrick specifically criticized the editors' penchant for propagandizing on behalf of socialism. This bias, he maintained, was inconsistent with experimentalism. Furthermore, he thought there was danger that the public might confuse the journal's obvious enthusiasm for socialistic programs with an attempt to gain converts for communism. To prevent such a misunderstanding, Kilpatrick served notice that the journal's policy of radicalism would not be allowed to continue. Wrote Kilpatrick: "As for the *Social Frontier,* I think it too should make clear that, while it may allow others to advocate either high-Marxism or Communism in its columns, it does not itself look to either as a way out of our American difficulty." [27] With this stiff reprimand, the journal ended its second year of publication.

Throughout 1936 less well-known educators, particularly within the NEA, were quietly attempting to rebuild society by preparing materials and study lists for social studies teachers. Men like Fred J. Kelly and Willard E. Givens of the NEA's Committee on Social-Economic Goals for America provided classroom teachers with important information on developments in the study of contemporary social and economic problems in school districts across the country.[28] Paul Hanna and Harold Hand of Stanford University, Edgar Dale of Ohio State University and H. L. Caswell of George Peabody College for Teachers continued to bring the study of American social conditions directly into the classroom through the *Building America* magazine. The magazine's 1936 issues treated such topics as "housing," "transportation" and "power" clearly and factually. Unlike the editors of *The Social Frontier,* the editorial staff of *Building America* left the individual students and teachers free to arrive at their own conclusions about methods of improving different facets of social life. However, by fostering a discussion of social issues among students, the sponsors of *Building America* were hoping that they would become social activists and thus make the school the fulcrum of social reform. This was social reconstructionism in a minor key, but it was still part of the larger movement that *The Social Frontier* was spearheading.

The social reconstruction group itself ended its nine-month struggle in a theoretical wilderness with its vision still blurred by the apparition of a class struggle. The split had finally developed because there was disagreement on the question of how to cope with the problems of a class struggle, and not because there was fundamental doubt that a class struggle was actually taking place. While the social reconstructionists were engaged in the protracted polemic over the issue of class warfare, Roosevelt's administration was changing the national economy and making steady legislative progress. The economy was definitely on the upswing; 6 million more people were at work in 1936 than in 1933; the national income, which had reached a low of $39.6 billion in 1933, stood at $64.7 billion in 1936. There were larger paychecks and a consequent decrease in social dissatisfaction. But the social reconstructionists did not mention this. They did not even acknowledge the significance of the Wagner Act, the Banking Act, and the Social Security Act, all drastic legislative innovations passed prior to September 1935, and all excellent examples that the social system, far from being doomed, was beginning to recover its vitality.

Though the social reconstructionists insisted that they used the experimental method, it was quite clear that their theorizing was removed, to an astonishing degree, from the social realities with which they were trying to cope. As they again recessed for the summer vacation, Roosevelt was preparing for the forthcoming national election. The election was to be, as he declared in his acceptance speech before the Democratic convention in June, "a rendezvous with destiny." Roosevelt was gaining an increasingly broad base of political support, including a new contingent of liberals and leftists, led by David Dubinsky, Sidney Hillman and Louis Waldman, who had defected from the Socialist party. The President could obviously look forward to the rendezvous with more optimism than the reform-minded educators who were still locked in a debate over theoretical questions that bore less and less relevance to American life.

NOTES

1. Arthur M. Schlesinger, Jr., *The Politics of Upheaval* (Boston: Houghton Mifflin, 1960), p. 393.
2. "Presidential Statement Upon Signing National Labor Relations Act, July 5, 1935," *The Public Papers and Addresses of Franklin D. Roosevelt,* compiled and collated by Samuel I. Rosenman (New York: Random House, 1938), vol. IV, p. 294.
3. Rosenman, *op. cit.,* pp. 312–13.
4. "Is Roosevelt Slipping?" *The New Republic,* LXXXIV (August 14, 1935), 6.
5. "CAPITALISM: MURDER," *Common Sense,* IV, 10 (October 1935), 2.
6. Norman Thomas, *The Choice Before Us* (New York: Macmillan, 1934), pp. 80–81.
7. The figures on the exact membership of the Communist party vary considerably; Arthur M. Schlesinger, Jr., has put it at 40,000, whereas Granville Hicks, who was a party member during this period, set it at nearly 100,000. See Granville Hicks, *Where We Came Out* (New York: Viking, 1954), p. 41.

8. I. D. Talmadge (ed.), *Whose Revolution?* (New York: Howell-Soskins, 1941), p. 97.

9. "Teachers and Labor," *The Social Frontier*, II, 1 (October 1935), 7, 8.

10. Quoted in "Teachers and the Class Struggle," *The Social Frontier*, II, 2 (November 1935), 39, 40.

11. Theodore Brameld, "Karl Marx and the American Teachers," *The Social Frontier*, II, 2 (November 1935), 54–56.

12. "Unity on the Left," *Common Sense*, IV, 2 (February 1935), 3.

13. "Crucial Strategy," *Common Sense*, IV, 9 (September 1935), 3.

14. "Mr. Roosevelt and the Liberals," *The New Republic*, LXXXIV, 1089 (October 16, 1935), 258.

15. *Christian Century* (April 10, 1935), p. 474.

16. Quoted in Paul A. Carter, *The Decline and Revival of the Social Gospel* (Ithaca, N.Y.: Cornell University Press, 1956), p. 176.

17. "Declaration of Principles," *American Socialist Quarterly*, 3 (July 1934), 4, 6.

18. Boyd H. Bode, "Dr. Bode Replies," *The Social Frontier*, II, 2 (November 1935), 42.

19. "Economics and the Good Life," *The Social Frontier*, II, 3 (December 1935), 72–73.

20. "Toward a United Front," *The Social Frontier*, II, 4 (January 1936), 104.

21. R. Bruce Raup, "Shall We Use the Class Dynamic?" *The Social Frontier*, II, 4 (January 1936), 109.

22. "Class and Social Purpose," *The Social Frontier*, II, 5 (February 1936), 135.

23. John L. Childs, "Can Teachers Stay Out of the Class Struggle?" *The Social Frontier*, II, 7 (April 1936), 222.

24. John Dewey, "The Meaning of Liberalism," *The Social Frontier*, II, 3 (December 1935), 75.

25. John Dewey, "Class Struggle and the Democratic Way," *The Social Frontier*, II, 8 (May 1936), 242.

26. John L. Childs, "Democracy, Education, and the Class Struggle," *The Social Frontier*, II, 9 (June 1936), 248.

27. William H. Kilpatrick, "High Marxism Defined and Rejected," *The Social Frontier*, II, 9 (June 1936), 274.

28. See *A Descriptive Bibliography of Social-Economic Education*, prepared by the Committee on Social-Economic Goals for America and published by the National Education Association (Washington, D.C., 1935), p. 93.

CHAPTER

5

Radicalism
in a Minor Key:
1937–1943

The social reconstruction group continued its search for a workable philosophy in the fall of 1936. Specific recommendations for social reform had, however, begun to give way to broad generalities, and with this change came a lessening of crusading zeal. This did not signify, however, that the leading interpreters of progressive education were having second thoughts about the advisability of urging classroom teachers to become social reformers. On the contrary, this was a settled issue; the discussion now involved the methods educators would use to carry out this self-appointed task. *The Social Frontier,* though seriously weakened by the internecine disputes over ideology, continued to be the primary avenue of expression for the social reconstructionists.

The journal began its third year of publication under less

auspicious circumstances than in previous years. The editorial staff remained unchanged—George Counts continued to approve the editorial statements of Norman Woelfel and Mordecai Grossman. Woelfel assumed the primary responsibility for publishing the journal. Grossman, who had received a small salary for carrying the major burden of editorial writing the previous year, was now assisting graduate students and doing free-lance writing in order to support himself. He was thus unable to devote much time to the journal. The loss of 1,000 subscribers, a gesture of disapproval that could be attributed almost entirely to the extreme radicalism of the editorials, was a serious blow to the whole enterprise. It is an indication of their dedication that the social reconstruction group continued to publish the journal even though it was no longer financially solvent. Editorial policy reflected the newly changed mood of the social reconstruction group. References to a class conflict were conspicuously absent. The debate over this issue the preceding year had threatened to split the group into two opposing factions. Such a split over procedural matters would have completely undermined their efforts to achieve the general goals upon which they all agreed—namely, creating a body of teachers who are conscious and effective agents of social change. The editors continued to remind teachers of their potential power to direct the nation's destiny, but for tactical reasons as well as the fact that the editors themselves were becoming tired of what must have appeared a hopeless cause, the content of the editorials was far less inflammatory. Discussions of uncontroversial educational meetings were published more frequently as the editors avoided taking definite positions on social issues. To allay fears of extremism, the editors printed a new policy statement that stated that the

> . . . editors owe no allegiance to any particular section of the country. . . . They have no personal or professional axe to grind. The view point of the journal is based on the fundamental Americanism of the Founding Fathers as that has been developed by changed material conditions. . . .

We would alter existing institutions by educational means until it is possible for everybody to enjoy the cultural opportunities now available only to a fortunate minority.[1]

The editors also announced that the Policies Commission of the NEA was formulating a program for American educators, one they hoped would enable the educational leadership to better understand the relationship of education to the "achievement of economic and social democracy under industrialism." The editors also believed the forthcoming report would help to "educate the great body of teachers and weld them into a democratic, comprehensive and militant organization prepared intellectually for cooperation with liberal political groups in the reconstruction of our economic and political life." [2] This faint echo of the previously militant radicalism still contained the old inconsistencies and an inflated optimism about the ability of educators to save society from a host of social evils.

The contents of John Dewey's monthly "Page" was further evidence that the social reconstructionists were losing their nerve and were beginning to abandon their controversial mission. After October 1936, Dewey ceased to dwell on the necessity of rebuilding society and turned his attention to an examination of the educational ideas of Robert M. Hutchins. Dewey criticized Hutchins' book, *The Higher Learning in America,* published in 1936, for its authoritarian tone. "I would not intimate," wrote Dewey, "that the author has any sympathy with fascism. But basically his idea as to the proper course to be taken is akin to the distrust of freedom and consequent appeal to *some* fixed authority that is now over-running the world." [3] Over the next few months the journal printed the running exchange between the two men in which Hutchins accused Dewey of committing the genetic fallacy, and Dewey charged that Hutchins had failed to argue the issues. The acrimonious debate ended with a final sarcasm: "I must ask his forgiveness," wrote Dewey, "if I took his book too seriously."

Dewey terminated his monthly "Page" in May 1937 with a

last discussion of the relationship between education and social change. He acknowledged that he had no new ideas; he wished only to once more put the issues into proper perspective. The relationship of education to social change, Dewey wrote, can be discovered by finding out what democracy means in its total range of concrete applications.

> If a sufficient number of educators devote themselves to striving courageously and with full sincerity to find the answer to the concrete questions which the [democratic] idea and the aim put to us, I believe that the question of the relation of the schools to direction [sic] of social change will cease to be a question and will become a moving answer in action.[4]

Dewey's article failed to give fresh insights to the social reconstructionists. Had Dewey argued the practical limitations of using the schools to reform society, he might have succeeded in convincing them to abandon their quixotic mission. Instead Dewey quietly withdrew to devote full time to working on his *Logic: The Theory of Inquiry,* leaving them with the idea that an adequate philosophy of social reconstruction would emerge if sufficient time and effort were expended on its formulation.

Throughout the remainder of the publication year (until June 1937) the journal continued to lose supporters and influence. By March, it had only 3,751 subscribers, and its financial condition was growing steadily worse. For its sponsors the real test lay ahead. If the social reconstructionists hoped to convince the classroom teacher that he should take an active role in social reform they would have to come up with new and compelling ideas. They had failed to win the support of the teachers during the worst days of the depression, and it seemed more and more improbable that they would be able to arouse teachers during a period of increasing prosperity. If the social reconstructionist educators had taken the time to analyze the group they were calling upon to shoulder the major responsibility for reforming society they would have realized from the outset that their efforts were doomed to failure. But it is one of the strange anomalies of this period that the social reconstructionists, in spite of all the lip service given to the principles of the experimentalist method of problem-solving, did not examine such important issues as the teacher's lack of job security or the folklore of the teacher that places education above politics. That the preponderant number of classrooms were taught by women who were not inclined to-ward social radicalism was yet another factor that was not taken into account. If the teachers had been able to overcome their deeply held belief that their work should be nonpartisan and had rallied to the challenge of the educational theorists they would have been dismissed from jobs that were already made precarious by the depression. The social reconstruction-ist educators overlooked the fact that the people, not the teachers, controlled the schools, and as long as teachers lacked real power and job security they would not be able to advocate social changes that were unacceptable to the people who paid their salaries. The teachers were aware of this fundamental reality and thus remained indifferent to the appeals of the social reconstructionists. Another reason that the classroom teacher ignored the heady proposals of the educational theorists is that in their own minds they could not accept indoctrination as the purpose of education.

Even more serious, many leading advocates of social re-constructionism were beginning to lose interest in the journal. The more moderate social reconstructionists began to give more of their time and support to the John Dewey Society, which had been formed in February 1935 for the study of education and culture. Kilpatrick acted as editor of the society's first yearbook, *The Teacher and Society,* which appeared in 1937. The yearbook included chapters by John Dewey, Jesse Newlon, George W. Hartmann, a professor of education at Teachers College, Ernest Melby, dean of the school of educa-tion at Northwestern University, George Stoddard, Dean of the graduate school at the State University of Iowa, Hilda Taba, a professor of education at Ohio State University, Goodwin Watson, and Laura Zirbes, a professor of education at Ohio State University, and contained the standard statement about the inseparability of educational and political policy. Although the yearbook took a more moderate position than the earlier editorials of *The Social Frontier*'s editorial position, it failed to go beyond *The Educational Frontier*.

The Social Frontier suffered another severe blow when it lost George Counts to the struggle between the supporters of Henry Linville and the Communists for control of the American Federation of Teachers' New York Local 5. In late 1936 Counts was becoming increasingly involved in organizing support for the coming struggle to oust the Communist-controlled locals from the A. F. of T. Counts' activities indicated that he had changed his opinion of the Communists. In 1935, when Henry Linville tried and failed to have the Communist-controlled New York Local 5 expelled from the federation, Counts and Reinhold Niebuhr tried to prevent any splitting of liberal and leftist forces. "If liberal and labor forces," they wrote in a joint letter, "cannot form a united front, if they weaken themselves in bitter factional and sectarian strife, there is no hope. But there are indications here and there on the social horizon that such a united front is possible." [5] The destruction of many prominent educators in the Russian purges had convinced Counts that he had been deceived about the value of cooperation with the Communists. In the spring of 1937, Counts resigned as editor of *The Social Frontier* to lead the anti-Communist fight within the newly formed local of college teachers, Local 537. Ultimately, Counts successfully defeated Jerome Davis as president of the A. F. of T. in 1939, and in 1940 he led the forces that ousted the Communist-controlled Local 5 from the federation, but his efforts to rid the A. F. of T from Communist influence left him little time to devote to the social reconstructionist cause.

In February 1937, an attempt was made to widen the journal's base of support. To give the faltering journal the appearance of being more widely supported by moderate pro-gressive educators, the new sixty-six-member board included almost all the leading progressives. The board included four professors of philosophy, John Dewey, Edward O. Sissons, Sidney Hook, and Harry A. Overstreet, the deans of the educational departments at New York University, Stanford, Northwestern, Ohio State, and Colorado State College of Education; and prominent professors of education like Edgar W. Knight, Kilpatrick, and Childs. This impressive group, however, proved little more than a front to hide the internal weakness of *The Social Frontier* enterprise. Reminiscing about the effectiveness of the board, Woelfel later wrote, "Grossman and I were pretty much disgusted with the Board members, who had now founded the John Dewey Society and seemed interested mainly in socially advanced news releases at con-ventions." [6]

The journal was on the verge of total collapse when both Woelfel and Grossman resigned as associate editors in June 1937. Feeling that lack of support had made the situation nearly hopeless, Woelfel left to take a teaching position at Ohio State University. Grossman was equally discouraged with the social reconstruction group and moved to Washington, D.C. The journal was salvaged by George W. Hartmann, an associate professor of education at Teachers College and a member of the Socialist party, who volunteered to take over the editorship. Kilpatrick became chairman of a ten-man Board of Editors that was established to assist Hartmann in deter-mining policy. The Board of Contributors was also reshuffled; Frank Baker, president of State Teachers College, Milwaukee, Wisconsin, Mordecai Grossman, and Frank K. Hart, a profes-sor of education at the University of California, replaced George A. Coe, Henry P. Fairchild, and Broadus Mitchell. The Board of Contributors continued to include original mem-bers Charles Beard, Boyd Bode, Merle Curti, John Dewey, Joseph K. Hart and Lewis Mumford, all liberal intellectuals. Untiringly, Kilpatrick offered to contribute a monthly "Page."

Although he had reached retirement age, Kilpatrick was finding it especially painful to sever his personal and professional bonds to Teachers College. His new responsibilities to *The Social Frontier* provided a welcome opportunity to give expression to his still tremendous personal energy.

Except for the personnel changes and a new sponsor, the John Dewey Society, *The Social Frontier* of October 1937, was little different from the issues of the previous year. The journal was still uncertain about the educator's role on the frontier of social change, and the drive to associate educational theory with a definite social program continued to lose momentum. Although the journal continued to print articles dealing with social issues, the liberal rather than the radical viewpoint received the major stress. The journal's pages no longer contained the accounts of those who debunked capitalism or articles that extolled the virtues of socialism. Earlier in the spring of 1937, the sponsors had printed as an editorial a telegram sent to President Roosevelt by the Fellows of the John Dewey Society and the directors of *The Social Frontier,* which stated their approval of his fight to change the composition of the Supreme Court and their hope that he would consider such men as Charles Beard, Eduard Lindeman, Robert F. Wagner and Henry Wallace, when he made his new appointments to the court. The collapse of the stock market in August, 1937, which signaled the beginning of a new recession, on the other hand, went entirely unnoticed. Nor did the social reconstruction group use the journal to applaud the New Deal's increasing concern with social legislation that followed the new breakdown in the economy. It simply ignored what Richard Hofstadter called the "social-democratic tinge" of the New Deal. Large-scale governmental responsibility for social security, unemployment insurance, wages and hours, and housing had become a permanent element of American political reformism, but the social reconstructionists did not take note of this fundamental change.

The flagging social reconstruction movement received an unexpected boost from, of all groups, the NEA's Department of Superintendence in 1937 when the department's fifteenth yearbook, *The Improvement of Education: Its Interpretation for Democracy* was published. Though others were beginning to retreat into the relative security of broad generalities, the reformist zeal of the superintendents remained, for the moment at least, undiminished. The yearbook commission had begun its work in November 1935, and the final draft of the yearbook was reviewed in September 1936, three months after Kilpatrick called for an end of radicalism in *The Social Frontier* and almost a year after the triumph of Roosevelt's second Hundred Days. The final report was a mixture of social radicalism, platitudes, and visionary thinking; it provided clear evidence that the significance of the events of the past year had gone unnoticed by members of the commission.

The commission reserved for educators the right of social leadership by branding elected political officials as selfish, weak, and uninterested in improving society. "Political life is," to use the language of the commission, "but a reflection and outgrowth of the underlying economic forces in society." At best it represents a method of compromise and evasion, and at worst, it is unusually susceptible to the influence of reactionary groups. On the other hand, educators "are far more independent and have greater leisure for fruitful meditation and the formulation of rational plans for social advance." Because educators possessed both superior wisdom and ability to act, the commission believed, they could avert the "collapse and decline in our culture" by formulating their "program of social change resolutely and courageously" even though this may result in a "desperate struggle" with the interests of big business and finance.[7] Their animus, which was really directed against the democratic process itself—though the commission included numerous platitudes about the value of democracy—was a cogent reminder that there was still a strong tendency toward social evangelism among certain educators.

The long-awaited and much-publicized report of the Educational Policies Commission of the NEA was a disappointment, however. Although Charles Beard had prepared the first draft and George Counts had been a member of the commission, the vapid contents of the report suggest that the moderate members like John K. Norton of Teachers College and Charles Judd, head of the department of education at the University of Chicago, had the decisive influence on the final version. In its finished form, the report, *The Unique Function of Education in American Democracy*, fell far short of providing the clear statement of educational goals that the leaders of the NEA and the sponsors of *The Social Frontier* had called for. Instead, it contained generalities about the teacher's responsibility to face the future and a great deal of sentimentally charged rhetoric about "the center of gravity in education—a treasury of knowledge, aspirations and values—that endures and is to be cherished against mere expediency." [8] Social reconstructionism was mentioned, but the Educational Policies Commission gave little advice to the educator in his role of social engineer except to state:

> As organized education turns to the future, then, it discards the theory of automatic democracy. It recognizes that rights to life, liberty, property, work, and the pursuit of happiness are shadows, unless those who claim the rights are competent and have the moral power necessary to the creation and maintenance of the social arrangements in which these rights may be realized. If this obligation is staggering in its dimensions, educational leadership must accept it, acquire the knowledge, and put forth the sustained effort calculated to discharge it. Here, too, in facing the future, education re-emphasizes the fact that it is not merely one profession among many, one branch of government among many. Its functions are all encompassing. Its duties are unique in their human aspects.[9]

In the same vein, the commission called upon the faithful to "prepare youth for associational life and activities." To this document the editors of *The Social Frontier* made no response.

The editors also failed to comment on two noteworthy little

volumes published in 1938. Dewey's *Experience and Education,* which appeared first, was intended to separate his educational ideas from the misinterpretations that had all but obscured his original position. Unless the progressive movement resolved the schism that existed between those who exalted the child's impulse and interest and those who were proponents of teaching fixed social beliefs, Dewey declared, the movement would fail. Although Dewey was addressing the whole movement, his warning—educators who think and act in terms of an "ism" become so involved in reaction against other "isms" that they become unwittingly controlled by their original dogmatic loyalty —was in part directed toward the members of the social reconstruction group. Several months later Boyd Bode published *Progressive Education at the Crossroads.* His message was similar to Dewey's. Bode believed that the progressive educators were contradicting themselves when they placed the individual at the center of the stage, yet continually criticized the competitive character of the present social order, which indicated that they really rejected the philosophy of individualism. If the progressive education movement could hope to unburden itself of its "heavy load of trivialities and errors," Bode counseled it would have to become an "avowed exponent of a democratic philosophy of education." Both Dewey and Bode were saying in effect that the two factions of the progressive education movement should unite and resolve their doctrinal differences.

The PEA: Philosophical Indecision

The most immediate problem facing the Board of Directors and editors of *The Social Frontier,* however, was finance; until this was settled the problem of determining the correct doctrine would have to wait. In the spring of 1937, the board reluctantly concluded that unless financial assistance was forthcoming from other sources, the journal would have to be discontinued. The board then decided somewhat naïvely that the John Dewey Society should appeal to the PEA to take over the sponsorship of *The Social Frontier*. The Board of Directors of the PEA responded to the request by setting up a special committee headed by Francis W. Foster to investigate the feasibility of such a merger. In order to determine how the membership felt about adopting the radical journal, Foster's committee sent out questionnaires to 750 PEA members. The results were a source of embarrassment to the committee because they revealed the vastly different ways in which the membership and officials of the PEA viewed educational policy. Money rather than radicalism proved to be the most important issue for the members. When asked if they would approve the merger if it entailed increasing membership dues to $4, a total of 236 members answered in the negative and only 92 were in the affirmative. However, when asked whether or not they would approve the merger if the dues remained at $3, the figures were almost reversed; 238 answered "yes" and 63 said "no."

The committee reported their findings to the PEA's Board of Directors in June 1937. Sidonie Gruenberg of the Child Study Association read the committee's report, which said that, although the committee was "sympathetic with the idea of cooperation and wishes to do everything it can to help *Social Frontier,*" it did not favor a merger at that time. To support this recommendation the report pointed out that a number of members had expressed doubts about the wisdom of becoming associated with the journal because of its history of radicalism. The committee also reported that *The Social Frontier* had operated at a loss of $6,570.18 in the last year; even though contributions had reduced the deficit to $1,915.59, the journal did not appear to be a sound financial venture. It was not difficult for the Board of Directors to reach a decision. The journal's financial deficit and radical tone, they concluded, would be detrimental to the interests of the PEA.

It was understandable that the PEA did not want to assume responsibility for *The Social Frontier* in the summer of 1937. Since the bitter fight over the report of the Committee on

Social and Economic Problems in 1933, the organization had been plagued by the inability of its members to agree on the purpose of the organization. The PEA's vacillation had been in vivid contrast to the speed with which the social reconstruction group was able to state its position, and this discrepancy had put the PEA at an even greater disadvantage when each group was striving to identify itself as the authentic voice of progressive education. Although it thus became imperative for the PEA to state its creed clearly if the social reconstructionists were not to preempt the organization's position as the chief spokesman for the progressive movement, in 1937, the PEA still had not formulated a distinct philosophy. As long as the PEA lacked a distinct program, it was unlikely that it would take over a journal that had a definite commitment to reconstructing society unless the members could agree that the PEA should become associated in the public mind with this same commitment.

The PEA had made repeated efforts to adopt a creed but had failed each time. After the association had refused to endorse the report, *A Call to the Teachers of the Nation,* President Willard Beatty had appealed for "a clearer understanding of the policies and purposes of the Association." "As our program and activities extend into new fields," he continued, in a speech to the Board of Directors of the PEA, "we must maintain our direction and be guided by a definite philosophy of education." At the same meeting Carleton Washburne began to answer questions and thus inadvertently revealed the inability of the PEA members to avoid getting bogged down in a welter of generalities and platitudes. Washburne responded to the specific question of whether or not the association's activities were consciously in line with any educational or social philosophy by saying that "while we did not have a set of definite principles for the schools, now we are committed to 'progressive' action, in the background of which there is still a philosophy." [10] In an unconscious prediction of the PEA's future difficulties, this 1933 discussion ended with the board's appeal for "the Association to develop a social philosophy to guide our activities."

The PEA established two special committees in 1936 and 1937 to work out a statement of principles. The first three-man committee, whose members were W. Carson Ryan, Jr., later to be president of the association, Lois Meek, director of the Child Development Institute at Teachers College and Theodore Newcomb, concluded: "It must be remembered, however, that what goes on in the education of children and adults is determined by the kind of society in which we live. The ideals of the controlling group dominate the scene; only as these ideals incorporate the welfare of an increasing number of people does education become, in the broadest sense, social." [11] When he presented the committee's findings to the Board of Directors, Ryan admitted that "the committee was not satisfied with the statement as it now stood but confessed that he was puzzled as to the next step." The 1937 committee also had little success. At the Midwestern policy meeting of the PEA in Chicago, still another committee was appointed to draft a statement of principles. When the committee reported back, however, instead of outlining a creed, it issued yet another warning: "The time has come for the Progressive Education Association to subject its procedures and its forms of organization to a critical examination and appraisal in the light of the social ideal to which it stands committed." [12] The committee failed to specify, however, the social ideal to which the PEA was supposedly committed.

In 1938, a resolutions committee sought to commit the association to cooperation with other organizations "in critically analyzing, projecting and supporting legislative measures increasing economic security—in organizing our agriculture and technological plant and equipment for continuous and capacity production of goods" and "in resisting the growth of authoritarianism and dictatorship in this country." [13] The members at the national convention listened intently to the committee's report and then began to raise questions: Were

these resolutions binding on all members? Did not these resolutions commit the association to a definite social policy? It
was finally agreed to use the committee's resolutions as material for study. A committee on philosophy of education was
next appointed, first headed by Orville Brim and later by
Harold Alberty, both of Ohio State University. After three
more national conferences, all held between 1938 and 1939,
the committee presented its final report to the national conference. This report, *Progressive Education: Its Philosophy
and Challenge,* was later published in the May 1941 issue of
Progressive Education. As one works his way through the
specific recommendations—"Education should deal directly
with the values individuals hold as they enter educative experiences"; "Educators should be interested in the history of
the growth and development of each individual"; "The educator should recognize more clearly that his efforts create
active patterns of behavior"; "The educator has the responsibility to help individuals select values and purposes in terms
of what may properly be called 'their surrounding reality' " [14]
—one gets the uneasy feeling that the committee had successfully avoided saying anything meaningful. There is no evidence
to indicate that this sober treatment of the mundane, which
the committee was attempting to present as philosophy of
education, was ever endorsed by the PEA.

In February 1939, the officials of the John Dewey Society
again asked the PEA to take over *The Social Frontier.* This
time the association was more receptive to the proposal—in
its search for a social creed the association was slowly adopting a position at a midpoint between the extreme child-centered
position and the social reformist position. Many members now
felt "strongly that teachers needed a vision larger than the
school house," as Frederick Redefer, an executive secretary
of the PEA, later recalled, and many thought that the journal
could now fill a need of the association. The softening of the
journal's tone also helped to make a rapprochement possible.
The meeting of the PEA's Board of Directors that decided in

favor of acquiring the journal was climaxed by a motion made by C. L. Cushman of the Denver Public Schools that the board go on record as "favoring unity of forces that are seeking to advance the frontier of social philosophy and educational practice." The vote on the motion was evenly divided until President W. Carson Ryan, Jr. cast the deciding vote. The association also absorbed the John Dewey Society and gave it the status of a commission. In June 1939, an announcement by President W. Carson Ryan, Jr. appeared in *The Social Frontier*. Ryan wrote in a conciliatory tone that "the age of infinitesimal division and separation has passed . . . beginning next fall the Progressive Education Association will continue the journalistic enterprise so ably initiated by the original Social Frontier group." [15] He also suggested that the journal might be a "great power for good" if its title were changed; suggestions were invited from the readers. The readers were not really being given an option on the question of whether or not *The Social Frontier* should be "rebaptized," however; the association had already stipulated that if the organization adopted the journal its name would be changed to *Frontiers of Democracy*. Supposedly this change would remove the taint of radicalism. The association also made the condition that a new board of editors would be constituted under the chairmanship of Kilpatrick.

Frontiers of Democracy appeared in October 1939 as a second journal of the association, although the official organ of the PEA was still *Progressive Education*. The journal's new governing body included a board of editors and four associate editors (Frank E. Baker, George S. Counts, George W. Hartmann, and Lewis Mumford). The bulk of the make-up work was done by James L. Hymes, Jr., the managing editor. In a lead editorial Kilpatrick announced that *Frontiers of Democracy* actually represented a continuation of the work begun by the original social reconstruction group in 1934. "This journal," he wrote, "has definite orientations, forming . . . a consistent outlook. It accepts democracy both as end and as means. By democracy as *end* is meant the highest possible regard for human personality. . . . By democracy as *means* is meant reliance upon free discussion and a free secret ballot to effect social changes." [16] Kilpatrick had obviously either forgotten the original goals of *The Social Frontier,* or he had misunderstood the journal's social philosophy. If he had recalled such opening statements as "The *Social Frontier* assumes that the age of individualism in economy is closing and that an age marked by close integration of social life and by collective planning and control is opening. For weal or woe it accepts as irrevocable this deliverance of the historical process," [17] he would have seen that his orientation statement had fundamentally different implications for education. In spite of Kilpatrick's failure to note this fundamental distinction, the PEA's sponsorship of the journal ended for the time being the split that had plagued the progressive education movement since 1933. This apparent amity, however, was actually only an uneasy truce between the two competing factions.

The reorganization gave the journal new life, and it began a new campaign to define the social goals of the schools. In their response to the continuing domestic problems and to the deepening international crisis, the educators indicated that they had learned little from the experience of the previous five years. They professed undiminished faith in the power of the public school to eradicate social evil by bringing about fundamental changes in the social structure and in the teacher's wisdom and social leadership qualities. They simply ignored the schools' singularly undistinguished record in achieving the goals of their reform program, and they continued to call upon educators to assume their social mission.

There was still plenty of evidence that social reform was badly needed. Although it had been ten years since the Wall Street crash, 9.5 million people were still without work. Worse yet, it seemed that Roosevelt had run out of new ideas for ending the depression. The most recent downturn in the economy indicated that the New Dealers had failed to restructure the economic system in a way that would eliminate rapid changes in the business cycle. The results of the 1938 election reflected the public dissatisfaction with the President's program; Republicans won seventy-nine seats in the House and eight seats in the Senate. Although the Democrats still controlled both houses by comfortable majorities, the President was unable to overcome the opposition from the coalition of Republicans and conservative Democrats. On the other hand, this opposition was not able to agree on any positive programs to replace the New Deal. At the same time that the battle between the executive and the legislature was producing this stalemate, the liberal cause was further undermined by renewed public credibility in the old idea that recessions were caused when the business community loses confidence in government. According to this theory, the cure for recessions lies in assuming a hands-off policy and letting the system correct itself. Under these circumstances the social reconstructionists set about to quicken educators to the task of social reform.

In his article "Creative America: Can She Begin Again?" Harold Rugg pondered the possible direction of social progress. Would it not be feasible, he speculated, to build a school program around the four ideas that constitute the crux of both social and educational reconstruction? Rugg felt that the ideas of "(1) potential abundance, (2) sustained-yield principle, (3) control efficient, yet democratic and (4) creative expression and appreciation," could serve as a guide to harmonize the potential of the physical environment with a planned society that would maximize individual expression within the confines of social responsibility. The cult of the values of profits and personal achievement that frequently eclipsed the value of responsiveness to the needs of others was not part of his vision of a democratic America. In essence, Rugg was proposing that the schools reconstruct society by making collective goals and social efficiency in obtaining these goals the fulcrum of the educational process. Although his educational ideas were shopworn from more than ten years of uncritical use in progressivist circles, Rugg was attempting anew to clarify the implications of the social reconstruction position for social revolution.

Harold Alberty, an educator on the staff of Ohio State University, was also concerned with the task of clarifying economic, political, and social aims in the classroom. Alberty felt that the growing emphasis on student-teacher planning was helping promote "democratic living at its best," and he was certain that this new stress represented a step forward. Alberty's arguments were especially significant because they were representative of the growing tendency of social reconstructionists to emphasize the process of socialization at the expense of individuality and subject matter. This preoccupation with the social value of democracy obscured the fact that the individual must first possess the ability to perceive and to respond from the depth of his own being before he can genuinely contribute to the social process. Alberty overlooked this basic fact in much the same manner as he had casually deprecated the logical organization of knowledge as a basis of learning. The abandonment of organized knowledge, he wrote, would enable the student to build his own organization of knowledge, oriented in terms of the values of democratic living.

The social reconstructionists continued to receive sporadic support from liberals who reminded their readers that the idea of social planning was an overlooked corollary of technological development and a proper adjunct of education. Henry Elmer Barnes, an eminent diplomatic and cultural historian, tried to put the idea in its historical perspective by showing that social planning had been advocated since the time of Plato. Barnes concluded that "the conception of planned social change has now triumphed in the contemporary world." But he warned the advocates of social planning that if they were not prepared "for the regimentation of economic life and the restrictions of complete intellectual freedom which effective planning must entail," they had better withdraw from the movement.[18] The editor of *Common Sense,* Alfred Bingham, wrote that democracy's major problem was reconciling the individual to the group, because, if this element of social cohesiveness were lacking, there could be little hope for social planning. Liberal individualism had long been a source of embarrassment to the social reconstructionists; they were undoubtedly reassured when such prominent liberals chose the well-being of the group over that of the individual.

Not all educators were satisfied with the progress the social reconstructionists were making in revolutionizing society. Theodore Brameld's laconic question "where are we going?" reflected both a feeling of bewilderment and a sense of agitation because educators so obviously lacked commitment to a specific social program. Brameld chided his colleagues for dropping their idea of planning for social welfare at the first sign of a business upswing (the business index was again edging upward after its disastrous fall in 1937, partly because Congress had passed a $3.75 billion measure for public works in 1938). Social reconstruction was meaningless unless educators set definite goals, he observed. Although the economy had partially recovered, the underlying social problems were still unresolved, and Brameld felt that educators should offer concrete proposals for solving these problems. He called upon them to give up the myth of inevitable progress, to forsake timidity, and to design an America where the people would control the economy collectively.

"What is holding us back?" asked Kilpatrick, who also sensed the general feeling of drift. The answer, he believed, lay in the impact of rapid social advance: "Many have been frightened and demand to go back." Kilpatrick, however, was in this case clearly obscuring the distinction between the social achievements of the New Deal and those of the social reconstruction group. Among the frightened and reactionary individuals who wanted to return to conservative ways of the predepression period, Kilpatrick listed Dewey's 1936 sparring partner Robert M. Hutchins and Mortimer Adler, a professor of philosophy at The University of Chicago. With the same facile analysis that characterized so much of social reconstructionist writing, Kilpatrick concluded: "What holds us back, then, is the need to consolidate our gains, to mop up the ground, to organize for the next advance. . . . At bottom, what holds us back is the time and effort that it takes to think." [19]

The War Years: The Social Reconstruction Movement Changes Focus

Ironically, the real obstacle to the social reconstruction group was the fact that they themselves had grown conservative. The sense of mission which had earlier found expression in the call for a class struggle still existed. Now, however, it was channeled into safer outlets and expressed through countless platitudes about the schools saving democracy from reactionaries at home and totalitarianism abroad. This change did not result from new doubts about the educators' ability to bring about social reform—the writings of the social reconstructionists continued to exude optimism and self-confidence, even as they searched for new social goals for the schools. Their retreat from social radicalism had instead been caused partly by their perception of the doctrine's diminishing appeal in educational and liberal circles and partly by their increasing preoccupation with the international scene. The threat to democracy in Europe gave the social reconstructionists a badly needed goal for the schools; and they promptly made its preservation contingent on the informed activities of educators. It was thus the imminence of war that finally saved the social reconstructionists from realistically assessing the bankruptcy of their earlier positions. However, the specter of war also confronted them with a new and more difficult challenge —reconciling their commitment to liberalism and the experimentalist philosophy with the demands for unity in the national war effort.

The social reconstructionists were in essence confronted with the same problem Dewey had faced prior to the United States' entrance into World War I. Like the liberals who were also faced for the second time with a moral decision about the use of force, they eventually ignored the lessons of that earlier experience. Prior to President Wilson's declaration of war on Germany, Dewey, as well as other reformers, had insisted that America's participation would mean involvement in a greedy struggle for world markets and power. Military involvement was therefore morally indefensible. In a few short months, however, the morally indefensible became the morally defensible as Wilson, using the progressive rhetoric of high moral idealism, justified going to war for selfless reasons. "We have gone in," he said shortly after the declaration of war, "with no specific grievance of our own, because we have always said that we were the friends and servants of mankind. We look for no profit. We look for no advantage." [20] After the President had reassured America that the war was being fought "to make the world safe for democracy," Dewey reversed himself and came out in full support. Pacifists, he wrote, showing his anger toward those whom he had supported just a few months earlier, "wasted rather than invested their potentialities when they turn so vigorously to opposing entrance into a war which was already all but universal, instead of using their energies to form, at a plastic juncture, the conditions and objects of our entrance." [21]

In *The New Republic* article, "Conscription of Thought," Dewey, once again admonished those liberals who were still committed to neutrality. If liberals did not join the war effort, he declared, they "shall have missed the great experience of discovering the significance of American national life by seeing it reflected into a remaking of the life of the world. And without this experience we shall have missed the contribution which the war has to make to the creation of a united America." [22] The editors of *The New Republic* also came out in support of the war. Their special contribution to the rhetoric of idealism was their characterization of the final outcome as "peace without victory." Even Charles Beard could write that the conflict was "not at bottom, or even potentially, a capitalistic war for colonies, markets and concessions."

Except for a handful of congressmen who claimed that joining the Allies had nothing to do with democracy and an almost equally small group of liberals who remained staunchly pacifist, the liberals of the progressive era found themselves supporting a war that was to end with the destruction of their reform movement, the Palmer Raids, which saw the illegal arrest and wholesale violation of the civil liberties of thousands of individuals who were suspected of being subversive, and the stifling of their own civil liberties. Randolph Bourne, deeply embittered by Dewey's failure to be true to the method of intelligence, made the most trenchant criticism of the liberals' support of the war and of Dewey's philosophy. He found the latter totally inadequate in times of emergency. In response to Dewey's claim that war could be used as an instrument for achieving socially useful ends, Bourne asked pointedly: "If the war is too strong for you to prevent, how is it going to be weak enough for you to control and mold to your liberal purposes?" Dewey's disciples, he continued, "have learned all too literally the instrumental attitude toward life, and, being immensely intelligent and energetic, they are making themselves efficient instruments of the war technique, accepting without question the ends announced above." [23] By attacking Dewey's philosophy for its inadequacy in the formulation of "ends," Bourne had laid bare its fundamental weakness. The conservative reaction that swept away reformism after the war and fastened on the American people the millstones of Prohibition, Warren G. Harding, and Calvin Coolidge established the correctness of Bourne's analysis.

In 1939, as progressive educators were preparing to apply Deweyan principles to yet another war crisis, liberals who remembered the disastrous consequences that had resulted from their failure to face the crisis of World War I came out strongly in support of an isolationist foreign policy. They were determined not to be burned twice. When the Soviet-Nazi non-aggression pact was exposed, the liberals were further disillusioned and became more wary of foreign involvement than ever. Many liberals who had become members of the Communist party, Granville Hicks later recalled in *Where We Came Out,* regarded the war as "clash between rival imperialists." The work of Hitler, Mussolini, Chamberlain, and Daladier at Munich seemed to justify their worst suspicions; it appeared that Europe was about to be sacrificed to fascism in order to provide a bulwark against the Soviet Union.

Prior to the actual outbreak of the war, certain liberals applied an economic interpretation to events in Europe and were convinced that America should retain its isolationism. This time Beard was a staunch isolationist; he maintained in *The Devil Theory of War* that "we shall be badly burned again if we keep on insisting that it is our obligation to do good in Europe." The imperialists should be left to fight it out alone, he said, and "we should concentrate our attention on tilling our own garden. It is a big garden and a good garden, though horribly managed and trampled by our greedy folly." [24]

The liberals did not abandon their conviction that the United States should remain neutral until after Hitler ended the phony war by sending his armies into Denmark, Norway, the Low Countries, and France. By June 25, 1940 he had conquered Western Europe and was seriously threatening Great Britain. The seventy-day blitz of Europe aroused the liberals to the danger of letting Britain fall. On the issue of lend-lease to Great Britain, *The New Republic,* which was representative of liberal thinking, began to reevaluate its isolationist stand. This time the editors—Bruce Bliven, Malcolm Cowley, and George Soule—did not attempt to justify their growing support for American participation in the war with appeals to idealism. We shall intervene, they claimed, to ensure that the country remains free and master of its own destiny, and they obviously hoped that this destiny would be shaped by liberal reformers. "At no matter what cost to ourselves," the editors wrote on March 17, 1941, "the wisest policy for us to pursue is to make sure England shall not fall." [25]

Isolationist sentiment was also discredited with the help of the blunt rebuke given liberals by Archibald MacLeish. In an article entitled "The Irresponsibles" that appeared in *The Nation* in May 1940, MacLeish pointed out that historians of the future would ask why scholars and writers of the 1940s witnessed the destruction of writing and scholarship in Europe without attempting to oppose it. Future historians would be forced to decide, he concluded, that writers and scholars were "too busy with rhetoric and ideals to concern themselves with the misfortunes of our generation." MacLeish warned that "the revolution of our age . . . is a revolution of negatives, the misfortunes of our generation." MacLeish warned that intellectuals must confront it head-on. By the time of the attack on Pearl Harbor the majority of liberals were strongly in support of going to war. Dewey did not comment on the shift of liberal opinion, and Beard could only remark: "Well, so now it's all morals and no economics, and we all rally behind the leader."

Educators went through the same process of re-evaluation, but unlike the liberals who were, in the last analysis, very pragmatic about World War II—Roosevelt called it a "war of survival"—they justified their position in highly moralistic terms that were reminiscent of the language used by Wilson in World War I. Both the NEA and the PEA favored neutrality when hostilities first broke out in Europe. With the outbreak of conflict in 1939, the NEA's Educational Policies Commission met in special session to consider what stand the association should take toward the events unfolding in Europe. The commission ended this session by issuing a policy statement which stated sanctimoniously:

> Those who are commissioned by society in the service of education should be the last to capitulate to the forces of

hatred, greed and fear. . . . When peace comes again, as come it must, the people ought to be prepared to play their part . . . in the process of rebuilding a world from which the threat of war and violence may be removed. Those who are to fulfill that mission can approach their task best if their hands are unstained by blood, their spirits uncorroded by hatred, and their minds uncrippled by months and years of wartime regimentation.[27]

Within a year the commission, partly out of fear of being regarded as unpatriotic, had abandoned this lofty idealism to defend the flag.

While other liberals were engaged in the painfully slow process of trying to reconcile traditional values of liberalism with going to war, the commission abruptly reversed itself by calling for a "bold and comprehensive program" of national defense. The commission made the traditional obeisance to democratic values but did not attempt to analyze the detrimental effects of war and unexamined patriotism on the educational process. The commission was so involved in planning how education could play a "central role" in the war effort that the danger that the classrooms would undoubtedly be flooded with war propaganda was not seriously considered. Outlining the immediate steps teachers could take in preparing the nation's defenses appeared far more important to the commission than engaging in an analysis of the moral issues raised by war. In July 1940, long before Roosevelt was able to get Congress to pass the Lend-Lease Act to aid Great Britain, the commission advised educators to act as catalysts to persuade the American public to accept national defense. The educators were urged to use the press and radio, to lead discussion groups, and to revitalize citizenship training "in the schools and coordinate the efforts of all local educative and public opinion forming agencies in a unified program for the defense of democracy." [28]

By January 1941, the commission, using appropriate militaristic terminology, was referring to the school as an arsenal for democracy. Although the Educational Policies Commission talked incessantly about the schools' role in the preservation of democracy, its support of "total defense" logically resulted in an appeal to the educators to de-emphasize social criticism in the classroom and to foster patriotism instead. The commission's study guide, "Suggestions for Teaching American History in the Present Emergency," spelled out the new danger that history teachers must avoid:

> The teaching of American history in the schools has sometimes reflected this general negative spirit and focused pupils' attention largely on the dilemmas of the nation. Over emphasis on the problems of American life, especially for pupils in their formative years, has sometimes created a hypercritical attitude, cynicism, and even submission to "the councils of despair." Such lack of faith in the American way of life rests on unwarranted distortion of fact and is now a danger to the national morale.[29]

In effect the commission was saying that the old liberal practice of criticism and protest, which the educators adopted so enthusiastically during the depression years, was incompatible with the present national interest. By urging educators to foster new social attitudes and loyalties that would ameliorate the immediate social crisis, the commission unconsciously revealed that it too regarded the educational process as a form of indoctrination.

The social reconstructionists, who were now also members of the PEA, were less eager to place the schools at the service of national defense. Their deep concern with the threat of fascism at home and abroad, which had preoccupied social reconstructionists for the five years immediately preceding the war, oddly enough, did not cause them to sanction United States' military intervention to stop the spread of fascism in Central Europe. The initial response of the social reconstructionists to the outbreak of hostilities in 1939 was an attempt to avoid all involvement. With almost Oriental fatalism, they reasoned that even though "civilized law and order among nations will for the time be destroyed," and that "Force and fear alone will survive . . . this war will end in time." Until it does the "United States will remain at a distance, unhurt by the fury." [30] If the United States were unscathed by the war, it would then be in a better moral position, they maintained, to act the role of the honest broker in establishing a lasting peace. The social reconstructionists refused to consider the possibility that the victorious powers might choose to ignore any plan for a world order put forth by the United States. For them the whole issue of war was a vague problematic situation, and they were sure only that it would somehow resolve itself. Using the occasion to explore the moral issues surrounding pacifism or to discuss the problem of using force to protect certain principles did not interest them nearly so much as resurrecting a nebulous policy that had been discredited since World War I and cloaking it in moralistic terms.

Not until October 1940 were the readers of *Frontiers of Democracy* urged to consider the necessity of building a practical defense program. Previously, understanding the meaning of democracy was still regarded by the social reconstructionists as the best means of defense. The October issue, however, clearly implied that the social reconstructionists were fast becoming "defense minded." It included the Teachers College faculty policy statement on "Democracy and Education in the Current Crisis," which recommended that the nation "must be ready to meet force with superior force." Furthermore, in an editorial directed toward neutrality minded liberals, Childs criticized the defeatist attitude that military defense against fascism would result in the United States' ultimate acceptance of the fascist pattern. "This defeatism," he wrote, "helps to bring about the very result that it fears. So long as liberals shun patriotism and recoil from programs for national defense they leave the field open to reactionary forces of the country." [31] It would be better for them to "define and put adequate content into patriotic efforts for national preparedness: social, economic, political and military," he concluded.

In December 1940, Childs belatedly appealed to progressive educators to clarify their thinking on how far the United States should go in aiding the Allied powers. And in January, the same month *The New Republic* recommended that the United States "give Britain aid—not too little, but amply sufficient to insure her successful resistance, and above all quickly," the journal announced that the time had come to make a sacrifice for the preservation of democracy. Editorialized Jesse Newlon: "We are going to aid England because our interests, whether narrowly or broadly conceived, demand that the British win." [32]

It was not until a year after Hitler had conquered the bulk of Western Europe that the social reconstructionists finally sanctioned the international application of the principle they had accepted earlier for settling domestic problems—the use of force. In October 1941, twelve of the fourteen members of the board of editors of *Frontiers of Democracy* signed the statement advocating "full responsible participation on the part of the United States in the democratic struggle against the Axis to the extent, if necessary, of actual participation in the war." [33] They now no longer regarded the war in Europe as a conflict between rival imperialistic powers. In the minds of the editors, the war had been transformed into a struggle between two conflicting ways of life—"the democratic-experimental vs. the totalitarian-authoritarian."

The reaction was immediate. Norman Thomas lost no time in ridiculing the editors for using the label "democratic-experimental" to refer to the Allied powers. He insisted that the Soviet Union was just as authoritarian as Germany and that if the Allies should win it would be Stalin, rather than Churchill or Roosevelt, who would dominate Europe. "Participation by *this* America in *this* war," he warned, "will make the achievement of the domestic program of *Frontiers of Democracy* impossible." The executive secretary of the American Friends Service Committee, Clarence Pickett, saw no reason to believe that getting rid of "Hitlerism" would automatically ensure permanent peace; nor could he accept the "notion that arming ourselves to the teeth for awhile in order to rid ourselves of totalitarianism will lead us to the point where intelligence, generosity and good will can create a new world." [34] Harold Benjamin and Harold C. Hand, the two members of the board of editors who refused to sign the statement, maintained that educators would now be urged to "beat the drum for another 'holy war,' " and that this crusade would pervert the purpose of the classroom. Robert J. Havighurst of the University of Chicago canceled his subscription to *Frontiers of Democracy* in order to protest what he feared would be an attempt on the part of the social reconstruction group to use the journal to win support among classroom teachers for their new position.

Havighurst's fears were indeed justified. After the editors decided to support the war effort, numerous articles appeared in *Frontiers of Democracy* explaining why it was imperative for the United States to enter the war. The articles contained almost no analysis of the economic, political, and moral issues that were at the center of the conflict. Instead, the social reconstructionists appealed to the reader's sense of nationalism and loyalty to democracy and reduced the war to a struggle between the forces of democracy and totalitarianism. As Childs put it, "Democratic civilization is in a struggle for survival throughout the world." "The Axis war threatens the continued existence of our nation, and, even more, our democratic way of life," editorialized the journal's board of editors.

The social reconstructionists apparently had conveniently forgotten that they had criticized the United States just a few years earlier for its lack of democracy. All their attention was focused on the struggle against the new villain. In fact, they were simply continuing their traditional practice of oversimplifying exceedingly complex problems so that good and evil could be easily identified through the use of slogans. During the depression the capitalists had been the villains and the workers could do no wrong. With the outbreak of the war, the conflict between democratic and totalitarian nations replaced the class struggle as the confrontation that the social reconstructionists viewed as extremely important. No matter how loudly and often they proclaimed themselves to be experimentalists, the social reconstructionists continued to be too easily swayed emotionally to make the penetrating and objective analysis of social problems demanded of a true experimentalist.

The educator's mission in the present crisis was, therefore, utterly clear to the social reconstructionists. The educator was destined to win the war and save democracy. Again, however, they gave little guidance to those who were supposed to achieve this objective. Childs talked vaguely about educators uniting with "forces concerned with the public welfare" to ensure that "the full productive energies of our nation are released so that the essential war and civilian needs may be adequately met." In a statement that indicated how little the social reconstructionists considered the interests of the individual at this time, Childs warned his readers, "Neither owners nor workers shall be permitted to limit our productive possibilities in this life and death struggle." Just how teachers were to ensure that everybody agreed on how the war should be prosecuted was not spelled out, but it was evident that their social responsibilities did not include fostering individual thought and initiative. In the name of democracy the war was to be a collective effort!

Kilpatrick envisaged essentially the same mission for the school, but he successfully obscured the exact role he thought teachers should play through generous use of jargon and clichés. "If then our schools are to do their part by this war," he wrote in March 1942, "they must have their pupils so live it that they grow best from what they thus live. . . . All alike must serve as best they can. Our schools will have helped the war-learning of their pupils in the degree that these do consciously and heartily serve the common cause." [35] In December 1942, the board of editors attempted to state the wartime goal of education:

Thus are our war aims and our educational aims part and parcel of one and the same effort: We wage war to fight off enemy attacks upon our civilization and the democratic way of life; we educate to upbuild what the war is to save— humanity, its ethical standards, and its hopes for world law and order and for an inclusive and truer democracy. . . . It is this vision which education must uphold. To make this vision so real in the minds and hearts of our people that it shall in fact prevail, this is the supreme mission of education during this war.[36]

Except for the objections raised earlier by Benjamin and Hand, the only major apprehension felt by the rest of the social reconstruction group was that the public might use the war as an excuse to curtail support of public education. Specifically, they feared that "the school program which is to prepare youth for our next-generation problems" was so new that the public, which had failed to grasp its value, would demand that the program that "stresses current life and its varied problems" be dropped as a needless frill. Such a public reaction could be avoided, according to Kilpatrick, if teachers and administrators "dig down deeper into the secret of learning, how it exists mainly to serve present living, how it comes best as one does really live, lives heartily and creatively." [37]

In 1943 the social reconstruction group turned its attention to the future problem of postwar reconstruction. The members of the group were determined that the events following World War I should not be allowed to repeat themselves. If future wars were to be avoided, they felt that it would be necessary to rebuild the world according to humanitarian principles. When they attempted to define the nature of the new world order, however, the social reconstructionists found themselves once again involved in deciding the ideal economic and political institutions. Furthermore, the old question of whether teachers should lead in the process of social change or adjust to it after the pattern had been established was raised once again. This time, however, the stakes were much higher; it was not just a nation that needed reconstruction, but a whole world.

Undaunted, social reconstructionist educators within the PEA and NEA, as well as members of the American Federation of Teachers, held conferences, wrote papers, and carried on research which focused on education's role in assisting in the immediate task of rebuilding whole societies after the termination of the war. The exciting prospect of playing a crucial part in this vital project revitalized the educators' sense of mission. Most of the leading members of the social reconstruction group headed committees set up to deal specifically with the problem. John Childs was head of the American Federation of Teachers' Commission on Education and the Post-War World; Kilpatrick headed the United States Committee on Educational Reconstruction; Carleton Washburne, as acting president of the PEA, organized the National Education Planning Commission; and Theodore Brameld chaired the Midwest Committee on Post-War Reconstruction.

Harold Rugg suggested that there were two problems to be resolved before postwar reconstruction could be expected to succeed; keeping the nation operating at its full productive capacity during peacetime and providing for a lasting peace. As a starting point, the editors of *Frontiers of Democracy* suggested that the nine freedoms, outlined by the National Resources Planning Board and called "A New Bill of Rights," be accepted as a "charter for our national life." These rights included:

1. The right to work, usefully and creatively through the productive years
2. The right to fair pay, adequate to command the necessities and amenities of life in exchange for work, ideas, thrift, and other socially valuable service
3. The right to adequate food, clothing, shelter and medical care
4. The right to security with freedom from fear of old age, want, dependency, sickness, unemployment and accident

5. The right to live in a system of free enterprise, free from compulsory labor, irresponsible private power, arbitrary public authority and unregulated monopoly
6. The right to come and go, to speak or be silent, free from the spying of secret political police
7. The right to equality before the law, with equal access to justice in fact
8. The right to education, for work, for citizenship, and for personal growth and happiness
9. The right to rest, recreation and adventure; the opportunity to enjoy life and take part in advancing civilization.

Translating these ideals into reality raised immediate problems for the educators, however. They were now faced with the problems of obtaining the people's consent and of determining how to educate the people to accept the idea of a planned economy.

In May 1943, just as the search for viable solutions to these problems was about to begin, Kilpatrick resigned as editor of *Frontiers of Democracy*. Because a long series of resignations had already drained the journal's editorial resources, Kilpatrick's resignation was an especially crushing blow. In October 1942, Harold Benjamin had left to take a commission in the army, and John Childs had withdrawn at the same time to become chairman of the Commission on Education and the Post-War World of the American Federation of Teachers. In the winter and spring of 1943, still more supporters of the Journal made the decision to join the war effort. Frederick L. Redefer left the directorship of the PEA, James L. Hymes, Jr., resigned his position as managing editor of *Frontiers of Democracy,* Carleton Washburne withdrew as president of the association, and Robert D. Leigh and other members of the journal's board of editors terminated their services.

When forced to choose between actively supporting the war effort and speculating on the role of educators in social reform, many educators, especially those who were not deeply committed to the social reconstruction movement, chose the former. The journal had been staffed by the moderate social reconstructionists since the PEA had first begun to support it, and it largely reflected their point of view; their departure thus created a crisis for the journal. Harold Rugg later recalled that "by the spring of 1943 it appeared that with the continued lukewarm attitude of a predominant block of the Board, *Frontiers of Democracy* would die."

Rugg offered to form a new editorial staff and save the moribund journal. With the tentative permission of the PEA officialdom, he formed a new board of contributing editors that included several of the most deeply committed social reconstructionists—Theodore Brameld, John L. Childs, George Counts, William H. Kilpatrick, and B. Othanel Smith, who had taken a doctorate at Teachers College and was now a professor of education at the University of Illinois. The October issue, which had as its theme "the struggle for power," was read and approved by the PEA's Board of Directors. On the surface at least the journal appeared to have the PEA's continued support. The association's President, Vinal H. Tibbetts, declared that ". . . it [*Frontiers of Democracy*] will continue under the editorship of Dr. Harold Rugg to be the same fighting journal for social improvement that it had been in the past."

Tibbetts may have understated the case somewhat, however, for Rugg immediately set out to use the journal as a vehicle for critical examination of the profit motive and contemporary social institutions. Rugg wanted to make *Frontiers of Democracy* more than a nominal "fighting journal." As he put it, "*Frontiers* will not be neutral. On every issue it will take sides . . . it will strive to let light in on the ugly and menacing forces and make plain the alternative courses of action." [38] Capitalism, the American Legion, and the formulation of United States foreign policy all came under criticism in the first issue under the new editorial policy. Rugg also argued the advantages of a planned economy at home and *"fostering democratic revolutions* in Europe and Japan." His declaration that "we are living in a world-wide social revolution" and his call to educators to become leaders in the struggle were apparently too radical for the PEA; the officials of the association were now forced to declare their real attitudes toward the journal. "Within a week thereafter," Rugg reminisced somewhat bitterly, "at the secret meeting of a small Executive Committee, to which I was not invited, the decision was made, on grounds of economy, to abolish the journal." [39]

The December issue carried a statement by Virgil Rogers, acting president of the PEA, explaining that the directors had voted 12 to 3 to discontinue publication of the journal. After stating that the association could no longer continue to publish *Frontiers of Democracy* at a deficit—the projected loss for the 1943–1944 school year was $2,200—Rogers reaffirmed the board's faith in the new program Rugg had outlined for the journal.

Rugg, enraged by what he regarded as the duplicity of the board, immediately suggested that the PEA had dropped the journal because the board members feared that controversy would threaten their professional security. He also castigated them for their failure to recognize the value of social studies. "As it has been for fifteen years, social study is still the bugaboo of Progressive Education." The board's plea for economy was also misleading, declared Rugg. *Progressive Education* was going to lose an estimated $2,700 for the year, yet the board had made no proposals to discontinue its publication. In answering Rugg's charge that the board was tired, timid, and interested only in balanced ledgers, Virgil Rogers replied with candor. He acknowledged that there was a modicum of truth in Rugg's accusations, but he wanted it understood that the PEA had no real obligation to continue the journal. It had been, in his estimation, a financial liability as well as a source of political embarrassment to the association. In fact, he wrote, some of the officers and directors had opposed the PEA's association with *Frontiers of Democracy* from the beginning.

Rugg made no further reply to the directors. Instead he promptly made inquiries among the original founders about the possibility of their refinancing the journal. Time was short, however, and Rugg found it impossible to round up sufficient support. The journal's former supporters were scattered, and the new battle that Rugg proposed to wage did not seem as urgent or as challenging as the old one. The readers were also directly solicited by the journal's research staff. They promised that the journal would be continued another year if the readers would contribute $5,000 before March 31, 1944. But this attempt, like Rugg's, ended in failure.

This phase of the educators' attempt to build a new social order thus ended amid the same acrimonious controversy that had been present when it began. The mistrust and bitterness that arose from the conflict between the two interpretations of progressive education philosophy—the child-centered theory and social reconstructionism—plagued the journal, as well as the progressive education movement in general, throughout its history. Sometimes the controversy was hidden behind a façade of friendliness and cooperation; at other times it came into the open to show the unresolved weaknesses of the progressive education movement. If an acceptable synthesis of the two interpretations of progressive education had been achieved in the years immediately prior to the founding of *The Social Frontier,* it might have found expression through existing educational journals. On the other hand, a wider base of support might have been attracted to *The Social Frontier* by such a synthesis, thereby diminishing the influence of the extreme radicals. Because the two factions could not agree, however, the journal represented a frequently insolvent but determined effort to evangelize educators to accept what was in reality only a part of Dewey's educational theory. The journal's attempts along these lines helped to discredit progressive education in the eyes of the public and to split the progressive education movement into factions that sapped the initial strength of the movement by their internecine fighting. The journal was not the only casualty, however. The PEA was greatly weakened and would shortly disappear as an effective force in American education.

The demise of *Frontiers of Democracy* did not mean that the social reconstruction faction thereafter ceased to be the most powerful force within the progressive education movement. It merely signaled the end of the loose alliance that politically minded educators had had with American liberals over the last ten years. Social reconstructionism would continue to preoccupy influential educational theorists for the next two decades, but the names of important liberals like Lewis Mumford, Sidney Hook, and John Dewey would no longer appear in their literature. The future thrust of the movement would be less in the direction of direct political action and more toward finding an adequate theoretical basis for a form of education that would incorporate the specific social and political values desired by the social reconstructionists.

NOTES

1. "Forked Roads," *The Social Frontier,* III, 19 (October 1936), 7.
2. *Ibid.*
3. John Dewey, "President Hutchins' Proposal to Remake Higher Education," *The Social Frontier,* III, 22 (January 1937), 104.
4. John Dewey, "Education and Social Change," *The Social Frontier,* III, 26 (May 1937), 238.
5. William Wattenberg, *On the Educational Front* (New York: Columbia University Press, 1936), p. 146.
6. Norman Woelfel, personal communication.

7. Department of Superintendence, National Education Association, *The Improvement of Education: Its Interpretation for Democracy* (Washington, D.C., 1937), pp. 113, 114, 117–18.
8. Educational Policies Commission, National Education Association, *The Unique Function of Education in American Democracy* (Washington, D.C., 1937), p. 72.
9. *Ibid.*, p. 92.
10. *Minutes of the Meeting of the Executive and Advisory Boards of the Progressive Education Association* (December 1–2, 1933).
11. *Minutes of the Meeting of the Board of Directors of the Progressive Education Association* (September 26, 1936).
12. *Report of the Board of Directors and Advisory Board of the Mid-Western Policies Meeting of the Progressive Education Association* (April 10–11, 1937).
13. Frederick L. Redefer, "Resolutions, Reactions and Reminiscences," *Progressive Education,* XXVI, 6 (April 1949), 189.
14. Harold Alberty, *et al.,* "Progressive Education: Its Philosophy and Challenge," *Progressive Education,* XVIII (May 1941), special supplement.
15. W. Carson Ryan, Jr., "Announcement," *The Social Frontier,* V, 46 (June 1939), 259.
16. William H. Kilpatrick, "The New Management: A Fresh Hold on a Continuing Effort," *Frontiers of Democracy,* VI, 47 (October 1939), 4.
17. "Orientation," *The Social Frontier,* I, 1 (October 1934), 4.
18. Henry Elmer Barnes, "Should Social Change Be Consciously Directed?" *Frontiers of Democracy,* VI, 50 (January 1940), 110.
19. William H. Kilpatrick, "What Is Holding Us Back?" *Frontiers of Democracy,* VI, 54 (May 1940), 232.
20. Ray S. Baker and William E. Dodd (eds.), *The Public Papers of Woodrow Wilson* (New York: Harper, 1925–1927), vol. V, p. 33.
21. John Dewey, "The Future of Pacifism," *The New Republic,* XI (July 28, 1917), 358.
22. John Dewey, "Conscription of Thought," *The New Republic,* XII, 148 (September 1, 1917), 130.
23. Quoted in Morton White, *Social Thought in America* (Boston: Beacon Press, 1947), pp. 169, 170.
24. Charles Beard, *The Devil Theory of War* (New York: Vanguard, 1936), pp. 117, 120.
25. "If America Stands Alone," *The New Republic,* CIV, 11 (March 17, 1941), 363.
26. Archibald MacLeish, "The Irresponsibles," *The Nation,* CL, 20 (May 18, 1940), 620.

27. Educational Policies Commission, "American Education and the War in Europe," *N.E.A. Journal,* XXVIII, 8 (November 1939), 225.

28. Educational Policies Commission, "Education and the Defense of America," *N.E.A. Journal,* XXIX, 6 (September 1940), 168.

29. Educational Policies Commission, *Suggestions for Teaching American History in the Present Emergency* (Washington, D.C., February 1941), p. 3.

30. William H. Kilpatrick, "The War: Our Country and the World," *Frontiers of Democracy,* VI, 49 (December 1939), 69–70.

31. John L. Childs, "Liberalism and National Defense," *Frontiers of Democracy,* VII, 55 (October 1940), 6.

32. Jesse Newlon, "How Shall We Aid England?" *Frontiers of Democracy,* VII, 58 (January 1941), 100.

33. "This War and America," *Frontiers of Democracy,* VIII, 63 (October 1941), 10–11.

34. Clarence Pickett, "Objection," *Frontiers of Democracy,* VIII, 63 (October 1941), 16–17.

35. William H. Kilpatrick, "Our Schools and the War," *Frontiers of Democracy,* VIII, 68 (March 1942), 167.

36. "The Mission of Education in This War," *Frontiers of Democracy,* IX, 73 (December 1942), 68–70.

37. William H. Kilpatrick, "Education in Wartime," *Frontiers of Democracy,* VIII, 69 (April 1942), 198–99.

38. Harold Rugg, "The Year of Decision: 1943–1944," *Frontiers of Democracy,* X, 79 (October 1943), 4.

39. Harold Rugg, *Foundations of American Education* (New York: World Book, 1947), p. 581.

CHAPTER

6

The Continuation
of a Tradition:
1943–1960

Although the small group of immediate supporters were reluctant to concede the point, the decision to terminate publication of *Frontiers of Democracy* was actually a merciful act that
immediately strengthened the social reconstructionist position
within education circles. The journal had been reaching a
steadily diminishing audience and it was only a matter of time
before it would have collapsed on its own. The abrupt can-
cellation of the journal liberated restless social reconstructionists from the constraint of participation in an organized group
that had been indelibly associated in the public mind with
radicalism. Henceforth, the social reconstructionists would only
be bound together by the general belief that the school should
anticipate the direction of social change. Educators who set
out to develop a few of the ideas that were implicitly contained

in the social reconstruction position and then to apply them in the classroom no longer risked rejection as radicals because of their association with the journal. The directors of the PEA had, quite unconsciously, given the classroom teacher an opportunity to reassess social reconstructionism, thus enabling individual reconstructionist educators to reach a larger and more receptive audience than before. As paradoxical as it may seem, the demise of the journal eliminated the major stumbling block to a rejuvenation of the movement.

The power of the social reconstructionists was further enhanced by the gradual decline of the PEA, which was still largely controlled by the child-centered educators. The once-influential organization continued to exist without purpose and almost without support. The PEA had refused to accept the report of its philosophy of education committee, even though its adoption would not have committed the PEA to anything more radical than Deweyan clichés about education for growth and democratic living. Board members were aware that something had happened, but as a reading of the board's official minutes reveals, they were perplexed about the causes of the association's plummet from its position of educational eminence. Ironically, they blamed the war for their plight. The war had, they claimed, put "the three R's and discipline . . . in the saddle." "Everywhere there is a trend toward regimentation which is unfavorable to educational experimentation." The officers of the PEA agreed that "the schools need vigorous leadership to guide them out of their perplexity" [1] but were at a loss as to how the PEA should go about it.

Of more immediate concern was the financial state of the organization itself. In the last year, 1942–1943, membership had fallen by 30 percent (there were only 6,987 members in 1943), and there was a corresponding decline in revenues from membership dues and research foundations as general interest in the PEA waned. Some felt the association would be able to survive the war as a publishing house, but others believed this estimate of the situation was overly optimistic. The officers of the PEA needed to raise $5,000 and to sign up 3,500 new members before September 1944; without the money, the association would not have been able to balance its budget. For an organization that had in an eight-year period received over $1.5 million in research grants from foundations, its present impecunious condition seemed pitiful indeed.

Instead of appraising the situation realistically and quietly administering the *coup de grâce* to the moribund organization, the officials engaged in a fruitless search for a new purpose for the PEA. Harold Rugg suggested that the association set as its new task "the assembling of the positive resources of this country and the world to make a program that is far-reaching and big." As always, however, he really wanted the PEA to take sides in the class struggle. At a board meeting that included a discussion of the future of the association, he stated flatly, "We must be specific—who are the persons and groups we must deal with as enemies?" Equally visionary was a suggestion by Arthur Keesler, treasurer of the PEA and a supervising principal in Glenwood Landing, New York. Keesler felt that the Board of Directors should take immediate steps to raise $500,000 and to acquire 100,000 members over the next three years. Both objectives might be achieved, he said, if the association would be willing to pay as much as $50,000 to an outside promotional agency. Others were more realistic. Ned Dearborn of the National Safety Council said that if the PEA continued to think of itself as an "aggressive fighting organization, we may as well resign ourselves at once to a numerically small group." Teachers will not carry banners, he told the Board of Directors. But if the association would give up its "aggressive posture" and turn to "education for complete human living" he thought the PEA could once again prosper. Roma Gans of Teachers College agreed that the new sources of funds could be found, but warned "we will not secure 'big money' unless we knuckle under."

It was not, however, all talk and no action. In the spring of 1944, the membership of the association voted by mail ballot to change its name to the American Education Fellowship. The decision to change the name of the PEA resulted from the awareness that the association was confronted with different kinds of problems than it had faced twenty-five years earlier. Vice-President W. Carson Ryan, Jr. candidly put the situation in perspective when he said other organizations were doing the PEA's old job "better than we can and that the PEA has no reason to exist unless it can step out in a new direction with vigor and imagination." [2] The new name was to symbolize that the association was "not retreating but moving ahead." In order to allay any suspicion that the association was in serious difficulty, the Board of Directors wanted to announce in *Progressive Education* that they were proud of their tradition and old name, "but there is a new, broader job to be done that no other group is undertaking." Just what this job included no one could say. The extent of their confusion is best demonstrated by the board's difficulty in deciding whether the word "education" should be included in the association's new name. The fear was expressed at a board meeting that it might limit the scope of the organization's future activities.

The association's preoccupation with the rudimentary problems of survival meant that it had ceased to be a leading interpreter of progressive education. The PEA had abandoned the field so completely that no effective voice remained to challenge the social reconstructionists as the only important theorists in the progressive education movement. Earlier the social reconstructionists had failed to attract a large following because of their extremism and because the classroom teacher had acknowledged the PEA's leadership in methodology. These limitations had now disappeared. As the educators began to reformulate the social reconstructionist philosophy, they were in a strategic position to exert a more powerful influence over classroom teachers who had been either unsympathetic or indifferent to the idea of a class struggle but who were more receptive to the idea of a community-centered school that fostered "democratic living."

The New Deal Social Reconstructionist Doctrine: A Shift in Emphasis

The social reconstructionist thesis was to undergo a profound change in the next decade and a half. It eventually became a much broader and more generalized doctrine that allowed for a new and seemingly more patriotic emphasis. A change in the leadership of the movement was partly responsible for this theoretical shift. Kilpatrick, Childs, Counts, and Rugg continued to write, but somehow their pronouncements seemed to be little more than a restatement of what had already been said. The new men who were responsible for carrying the movement on in the forties were mostly educators who had been close to R. Bruce Raup at Teachers College and who, for the most part, had not taken a prominent role in the earlier and more radical period. Kenneth Benne and William O. Stanley, along with Raup, were the leaders of this group. Both Benne and Stanley had taught high school in Kansas before taking their doctorates in education at Teachers College under the tutelage of the old-guard reconstructionists. Both men went to teach at the University of Illinois in 1941 and 1942, respectively. Theodore Brameld, who had been active much earlier, was also part of the innovating group.

The old guard continued to call upon teachers to be on the cutting edge of social change, and new voices like Isaac Berkson continued to support the same idea. In *Education Faces the Future,* Berkson argued that interdependence, a planning society, and international order were the key concepts of the "new era" toward which teachers should work. But somehow these continual exhortations to create a better world seemed dated and preachy. If the schools were to be genuinely in the forefront of social change in the 1940s, the teachers needed less visionary exhortation and more concrete methodology that would incorporate the tenets of both factions of the progressive education movement. R. Bruce Raup, George E. Axtelle, a professor of education at Northwestern University,

Kenneth Benne, and B. Othanel Smith took a major step in this direction when they realized that a new method had to be found for solving social problems democratically.

Like the earlier reconstructionists, these men started with the thesis that the growth of science and technology is the "chief dynamics" of social change. These forces had made society a highly interdependent, specialized, and delicately balanced system. The reconstructionists believed that such a society could not tolerate individuals who were not aware of the social implications of their actions. The continual contest between private and public interests threatened to slow the advance of technology and to ultimately lead to the disintegration of society. The only way to avert the social crisis that would result from the inability of individuals and groups to reach agreement on social issues was to find a method for solving problems in a truly democratic manner. The problem, as the reconstructionists saw it, was primarily one of education. People would have to be taught new methods of thinking and new techniques of cooperation and more effective communication in groups. In short, people would have to learn the method of what the reconstructionists called "democratic deliberation."

In the earliest formulation of social reconstructionist philosophy there had been a pronounced tendency to disparage individualism as a threat to society and to exalt collective behavior. The social ideal embraced by Raup, Axtelle, Benne, and Smith represented a logical extension of the early analysis. The new society was to be an "uncoerced community of persuasion." This somewhat awkward phrase meant that social policy would represent the collective thought, and eventual agreement, of *all* who were affected by it. This application of what these men called social intelligence to social problems would represent democratic planning at its best. These latter-day social reconstructionists were, however, extremely utopian in their thinking. Not only did Raup, Axtelle, Benne, and Smith believe total agreement on social issues was possible, but they also insisted that this harmony would eventually be achieved without resorting to compromise. In fact, the use of compromise was rejected on the grounds that it "possesses all the long-run faults of the method of compulsion. The minds and characters of parties to a compromise do not grow immeasurably through intercommunication with each other." It is important to note here that to these later reconstructionists "growth" meant giving up one's own individually held values and ideas and adopting instead the collective judgments of the group.

When translated into more concrete terms, their ideal of democratic planning would entail a radical change in the nature of political and economic institutions. "Our need," Raup, Axtelle, Benne, and Smith wrote in *The Improvement of Practical Intelligence,* a book that they jointly authored in 1943, "is for economic and political institutions which embody the reality and sense of community, institutions which provide that *whoever may be affected by a decision or policy shall in some way have a part in shaping it*." [8] Given the four authors' organic frame of reference, it is difficult to see how society, as we know it in America, could function at all. Not only would the task of polling the ideas of all affected individuals be virtually endless, but such a project would also demand an equally protracted process of reeducation. Without both it would be impossible to achieve the uncoerced community of persuasion. The authors' naïve assumption that all social problems could be solved through democratic action further compounded the difficulties in applying their ideas.

The schools, Raup and his colleagues maintained, could facilitate the extension of "democratic deliberation" into all areas of society by educating students with a "profound sense of community in which the self becomes identified as a functional part of an organic process." Until the values of students are reconstructed, the authors of *The Improvement of Practical Intelligence* warned, "planning will continue to meet great resistance from the individualistic mentality, jealous of its vested interests and selfish opportunities." It is extremely significant to note that the authors were deeply suspicious of the individual who refused to go along with the decisions of the group. Ironically, they regarded the individual who possessed the courage to remain an individual as undemocratic. Democracy, in their view, was completely identified with collective action and the group mind.

That democracy could also be interpreted to mean protecting the individual from the tyranny of the majority did not occur to the authors. In their concept of society, the tension that exists between the individual and the group was regarded as something that would have to be eradicated. There was to be no nonsense about the private area of one's life. Man is social and all his problems are social and thus potentially capable of being solved efficiently and quickly through the collective intelligence of the group. This attitude, which ignores the importance of protecting the individual's rights, underlies the naïve faith of Raup and his colleagues that all problems are soluble. Reliance on man's social nature also explains the lack of references in the writings of the social reconstructionists to the existential problems experienced by the individual who takes seriously the problems of determining who he is, what he values, and how he should determine his life. These problems, which the new reconstructionists considered a matter to be left to the individual, are simply ignored. Worse yet, the social reconstructionists succeeded in casting suspicion on the individual who shows any inclination to grapple with these basic issues by their many references to individualism as basically selfish and antisocial.

"Men have an almost unlimited capacity for dedication to common ends and ideals, for devotion to a common cause," wrote Raup and his associates as they set out to outline the new methodology that they hoped would enable teachers to educate students for "democratic living." The classroom teacher was expected to help students become "integral, socialized, and objective." Discipline in what the four authors called "the method of practical judgment" would produce this type of character in students. The method itself was actually only a slight revision of Dewey's five steps to problem-solving, although Raup, Axtelle, Benne, and Smith did place new emphasis on the social implications of the method. The four men focused on the ways the collective approach to problem-solving modifies the social values of all participants by making them both more aware of group decisions and more amenable to the collective will. As Raup and his associates put it, ". . . in a democratic culture the ideal of deliberation is to rebuild mind and character as well as overt behavior, and the judgmental process should, therefore, be directed toward the reconstruction of common persuasion as the basis of common actions."

For the teacher who might wonder about how he should deal with the student who refuses to lose his identity in the group, the authors of *The Improvement of Practical Intelligence* had a ready answer. "Recognition of conflicts in character as important features of practical situations does not leave us in a maze of subjectivity if the 'inner' conflicts can be symbolized, communicated, and submitted, directly or indirectly, to a process of group consideration." In short, those students who do not conform would themselves become the object of reconstruction by the group. The authors ignored the fact that there was a danger of "reconstructing" an individual who might, in fact, have a clearer understanding of the truth. For Raup and the others, truth and social consensus were indistinguishable.

Stripped of excess verbiage, the method of practical judgment involved learning how to cooperate with others in solving the everyday problems of life. And the best way to give students the ability to make practical judgments was to organize the curriculum around the experiences that are vital to the learners themselves. Only in these situations would the student be forced to make value judgments that were personally meaningful. The discovery of facts would thus be more than a sterile exercise of the mind. Furthermore, such an approach would overcome the discrepancy that Raup and his associates thought existed between what the student learns in the classroom and what is useful in his daily life. The four social reconstructionists complained that the curriculum of the schools was still dominated by university professors who did not understand the importance of being able to make practical judgments, a statement that revealed an unmistakable anti-intellectual strain in their thinking. This bias is also clear in the authors' statement that "the foremost obstacle to the shaping of personal characters for effective membership in a democratic order is the almost exclusive commitment of the educational program to theoretical disciplines." To continue such a practice was to invite the destruction of democracy, they warned.

Although Rugg and his associates never adopted the extreme proposals of some of their colleagues, the four men nevertheless believed strongly in the school's power to regenerate society. In particular they felt that educational programs that did not teach the students the value of collective behavior were at best misguided attempts at objectivity and at worst the pernicious efforts of reactionaries to retard the advance of society. Programs that divided subjects into mathematics, history, English and so on as well as those that sought to "steep the minds of persons in the ancient liberal arts and in the world's great classics" were also considered a threat to democratic institutions. On the other hand, if the schools would work to "generate vitality and develop responsibility and effectiveness in social membership by bringing the school, the children, and the adult community together in all conceivable ways—sightseeing excursions, expansion of vocational education, and common participation in the promotion of general community understandings," [4] they would be doing their part in directing social change and ensuring the continuation of democracy.

If *The Improvement of Practical Intelligence* represented the most important social reconstructionist statement of 1943, Kenneth Benne's *A Conception of Authority* was a close second. Benne's book had originally been a Teachers College doctoral study written under the direction of Raup. In the preface Benne observed that a revolution was basically a major shift of allegiance from one set of bearers of authority within a social group to another. As partisan "authorities" competed for control of the minds and hearts of the masses, the public tended to grow confused and insecure. This confusion frequently led the masses to support a "strong man" who promised security through the imposition of order and the suppression of conflict and thus to give up the authority that rightly belonged to them as a group. Benne's study sought to define the social nature of authority, which he regarded as the legitimate possession of the group as a whole, and to show how it could be used by teachers.

The function of authority, Benne thought, borrowing from Yves R. Simon's definition, was to assure the unity of action of a group that aimed at a common good. If authority is shared by the members of the group, it will allow democracy to function and, in the process, ensure each of the members an opportunity to work toward a common end. When Benne maintained that "wholeness of personality is consonant only with fullness of membership in the human community," he laid the basis for legitimizing the coercive power of the group over the individual. For Benne contended, quite paradoxically, that men become whole, mature, and self-directing only when they submit their own thoughts and actions to the control and demands of the community. Even the teacher must derive his authority from the community, and it must be exercised with constant attention focused on the common good. The teacher who seeks to provide students with subject matter alone is, therefore, in error. For his decisions in the classroom must reflect the social needs of the community from which he derives his authority. Conducted properly, the educational experience would involve students in the "common life process" of the larger community, with a heavy emphasis on group activity and decision-making.

Benne's discussion of the teacher's ideal use of his authority was not entirely consistent. In maintaining that the teacher must ensure that the "educative enterprise fit rather than unfit his pupils for active and responsible membership in the community," Benne seems to be suggesting that the teacher should work toward those ends that the community has already decided collectively. Occasionally, however, he reverses the teacher's role. Instead of the servant of the community, Benne suggests that the teacher should be a benevolent leader who has "a conception of the type of personality consonant with the community which is in the making." [5] By anticipating the direction of social change and molding the character of the student accordingly, the teacher thus takes the initiative and no longer waits for the collective decision of the community as to appropriate goals. Benne and his colleagues were indifferent to the paradox inherent in their position. For as individuals writing about the needs of society, they exemplified this very paradox. Even though under contemporary conditions it was admittedly impossible to determine the collective will of society, the educators advocated, in the name of society, that the schools create a new type of individual for the emerging age.

The educational vanguard was giving social reconstructionism a new image. The old appeals to mount the barricades and throw the capitalists out had, happily for the classroom teacher, been forgotten. The leading theoreticians of progressive education were advocating a new doctrine that was far more seductive. What teacher could resist striving to attain the new goals? Education for democratic living, democratic cooperation, democratic deliberation, and democratic planning all possessed a magnetic appeal because they expressed loyalty to the ideal of the country. The new collectivist meaning that the social reconstructionists had given democracy did not seem to disturb the teachers who were busily trying to give the new educational slogans concrete expression in the classroom. Unfortunately for the students, the rigorous demands of teaching democracy did not leave the average teacher sufficient time or energy to examine the nuances of the term with any precision. As a result, through the use of slogans like "education for democratic living" (the "uncoerced school-community of persuasion" had proved too awkward and ambiguous) the social reconstructionists were able to exert a significant influence on the classrooms across the country.

Vulgarized and oversimplified as it was, the concept of democracy had been decisively associated with social reconstructionism. Thus, while teachers adopted the reconstructionist methodology along with the slogans, the unimpeachability of the slogans seemed to legitimize the methodology and eventually the social goals of the reconstructionists. For individuals who may have been alarmed about the anti-intellectualism and the equalitarianism of the group ethic, the close identification of the collectivist concept with democracy made criticism of the social reconstructionist educator difficult, if not impossible, during the war and the cold war crisis that followed. Between 1943 and 1950, when the social reconstruction movement was exerting a profound influence on the direction of American education, there were thus virtually no important critics within the field of education.

The Life-Adjustment Educators

During this period the group that implemented the important tenets of the reconstructionist doctrine were the life-adjustment educators. They were concerned, almost to the point of obsession, with the practical aspects of living. Given their practical frame of reference, it is quite natural that they left to others the task of theorizing about the aims and methodology of education. The life-adjustment educators were primarily practitioners. When they did make statements about their ultimate aims, these educators showed their indebtedness to work done by the moderate reconstructionists during the thirties, particularly to Kilpatrick, and, in the forties, to the ideas of R. Bruce Raup, Kenneth Benne, and William O. Stanley.

Because of this obvious intellectual dependency, it would be a mistake to regard the life-adjustment educators as the leaders of a separate movement. Evidence indicates that they were actually members of the broad social reconstruction wing of the progressive education movement that had numerous adherents among the more moderate educators in the PEA and the NEA. Any other explanation would have to ignore the similarity between the basic tenets of life-adjustment education and those of moderate social reconstructionism and the fact that a number of reconstructionists were members of commissions that produced reports in support of life-adjustment education. For example, George D. Stoddard, dean of the graduate college at the State University of Iowa, was a member of the Board of Directors of *The Social Frontier* and participated in the Educational Policies Commission of the NEA that issued the report, *Education for All American Youth*. The Virginia state superintendent of public instruction, Sidney B. Hall, was also connected with both these organizations, as were Ernest O. Melby, the dean of the school of education at Northwestern University and George Counts. J. B. Edmondson, dean of the school of education at the University of Michigan, also exemplified this interrelationship. He had collaborated on the NEA yearbook, *Education and Social Change,* and was a member of the National Conference on Life-Adjustment Education.

The creed adopted by the Commission on Life-Adjustment Education for Youth, which had been appointed by the United States Commissioner of Education, John W. Studebaker, in 1947, is strikingly similar in tone to the Raup-Benne-Axtelle-Smith interpretation of social reconstructionism. The primary goal of life-adjustment education, the creed stated, was to equip "all American youth to live democratically." More specifically, life-adjustment education was defined by the following characteristics: "It is concerned with the present problems of youth as well as with their preparation for future living"; "It respects the dignity of work and recognizes the educational values of responsible work experiences in the life of the community"; and it teaches students "to think of government as an instrument, which people use to do things collectively for the common good." [6]

All of this has a familiar ring. In his Inglis Lecture delivered at Harvard University in 1939, Charles Prosser of the Dunwoody Institute of Minneapolis, an agency-school of industrial education, laid down a maxim of life-adjustment education that was also fundamental to social reconstructionist thinking. Said Prosser: "The general rule seems to be that the younger any school study, the greater is its utilitarian value in affairs outside the schoolroom, and the older the study, the less the usefulness of its contents in meeting the real demands for living." [7] Raup and his associates stated the same principle more succinctly when they wrote, "The method of practical judgment is the method of democratic living." [8] From the student's point of view it would not make any difference whether the label "life-adjustment" or "social reconstructionism" was used to describe his educational experience; the outcome would be the same. In the classroom he would learn "life values," his future would be directed toward "democratic living," and he would emerge from his educational experience as a "whole child." Furthermore, the student would possess the reassuring knowledge that regardless of the nature of his problem he could always take it to the group for "collective deliberation."

The slight differences between the two groups involved the life-adjustment educators' greater emphasis on practical training in the "arts" of family membership (for example, dating, marriage, parenthood, and parent-child relationships) and on vocational education. Social reconstructionism, on the other hand, emphasized the importance of training for efficient membership in the community that largely ignored this 4-H aspect of education. It should again be stressed, however, that the principles of life-adjustment education are easily derived from social reconstructionism. Democratic solution of problems, the value of collective behavior, the importance of immediate experience as opposed to historical experience, and the value placed on general education with the corresponding devaluation of specialization as somehow undemocratic, were all integral to both approaches. The life-adjustment educators also possessed the same deep sense that it was their mission to shape the character of their students in accordance with their own vision of the good society. And had life-adjustment education been implemented more fully throughout the country, it would have undoubtedly resulted in a major transformation of American society.

Originally, the principles of life-adjustment education grew out of the work of the Commission on the Relation of School and College that the PEA established in 1932 to study the feasibility of applying the theories of progressive education to the secondary schools. This change in emphasis from elementary to secondary education came at the same time the child-centered educators, who had been largely connected with small private experimental schools, were being challenged for control of the PEA by the professors of education, particularly those associated with Teachers College. In 1932, members of the PEA were also urging their association to state clearly what it thought should be the social responsibilities of the school. The commission itself, which was originally called the Committee on College Entrance and Secondary Schools, was set up to explore ways in which colleges and secondary schools might work more closely together in improving the quality of education. The main concern, at least on the part of the educational theorists, was to free the high school curriculum from excessive attention to college entrance requirements.

At the first meeting of the commission (its members included Bruce Bliven of *The New Republic,* President Robert Leigh of Bennington College, Harold Rugg, Jesse Newlon, and Goodwin Watson) it was decided that something more was required than simple tinkering with college entrance requirements. "Nothing less than a complete remaking of the whole secondary-school curriculum, organization, and procedure seemed in order." As the commission set out to determine the needed changes, they assured educators that there would be no lowering of academic standards in creating "conditions by which it will be possible to shape each student's course throughout school and college so that it will be best fitted to his needs." [9]

The commission proposed that twenty leading secondary schools be invited to participate in an experiment in which the curriculum would be revised to achieve (1) mastery of the skills of reading with speed and comprehension and organizing and stating ideas concisely, (2) more continuity of learning, (3) the releasing of creative energies through art experiences, (4) a clearer understanding of contemporary society by including current problems in the curriculum and by making an effort, individually and collectively, to solve these problems, (5) better teaching materials, and (6) better individual guidance of students. Willingness to cooperate in such an experiment was greater than had been expected. Thirty secondary schools eventually took part and over three hundred colleges agreed to waive their formal admissions requirements for recommended graduates of these schools for the duration of the experiment. The Commission's Eight-Year Study also gained substantial foundation support. Between 1932 and 1940 the Carnegie Foundation made grants totaling $70,000 and the General Education Board gave $622,500.

The Commission on the Relation of School and College's proposal to the colleges claimed that it was "trying to develop students who regard education as an enduring quest for meaning rather than credit accumulation." Neither this appealing statement nor the commission's list of goals could, however, hide the anti-intellectual implications of the commission's philosophy of education. The PEA commission was actually arguing that the content of the curriculum should be flexible enough to allow each student's education to "grow out of his capacities, interests and needs." This life-adjustment philosophy was clearly expressed in the commission's progress report to the membership of the PEA. The report included the claim that "most, if not all, thoughtful educators think that all students in schools and colleges should have abundant experience in living in a democratic society." The commission's contempt for any systematic acquisition of knowledge was indicated when its evaluation committee placed special importance upon "the use of life situations as test situations." The progress report also boasted that content of "doubtful value" was being eliminated from the curriculum in the experimental schools. "In mathematics, for instance, there is much less abstract manipulation and much more study of life situations involving the use of mathematics." One school was reportedly offering a course entitled "Mathematics of Everyday Life" that dealt with the financial relationships of children and parents. The commission's report also referred frequently to the attempts toward fostering group activity in the experimental schools.

The PEA also established two other commissions to deal with the problem of "upgrading" secondary education. The Commission on Secondary-School Curriculum, established in May 1932 and financed by generous grants, totaling $360,000, was supposed to suggest curriculum changes that would be in harmony with changing economic and social conditions. This commission adopted the view that the primary aim of secondary education was to reorient the student's values and personality so that he could function more effectively in the emerging society. This aim could best be achieved, concluded the members of the commission, when the needs of youth are identified and used as the criteria for "the selection and organization of educational experiences and the organization of the life of the school." [10] To answer the question "For what type of adjustment are we working?" the commission outlined what it regarded as the ideal behavior in terms of the student's relationship to his family, group, individual friends, the opposite sex, and society in general.

The task of improving the quality of social and family life through revisions in the secondary curriculum was also the primary goal of the Commission on Human Relations, which the PEA created in 1935. The achievements of the commission included the preparation of four books: *Life and Growth, Do Adolescents Need Parents?, The Family Past and Present,* and *Literature as Exploration.* The volume with the provocative title *Do Adolescents Need Parents?* was rated by *Parents Magazine* as one of the eight most important books of the year and set the tone for a whole generation of life-adjustment textbooks with its chapters on "Making Friends," "Finding Work," "Finding Love," and "Understanding."

In addition to the impetus that the PEA's three commissions gave life-adjustment education, the NEA also provided active encouragement for this philosophy, although the association at first did not mention it by name. In 1934, the NEA's Department of Secondary School Principals issued the report of its Committee on the Orientation of Secondary Education. The report dealt thoughtfully with the basic issues of secondary education—finance, attendance, curriculum, and the responsibility of the school to work directly for social change. Unfortunately, the committee also succumbed to the appeal of the goals of life-adjustment education. The report urged that the social interests of students be used as the criteria for organizing the curriculum. However, it recognized that even though the "tool" courses (French, algebra, and so on) seemed not "to have much relation to the problems which at the moment confront high school youth," they still had value for those intending to go on to higher education. The committee did not offer solutions, however, for a basic problem: How were the schools to provide "tool" courses in a curriculum organized specifically to promote "social intelligence" and vocational education. On the issue of social reconstruction, the report stated that "through cooperative endeavor aimed at thoughtful participation in them [the social goals of the NEA committee]," the schools could ensure that the students understood the social goals of the NEA's Committee on Social-Economic Goals for America.

In 1940, the NEA's Educational Policies Commission

established itself as a leading spokesman for life-adjustment education with the publication of its casebook study of civic education, *Learning the Ways of Democracy*. This volume contained accounts of experiments in democratic education in ninety schools throughout the country. The book was intended to stimulate other educators to make education for democratic living their primary aim. Glowing reports were given of students who translated their increased understanding of democracy into direct political action. The commission especially acclaimed the attempt of students at Theodore Roosevelt High School in Des Moines, Iowa, to bring about a change in city government. After studying the situation and deciding that the city should have a city-manager form of government, the students had circulated a petition calling for a change in the city's charter. During their campaign, the students had worked closely with interested pressure groups. The students had also initiated a get-out-the-vote drive during a civic election. The volume was more than a compilation of shining examples of "democratic education," however. It promoted, in addition, a concept of democracy that reflected the ideological bias of the social reconstructionist educators: Democratic education would summon "youth to service in a great cause"—to complete the task of improving the "welfare of all the people."

A later report of the NEA's Educational Policies Commission, issued in 1944, eventually became the bible of life-adjustment educators. Although, as one devotee stated, it did not present anything essentially new, "it was so authoritative in character as to receive wide acceptance among educational leaders." [11] The report, *Education for All American Youth,* went through eight printings and was reissued in 1952 by the commission, which was then chaired by James Bryant Conant. The express purpose of the 1944 report was to provide a blueprint of the kind of education that would be needed five years after the end of World War II. To make this projection, the commission reduced the needs common to all youth to seven broad categories and then suggested that the fulfillment of these needs be made the goal of education. As the categories ranged from civic training and instruction in family life to introducing the student to the main elements of the culture and providing occupational guidance and training, the commission was placing a Herculean burden on the secondary schools.

The report's suggestion that the schools perform educational functions normally carried on by other institutions, such as instructions in family life and occupational training, could only have had the effect of spreading the resources of the school so thin that the teaching of concepts and skills would be reduced to an almost superficial level. Furthermore, the philosophy of education promulgated in the report was predicated on the questionable assumption that the good life can be achieved solely through efficiency in solving the problems of everyday life and through acting democratically. Conspicuously absent from the report, and for that matter from the other educational writings of the 1940s, was any awareness of the mystery and paradox that surrounds the meaning of existence. The report recognized no aristocracy of subjects: "Mathematics and mechanics, art and agriculture, history and homemaking are all peers." Similarly, there was for these educators no hierarchy of values, nor of ideas. The commission equated discovery of the meaning of self-determination or questioning the underlying premises of one's culture with mastering the technique of good grooming. Actually, practical studies even had an advantage over those that might liberalize the student's mind. Educators who subscribed to the doctrines of *Education for All American Youth* would necessarily determine the subjects to be taught on the criterion of practical application to actual life situations.

In a discussion of what education might be like in the future, the commission's report optimistically speculated that after the ninth grade advanced mathematics would be "taught to all as needed in connection with agriculture, mechanics, business education, and homemaking." Government, economics, history and literature were to be dealt with in a single course called "Common Learnings." This would be a five-year course, starting in the tenth grade and extending two years into an institution of the future that the report named the community institute. This course, promised the commission, "consists of learning experiences which *everyone* needs to have, regardless of what occupation he may expect to follow or where he may happen to live." The school of the future would also undertake the job of building a society that would provide everybody with the same economic and social opportunities. Differences in opportunity still exist, concluded the report. But they could be "measurably reduced by wise educational leadership and administration, and by the objective study of community problems in the schools." [12]

The recommendation that the offerings of the secondary school be drastically revised obviously implied that their present academic orientation was inadequate for a large fraction of the country's secondary students. Just how many students were not having their "needs" met was a matter of conjecture until Charles Prosser suggested the figure of 60 percent. Basing his estimates on the work of psychologists who were working on IQ tests, Prosser claimed that only 20 percent of all secondary students would benefit from academic preparatory work in high school and that another 20 percent had sufficiently high IQ's to succeed in vocational education courses. For the other 60 percent, secondary education, as it was then offered, was a waste of time and energy.

The work of the PEA and NEA commissions had helped to reinforce the idea that American secondary education was greatly inadequate and that if something was not done quickly the very foundations of democracy would be seriously threatened. This challenge was therefore promptly taken up by the Vocational Division of the U.S. Office of Education in January 1944. The division initiated a study entitled "Vocational Education in the Years Ahead" that took 150 prominent educators a year and a half to complete. At the final meeting of the study group in May 1945, Charles Prosser presented a resolution requesting that the U.S. Office of Education call a series of regional conferences to determine what could be done about ensuring that "the remaining 60 percent of our youth of secondary school age will receive the life-adjustment training they need and to which they are entitled as American citizens." [13] The resolution was promptly passed. No one had even questioned the adequacy of the scientific research that Prosser had used to justify the appalling figure of 60 percent or the wisdom of placing so many in the category of the uneducable. Acting upon the resolution, the U.S. Commissioner of Education, John W. Studebaker, set up regional conferences to study possible new programs to help the nation's slow learners. In 1947, a National Conference on Life Adjustment Education was called to devise ways of implementing the principles of life-adjustment education at the local level throughout the country.

The term "life-adjustment" was not adopted officially until after the U.S. Office of Education acted on the Prosser resolution, but the philosophy of education that it came to symbolize had already been worked out by the many PEA and NEA commissions. And these commissions had, in turn, drawn upon the more moderate tenets of social reconstructionism for their reform proposals. Proof of the fact that the conferences on life-adjustment education did not originate any new ideas can be seen by comparing the platform of the National Conference on Life Adjustment Education with the policies set forth by the earlier PEA and NEA commissions. Even much of the wording that these groups used to describe the aims of education was the same.

The AEF in Crisis

As life-adjustment education was gaining more and more converts, the social reconstructionists who favored a more direct form of social action were quietly taking over the derelict American Education Fellowship, which was all that remained of the once-vigorous PEA. Getting the AEF to adopt reconstructionist social policies was not marked by the same bitter struggles that had accompanied previous attempts. By 1947, when the national convention of the AEF unanimously endorsed a social reconstructionist policy statement, the child-centered educators who had controlled the old PEA had become largely indifferent to the future of the fellowship. The half-hearted and futile attempts these educators made after 1944 to define the purpose of the AEF vividly indicated this loss of interest.

For instance, at one meeting, the AEF executive committee seriously considered affiliation with the CIO. The director of the AEF, Vinal H. Tibbetts, thought that both organizations would benefit from the union of forces; the AEF would prepare written materials for use by the Educational Division of the CIO and confer with members of the division on educational matters. In exchange, the CIO would make its mailing lists available and aid in organizing local chapters and conferences. A representative of the CIO who was present at the meeting agreed that the labor movement as a whole did not know what constituted good education and that the fellowship thus might serve a useful purpose by educating the movement to know what to expect from the schools. However, he cautioned the educators that any direct affiliation with the CIO would seriously limit the effectiveness of the AEF. Unlike many educators, the CIO representative appeared to fully realize that the public would react unfavorably to any educational organization that identified itself too closely with any one segment of society. But he did agree that the possibility of some form of cooperation between the two organizations should be explored further. As the door had not been firmly shut on their aspirations, the executive committee then passed a resolution authorizing Tibbetts to enter into direct negotiations with the CIO. At the same meeting Harold Baker and Elinor Gimbel both suggested that the AEF also consider some form of cooperation with the A. F. of L. and similar liberal groups. As far as can be determined, these incredible proposals to save the fellowship were eventually shelved.

A rapidly dwindling membership and near bankruptcy were the underlying reasons for the executive committee's willingness to establish close ties with the labor movement. Although the proposals showed a lack of political realism and a disregard for the organization's long tradition of neutrality, it at least had some merit as a last desperate move. Other proposals for saving the fellowship were even less practical and were symbolic of the AEF's real difficulty: its inability to give new direction to the missionary zeal of its members. The recommendation of Margaret Lewisohn, a member of the executive committee and director of the Public School Association in New York, is an excellent example of the fellowship's lack of realism. "We must enlist the active support of young people," she declared, "and give them two things: (1) a feeling that this is a crusade in which they are vitally important, and (2) a concrete program to work on." [14] It was much easier to talk about crusades than to formulate concrete programs. A special committee that had been appointed in 1944 to draw up a new constitution for the fellowship was forced to admit that this lack of purpose was still the organization's nemesis. The only thing the committee could recommend was that the fellowship should take care of its organizational problems before it tried to adopt a statement of principles.

Throughout 1945 and 1946 the executive committee labored to resolve the financial crisis. The problem became so serious that at one point Vinal Tibbetts warned that if $4,000 were not raised within six months the organization would be forced to disband. Unable to find other sources, Tibbetts finally sent a letter to every member of the AEF asking each to contribute a dollar. The irony of the situation was that even though no one could state the purpose of the fellowship, the officers were determined that it should continue to exist. At one of the special meetings called in an attempt to avert complete financial disaster, Robert Speer, a professor of education at New York University, suggested that the AEF might be able to raise money by becoming a distributing agent for commercial publishers. This proposal was dropped as too impractical. And a new plan that Tibbetts proposed experienced the same fate. He wanted the fellowship to establish a teachers' bureau that would supply school boards with progressive teachers. The fees for this service would, he thought, be sufficient to keep the fellowship from going under entirely. The paralysis continued into 1946, as the leadership continued their fruitless quest for funds. The end seemed at last to have arrived when the executive meetings began to resemble the deliberations of a small group of embattled crusaders holding out against overwhelming odds. The crisis is dramatically shown by the following dialogue between Robert Speer and the clerical staff of the AEF:

MISS GHAI (*a staff worker*): It is absolutely impossible for one person to handle finances, circulation, publications and membership.

DR. ROBERT SPEER: Of the four ideas I have outlined any two or three will take care of the disparity of $2,000. Any organization lives from hand to mouth. You don't have to have dollars to survive, you have to have ideas. My own conclusion is to breathe some life into the organization. I do not preside at the burial of organizations.

MRS. PEET (*another staff worker*): How are we going to meet this payroll and expenses?

DR. SPEER: If we cannot come through on at least two of the propositions within the next sixty days then I say collapse. The amount we need is $1,800. Mr. Tibbetts has offered to surrender his pay for the month of October. That is $500.

MR. BAKER (*a member of the Executive Committee*): Now how about office personnel? Just how long can Fred and Diana hold out here?

MR. BARNES (*staff worker*): I am aware that the agenda states Diana and I will have to resign immediately. However, we can't quit and leave the fellowship in a hole.[15]

But somehow the fellowship managed to keep going, and in 1947 a national convention of the AEF was held in Chicago on Thanksgiving Day. It was the first such convention in five years. As the delegates gathered at the Stevens Hotel to decide on a statement of purpose that Ernest O. Melby's policy committee had drawn up, they must have been inclined to doubt whether they were to witness a burial or a resurrection. The mood of the gathering had been anticipated by AEF President John J. DeBoer. "Progressive education," he wrote a month before the meeting, "has been wishfully 'buried,' with appropriate obsequies, so many times during the last five years that one wonders what fantastic definitions its enemies are giving to the term." [16] To ensure that the delegates came to the convention properly motivated, DeBoer appealed to them to make the fellowship a fighting organization and to put it in "the forefront of research and leadership and social action." He also used his welcoming address to revive the delegates' sense of mission, which had been severely strained by the recent financial crisis. Declared DeBoer: "The temper of the American Education Fellowship today . . . is one that calls for courageous advance."

But in what direction should the AEF advance? Some delegates believed that the battles of progressive education had already been won and that the continued existence of the fellowship would only be justified if bold new objectives could be found. This view, it should be noted, was only partially correct. Although it was true that the widely implemented life-adjustment education embodied many principles of progressive education, the majority of professional educators had not yet unequivocally agreed to support a specific program of social reform. Until this happened the achievements of life-adjustment education would continue to fall short of the full promise of progressive education. However much life-adjustment education may have been oriented toward solving community problems through collective action, it lacked the sharp cutting edge of a disciplined and dedicated social reform movement. Furthermore, whatever social changes the life-adjustment philosophy managed to effect had been largely restricted to the community level. The local communities might be beautified by newly mobilized students, their government officials made honest by the watchful eye of the educational theorists, and family life democratized; but the larger and more fundamental economic and social problems that affected the country as a whole remained untouched by this approach.

The objectives that Ernest Melby's policy committee put before the delegates to the AEF national conference for endorsement turned out to be a restatement of the social reconstructionist program of the radical thirties. Theodore Brameld was responsible for drafting the statement of policy that was intended to infuse the fellowship with a new sense of purpose. After praising the achievements of the old PEA, Brameld pointed out that "the responsibilities which education faces today and tomorrow are vastly more serious [sic] more compelling, than after the first World War." [17] The two problems that demanded the immediate attention of educators, according to Brameld, were the unstable economic system and the threat of another nationalistic war. The "vanguard task" of the AEF was, therefore, to return to the incomplete job of reconstructing the economic system and to take up the challenge of using the classroom to build a world government.

Although the policy statement was extremely unrealistic, both because the weakened condition of the AEF made it impossible to implement and because it had potential divisive effects, the delegates were enthusiastic about committing the fellowship to what was, in effect, a political program. Although a few delegates did express reservations, these were easily overcome. The question of whether or not the adoption of the policy statement would represent a departure from the traditional position of the old PEA was raised but the convention ignored it. One delegate touched upon a more important issue when he asked if the fellowship were not actually committing itself to a program of indoctrination for a socialized economy. After he was assured that such commitment was not implied by the policy statement, another delegate expressed concern that the policy statement did not make the fellowship's commitment to democracy explicit enough. The policy statement was revised slightly to meet this objection and then endorsed unanimously by the delegates. This move signaled the end of the social reconstructionist educators' fifteen-year struggle to win the PEA and its successor to their interpretation of the true social purpose of progressive education.

A short time later the AEF formally adopted by mail ballot of the membership, and without further debate, the social reconstructionists' policy statement. The fellowship thus transformed itself into a parapolitical body with a party platform that would have aroused the envy of many an old-time Socialist. Although a few months earlier it had been struggling to pay the salaries of its small clerical staff, the fellowship readily took on social burdens of monumental proportions. The alchemy of the policy statement was so effective that the fellowship coolly faced the task of proving "to teachers, parents, students, administrators, and to the public, that civilization itself has never been in greater jeopardy" and accepted the challenge of rescuing it. The threat to civilization was to be met on two fronts. The fellowship set as its immediate targets the creation of a socialized economic system and the promotion of a new world order in which national sovereignty would be subordinated to a world authority.

The classroom teacher was not left without a battle plan, however. Specific proposals for transforming the classroom into a center of direct social action were also adopted:

1. The curriculum was to be reorganized to include a study of evolving political and economic systems.
2. The attempts to establish a world order were to be carefully studied.
3. "Realistic materials" dealing with economics and providing "skill in penetrating propaganda" were to be created.
4. Steps were to be taken to "develop consciousness in students, teachers and other citizens of the meaning and con-

tent of the values which should govern new social arrangements and purposes."

5. "Extensive educational practice in building detailed social 'designs' " was to be given.

6. A new democratic conception of discipline—intellectual, moral and social—was to be developed in the classroom.

7. A reexamination of the complex problems of enriching the "qualities of personal and family living" would be required.

8. Contributions of the arts and sciences would be integrated with social studies in such a way that students would see the social potentialities of science for health and home designing as well as understand the value of community planning.[18]

In addition to recommending that students be taught to understand the importance of "world citizenship," the policy statement also mentioned the need for close cooperation with UNESCO and for support of "the democratic potentialities of the labor movement." The last of the sixteen points included the proposal that the editorial content of *Progressive Education* be changed to support the social program of the fellowship.

The AEF membership was assured that the new goals of the fellowship would not result in the abandonment of traditional progressive educational values. "It will continue to emphasize," the policy statement stressed, " 'learning by doing,' 'community schools,' 'the integrating curriculum,' 'teacher-pupil planning,' 'child development' and other objectives of 'progressive education.' " [19] As these principles were now the mainstay of life-adjustment education, the fellowship was in effect giving its blessing to the milder form of social reconstruction that was actually being applied in the classroom, though it chose for itself a more radical approach.

Of the old guard only Harold Rugg and Goodwin Watson played a prominent part in persuading the AEF to adopt the new policy. Kilpatrick had long ago disavowed social radicalism and had not taken an active part in the 1947 convention. When his *Philosophy of Education* appeared several years later, he did not even refer directly to using the school as a lever of social change. Instead, Kilpatrick's book supported the worst form of life-adjustment education. The school, as he now envisaged it, "must be a place of living what is to be learned; for each one learns what he really and truly lives." He carried this learning-by-living idea to an almost ludicrous extreme by insisting that "primary children gradually *live* reading." [20] Anything that might create "divisive cleavages" and disrupt the harmony of "social living" was, he counseled, to be eliminated from the curriculum.

Both Childs and Counts continued to defend a planned society and the idea that the educator must practice a form of statesmanship, but their writings lacked the radicalism of former years. Childs and Counts had forfeited the theoretical leadership of the social reconstructionist movement to men like Raup, Benne, Axtelle, Smith, Stanley, and Brameld. Their effectiveness as leaders was further compromised by the prominent nationalistic emphasis that their writings contained in the latter half of the nineteen-forties. In *Education and the Promise of America* (1945), Counts' new conservatism led him to extol the greatness of the American military tradition: "Our military leadership has equalled the best in our history." "Our fighting men," he continued, ". . . have added fresh laurels to a long tradition of heroism." [21] Patriotism had also become important to Childs. In *Education and Morals,* which appeared in 1950, he wrote ". . . we are nevertheless in accord with the view that our schools should be deliberately used to prepare the young for their roles as patriotic citizens." More important, Childs was slowly moving away from a curriculum centered on social problems and toward the more traditional view that emphasized learning fixed bodies of subject matter. Childs eventually criticized progressive education itself and declared that the "American school indubitably has an obligation to acquaint our young with the essentials of this spiritual heritage; its classics, its histories, its great documents, its songs, its symbols." [22]

The Preeminence of the Group: Individualism Denied

Following the reorientation of the fellowship there was a renaissance of activity among the social reconstructionists, who were now following the theoretical leadership of Kenneth Benne, William O. Stanley, R. Bruce Raup, and Theodore Brameld in trying to more thoroughly define the movement's philosophical basis. This phase was in many respects the most detrimental to education in general and to the students in particular, because the classroom teacher who had a professional commitment—one might almost say religious devotion—to using the group as the basic unit in the learning experience received both encouragement and a theoretical justification for their preference. Because most teachers accepted the new educational theory without question, the situation was even more serious. The longing of the average teacher to know that his efforts counted for something was more than fulfilled when he was told repeatedly that the responsibility for preserving democracy was his alone. It did not occur to most teachers that what they were doing in the classroom in the name of democracy threatened to destroy its very roots. As incongruous as it may seem, at the same time the social reconstructionists canonized democracy as the supreme good, they were also declaring war on individualism.

From the beginning of the movement individualism was a source of embarrassment to the social reconstructionists. In their more charitable moments they either made the perfunctory genuflections before the altar of individualism by praising the value of growth or they remained silent about the issue altogether. At worst they viewed individualism as antisocial and undemocratic. In 1949, when they were attempting anew to justify the transformation of the classroom teacher into a "social engineer," they finally overcame their ambivalence and relegated individualism to the scrap heap of history.

Although the social reconstructionists insisted that they were theorizing about improving the quality of social living through education, they were actually making a direct assault on the value of individualism. They argued that "the democratic ideal imposes a public dimension on all problems regardless of their origin or degree of apparent privateness." Hubert M. Evans, an associate professor of education at the Horace Mann-Lincoln Institute of School Experimentation at Teachers College, stated the social reconstructionist position with even greater succinctness by declaring that "there is little to be gained by further attempts to separate private problems from social problems."

Once the educator accepts the lack of distinction between public and private, the school becomes justified in extending its benevolent control over the student's total life. Consequently, any problem that might arise in connection with the individual's behavior or needs automatically becomes a matter of concern to both the teacher and his fellow students. Not only does the student thus lose any claim to privacy, but his problem also becomes the source of an educational experience for the whole group. Furthermore, the removal of this fundamental distinction between the private and public areas of the individual's life makes him more amenable to social control and discipline. To answer the question, "What 'individual-centered' roles must be eliminated if a group is to grow and to solve problems effectively?" Kenneth Benne approvingly wrote, "It seems to be clear that a group goes through some kind of a process of development as it changes from a collection of individuals to a social organism capable of common purposing, feeling and thinking." [23] Because Benne also thought of democracy as a "social organism," one can only infer that he regarded this transformation as an essential responsibility of the school.

The social reconstructionists further undermined the autonomy of the individual by claiming that his biological and psychological needs could be met only when he participated in the social group. Before the individual can determine and rank his values and needs, he must first consult the thinking of the group to ensure that he is conforming to the basic pattern of the collectivity. He must also derive his sense of identity from the same omnipresent source. The "social organism" thus becomes the dominant reality, whereas the individual is relegated to a subordinate and dependent role. This view of man represents a clear break with the Western humanistic tradition that had focused concern on the nature and meaning of man and only dealt indirectly with the characteristics and purposes of the social group. Furthermore, although the social reconstructionists would have vehemently denied it, their philosophy represented a rejection of the American liberal struggle to defend the individual from coercive interference in his social, economic, and political life. Instead of upholding the value of a free individual conscious of his capacity for unfettered development and self-expression, the social reconstructionists adopted, in the name of the common good, a monolithic view of man and society.

To support the reconstructionists' view of man it became necessary to "reconstruct" the traditional concepts of responsibility and discipline, though their efforts in this direction proved to lack originality. Assuming that responsibility "has no meaning outside of a social context," Hubert Evans stated: "Individual responsibility grows and develops out of experience in helping others and in working together. Responsibility always implies mutuality and interrelationships with others. In this sense, responsibility for one's self in a context of pure individualism is not a very useful concept." [24] Discipline was also reduced to a purely social process and the older idea of self-discipline was summarily engineered out of existence. Self-realization in the society of the future would require, according to the reconstructionists, a new kind of discipline that demanded that the individual recognize, accept, and act upon the standards of behavior deemed acceptable by his social group. Milosh Muntyan, an assistant professor of education at the University of Delaware and a member of the editorial board of *Progressive Education*, had obviously been influenced by this concept when he wrote that

> . . . the problem lies in making the group and the group process—the necessarily imposed discipline of unavoidable membership in the group—meaningful and understandable to the child so that he can intelligently interact with the group and help in reconstructing such elements of current group discipline as are incompatible with the best that the group believes or would profess to believe.[25]

The problem of persuading the individual to conform to group norms had been given extensive treatment by Raup and Benne and their associates in the early forties. After 1949, however, the social reconstructionists were finally ready to provide teachers with "engineering concepts" that could be used in teaching "democratic living." In the past the student's attitudes and values had been developed through the educator's careful use of a well-planned curriculum and the traditional method of intellectual inquiry. In the future, the reconstructionist educators contended, a more reliable technique would be needed, one that would ensure that the student did succumb to the "miseducative" influences outside the classroom. To guard against such capitulation, the total educational experience should be organized in a way that would mold the student's attitudes through participation in a specific way of life. William O. Stanley asserted that "this means nothing less than that every aspect of the organization and life of the school, and every activity in which it engages, provided that they directly or indirectly touch its students at any point, are a part of the teaching program of the school." [26] The most effective way to guarantee that all learning experiences are brought under the control of the educator is to make the educational process a form of group living and to extend it beyond the school building to include all activities in the community. The educator thus becomes responsible for influencing the values of the larger community in accordance with his vision of the good society. This recommendation was, of course, consistent with Dewey's idea that the artificial barriers between the school and community must be broken down. Benne indicated the strength of this approach when he pointed out that the individual's values and attitudes could be most effectively changed when he was subjected to the pressures of the group. Another benefit of this method was that the student would find it difficult to escape these pressures after school hours.

For dealing with those individuals who are the problem members of society, the reconstructionists had a number of helpful suggestions. It is important to note that they relied heavily upon techniques already developed by the students of group dynamics. The authors of the *Guide to Study and Experimentation in Cooperative Planning in Education,* issued by the Horace Mann-Lincoln Institute of School Experimentation, noted that a problem member may be reluctant to contribute to the group, talk too much, not show interest, be a slow learner, or be an "out and out scrapper." The study made a number of suggestions for coping with each deviant, but the advice given for dealing with the "scrapper" was especially significant. The teachers were told that this type of nonconformist might be effectively "disarmed" by soft voices or by being given some small task that would bring him prestige in the group. The possibility that the individual might be justified in resisting the pressure of the group for valid moral, political, or social reasons was ignored by some reconstructionists and categorically denied by others. Benne, for example, left the teacher free to decide on the appropriate coercive technique, but he left little doubt that coercion should be used if necessary. Wrote Benne:

> The methodology of planned change which is consistent with democratic ideology must elevate informed and experimental collective judgment over unchecked private judgment. A methodology of training for participation in planned

change must emphasize the development of skills necessary for creating common public judgments out of the disciplined conflict of "private" points of view. It must develop persons who see non-influenceability of private convictions in joint deliberations as a vice rather than a virtue. It is in this sense that democratic planning for change must be anti-individual-istic.[27]

This statement was made in the provocatively entitled article "Democratic Ethics in Social Engineering," which appeared in the May 1949 issue of *Progressive Education*.

Exalting the group as the new educative unit put the social reconstructionists on surer ideological ground than they had enjoyed during the radical thirties. It no longer seemed neces-sary—indeed, no longer democratic—to effect social change by aligning the school with the oppressed classes in a class struggle. Furthermore, the old approach had possessed the added disad-vantage of placing the educator-statesman in a position of open opposition to the class he wished to reconstruct. As a result, whatever educative influence the teacher might want to extend over the opposing class would be constricted while, at the same time, friction and hostility would increase. The new theory of social engineering was more seductive and ostensibly more democratic because the educator's expressed goal was to create consensus.

Theoretically, the size and geographical boundaries of the group could now be arbitrarily manipulated by the educator to encompass any number of people he deemed desirable. It there-fore became possible for the reconstructionist to appear to be removed from any controversy and to quietly influence the group's behavior without ever appearing to take sides. Instead of pitting class against class, the new and more subtle approach made social engineering a matter of changing the behavior and values of the group. And the reconstructionist could, in the name of democracy, play the role of the dis-interested mediator.

The educator's apparent detachment was, however, misleading, for in order to achieve group consensus, he would have to use the psychological and social pressures of the group to create the desired consensus on the particular social issue. In a moment of candor, Benne described the real role that the educator would play in engineering social change. "In other words," Benne wrote, "the improvement of a group is a process of social change in miniature . . . strategic social change is accomplished only as the forces supporting and the forces resisting movement to a new level of behavior are analyzed and as ways of increasing supportive forces and reducing or eliminating resisting forces are planned and carried out." [28] Regardless of whether this process was termed "democratic leadership" or cloaked in benevolent-sounding jargon, the educator was actually being called upon to decide the appropriate direction of social change and to manipulate unsuspecting individuals—we can use Benne's terminology and call them the "resisting forces"—in order to gain his own objectives. The reconstructionists still conceived of education as an ideological weapon, one that could be used to fuse the individual to the group rather than to emancipate him as the earlier forms of education had sought to do.

Between 1948 and 1951 social reconstructionism reached its peak of influence in educational circles. It enjoyed wide support in colleges of education throughout the country, particularly at the University of Illinois. Furthermore, social reconstructionism influenced and was influenced by developments taking place in the field of educational psychology. Both educational theorists and educational psychologists found that important educational powers were inherent in the group dynamic. The educational theorists' desire to use these forces to change society was accepted, even encouraged, by many important psychologists. For example, a leading educational psychologist at the University of Chicago, Herbert Thelen, wrote an article dealing with "foreseeing, diagnosing, and treating" individuals and groups who resist social change. Social reconstructionism exerted an equally strong influence on curriculum development. The popular *Fundamentals of Curriculum Development,* written by B. Othanel Smith, William O. Stanley and J. Harlan Shores in 1950, represents the standard social reconstructionist statement. Although the authors regarded the development of curriculum as a form of social engineering, the book remained until recently one of the standard texts in the field, even though the influence of social reconstructionism in other aspects of education began to wane over a decade ago. The close connection between life-adjustment education and social reconstructionism was frequently acknowledged in the literature during this period. Books like *Education for All American Youth* could be found on the suggested reading lists of social reconstructionist professors of education. Though it was still possible to distinguish between these two mutually supportive movements, their combined doctrine was the dominant force in American education at midcentury.

But this doctrine did not go entirely unchallenged. In February 1951, the AEF held a "mid-century conference" to chart the fellowship's future course. The reconstructionist educators went to the conference optimistic about the outcome. With the issue of policy already decided, it seemed fairly certain that the fellowship could once again become the leader in public education that the PEA had been. Instead, the whole issue of the organizational purpose was reopened when a group led by Roma Gans and Carleton Washburne challenged the newly adopted policy of the AEF. They cited the policy statement's many limitations, including what they believed to be its one-sided analysis of the world situation. Although the policy statement contained sharp criticisms of the American social and economic system there was, they pointed out, no mention of the Soviet Union's ruthless disregard for civil liberties. A more fundamental weakness, Gans and Washburne declared, was the statement's attempt to arrogate to the fellowship the right to determine the nature of social problems and to provide for their solutions. Turning the AEF into an instrument of social action would, they insisted, force administrators and teachers who were subject to pressure from school boards to leave the fellowship. The membership would thus be reduced to the tenured professors of education who had written the document.

Willard B. Spalding made the most penetrating criticisms in his speech to the convention. Like a number of other educators, Spalding who was the dean of the College of Education at the University of Illinois, had withdrawn from the AEF in protest against its avowed political orientation. He was concerned because progressive education had become stereotyped in the public's mind as a form of education that lacked subject content, failed to produce disciplined people, showed a general disregard for moral values, and was conducted by teachers who aimed at indoctrinating students with socialistic values. This negative image had been projected, Spalding thought, because the progressive educators had not adhered to one of the original goals of the PEA—the development of a science of education. Had this goal been kept clearly in mind, he declared, the fellowship would have concerned itself with discovering the scientific principles of learning necessary for increasing the student's level of intellectual competence and achievement. Instead, it had concentrated on propagandizing for a welfare state.

"An organization which defines the good and seeks to convert others to the good, necessarily uses new and old devices for propagation of the faith. This is," he warned, "an inevitable consequence of substituting dogma for scientific inquiry." [29] If society needs changing, and Spalding acknowledged that this might indeed be the case, it would be far better for the educator to improve the student's knowledge of subject matter and mastery of intellectual skills so that later, as an adult, he could effectively cope with social problems in his own way. Spalding bitterly objected to the capture of the progressive education movement by educators who were more interested in changing society than in improving the quality of learning in the classroom. He believed that the new leaders had deliberately excluded those educators who still adhered to the original goals of progressive education. He concluded his speech by calling upon the AEF to take up anew Dewey's challenge to develop a true science of education.

The board of the AEF responded to these criticisms by asking the membership to suggest ways to bring the policy statement into greater conformity with the thinking of the membership. In the spring of 1952 the board also appointed a Committee on the Revision of the AEF Policy Statement under the chairmanship of Miles E. Cary. Cary was the director of the Ethical Culture Schools in New York City and had not been too closely identified with the more vociferous spokesmen of social reconstruction. Unfortunately, the committee failed to overcome the impasse that had developed within the membership. Over the next two years the committee presented two different proposals for revising the policy, but neither was ever acted upon. The two factions had become so sharply divided that a compromise was no longer possible. Brameld, who had become one of the more important members of the social reconstruction group, wanted to retain the 1947 policy statement in its original form. The others, led by Washburne, were fully convinced that "building an uncoerced community of outlook and belief in crucial areas of conflict and tension" was only a euphemistic way of saying "so organize the schools that students will come out believing as we do in regard to controversial issues," and they emphatically rejected this form of education. The only concrete achievement in two years of debate was the readoption of the name Progressive Education Association.

The Demise of the AEF-PEA:
Progressive Education Indicted

On June 25, 1955, PEA President H. Gordon Hullfish met with the vice-president and together they passed a resolution to terminate the existence of the association. A meeting of the membership was held on July 23, and the seven who attended, as well as 188 of the members who registered their votes by proxy, voted for the resolution. Only six members voted to continue the association. Aside from *Newsweek,* which eulogized, ". . . when the PEA voted to dissolve last week, it was signalling its greatest triumph," few Americans took the time to notice its demise.

As the last battles were being fought within the PEA, a heavy barrage of criticism was being leveled at progressive education by an awakened and highly concerned public. Dissatisfaction with progressive education had been growing among interested and vocal members of the American public since the early forties, but it was not until 1949 that they began a direct assault on the philosophy and practice of progressive schools. The attack was so sweeping that little escaped condemnation, yet the critics were so busy indicting progressive educators in general that they failed almost completely to single out social reconstructionism for special attention. Some even failed to recognize that progressive education had undergone a profound change in the thirties and forties and that the slogans of the child-centered classrooms had been replaced by the politically charged terminology of the reconstructionists.

Mortimer Smith's trenchant little book, *And Madly Teach,* was typical of the critics' attacks. Although his criticisms of what he called the "doctrines of modern education" were devastating, he did not include on his list of questionable educational practices and goals the fundamental reconstructionist goal of building a new society. He thus ignored an educational objective sanctioned by such prestigious bodies as the Educational Policies Commission (1944), the President's Commission on Higher Education (1947), the American Association of School Administrators' Commission on Schools for a New World (1947), and, in the same year, the AEF. Many of Smith's strictures were valid. For example, he stated that progressive education is totalitarian to the degree that it extends the control of the teacher over the total education of the students; it lowers intellectual standards by spending more and more of the student's time on matters that could best be learned outside the schools; educating for life situations saps the vitality of both the educational program and the student's intellectual powers. But he nevertheless seemed to be grappling with issues that had been superseded by new and even more important ones.

However, in his later work, *The Diminished Mind* (1954), this omission was corrected, and Smith specifically criticized social reconstructionism. Unfortunately, he vitiated the impact of his remarks by incorrectly stating that this philosophy of education had been a good deal more popular twenty years earlier. Smith found the reconstructionists' interpretation of democracy especially peculiar and suggested that it "might be called by other, perhaps uglier, names." He called the authors of social reconstructionist textbooks "zealots and reformers who are writing propaganda." Smith failed to understand how widely social reconstructionist principles had become accepted by educators, especially those who were supposedly leaders, because, like a number of other critics, he saw life-adjustment education as a separate movement. He failed to understand that the name life-adjustment was a misnomer, attached belatedly to a movement that was actually fostering social reform by controlling the values and skills of the students in accordance with the educator's own vision of the emerging society. Smith thus mistakenly assured his readers that "reconstructionism is probably a good deal easier to combat than Life-Adjustment for its tenets and the coercive methods essential to their fulfillment are probably still repugnant to a large body of Americans." [30] Obviously, Smith was still thinking of the radical educators of the thirties who had accused their colleagues of a failure of nerve.

Of the other important critics, Arthur Bestor, a professor of American history at the University of Illinois, failed even to mention reconstructionism in his strong indictment of progressive education, *Educational Wastelands* (1953). It did not, however, escape the attention of Robert M. Hutchins. In *The Conflict of Education* he observed that the "doctrine of immediate needs" and the "doctrine of adjustment" were substantially identical to social reconstructionism. Hutchins felt, however, that the social reformer is restricted to adapting the education of the rising generation to social changes already agreed upon. This approach, he maintained, undermined the student's ability to learn to think for himself by placing in the hands of the educator too much control over the student's life. Furthermore, once the idea of the school as an agent of social reform is accepted, the educator must be prepared to tolerate reforms that he dislikes, as well as those he likes. The type of reform will necessarily be determined by the amount of pressure various groups are able to exert on the educational system. In essence, Hutchins was saying that the community rather than the educators would be responsible for initiating reforms. Instead of directing change, the educators would have to react to these pressures by carrying out the programs of the group that managed to exert its dominance in school affairs. Hutchins scored on another important point that had been overlooked by the reconstructionist educators. He acknowledged that he too thought the improvement of society should be the goal of education; but, he warned, "to make this view effective you have to know what improvement is, and you have to recognize the limitations, as well as the possibilities, of education." [31] Failure to examine seriously the limitations of education was, he charged, the chief shortcoming of the social reconstructionists.

The most direct criticism leveled against social reconstructionism was made by Frederic Lilge, a professor of education at the University of California. In a comment on *Patterns of Educational Philosophy,* a volume that had established Brameld as the chief exponent of the reconstructionist philosophy, Lilge took the author to task for transforming philosophy into ideology and then using it as a weapon to further the designs of certain social groups. For the social reconstructionists, Lilge noted, philosophy no longer had anything to do with contemplation, the search for the good, or even inquiry. The philosopher as spectator had been forced to yield to the philosopher as social agent.

This interpretation of the role of philosophy had clearly resulted in the social reconstructionist's definition of truth as social consensus. Brameld had written that the "principle of truth-seeking as social consensus may be defined, in preliminary fashion, as follows: the truth of those experiences most vital in the social life of any culture are determined not merely by the needful satisfactions they produce, but also by the extent to which they are *agreed upon* by the largest possible number of the group concerned; without this factor of agreement or consensus, the experience simply is not 'true.' " [32] This definition of truth, Lilge rightly contended, "is an invitation to hold as true that which men like to believe and what they wish to happen." Referring to Brameld's practice of dismissing ideas as expressions of reactionary societies, past and present, Lilge warned that "this whole manner of thought, of which reconstructionism is but an extreme example, holds no future for education but leads into the dead end of antirationalism." [33]

Only a handful of critics joined Lilge in challenging the philosophy of social reconstructionism during the period that Dean Hollis L. Caswell of Teachers College called "the great reappraisal of public education." Nevertheless, the movement itself rapidly lost supporters as association with any form of progressive education became increasingly unpopular. The fusillade of criticism aimed directly at the tenets of life-adjustment education precipitated a general retreat from these principles. By 1954, the application of moderate reconstructionist principles in the elementary and secondary schools had thus effectively ended. When the life-adjustment educators disappeared from the national scene, the social reconstruction movement was reduced to a small coterie of theoreticians, lacking an organized following. The public—the vast body that apparently had not been sufficiently "reconstructed" to accept the social leadership of educational theorists—reasserted its interest and control over the destiny of public education. In the process, the public once again demonstrated how little power educators really had over educational policy, much less over social and political policy. The orbiting of the Russian satellite in 1957 further sealed the fate of the movement. With national security and honor seemingly at stake, the government could no longer remain indifferent to the condition of its schools, much less leave them in the control of educators whose egalitarian doctrine had distinctively anti-intellectual overtones. Through massive financial support of science programs, particularly at the university level, it was made clear that science and mathematics were to be given greater priority in the public schools and that henceforth the schools themselves were to play an important part in national policy. Politics and education were once again being fused in the name of national survival. In this politically charged atmosphere, as in the 1930s and 1940s, less thought was given to the kind of education that humanizes the individual than to socializing him to become more efficient in meeting the needs of the state.

Ironically, although the public had shown that educators could only make a pretense at possessing real social power, a few prominent reconstructionists refused to abandon their Promethean mission. Isaac Berkson, a professor of education at The City College of New York, was one of these. In his attempt to correct what he regarded as one of the main weaknesses of the reconstructionist doctrine—its future orientation —he argued in *The Ideal and the Community* (1958) that social change cannot simply be regarded as a matter of correcting existing errors. Cultural heritage must be taken into account in order to ensure the continuity of reform. By broadening the responsibilities of the school to include the transmission of the cultural heritage, the reconstructionists would be able to avoid the overly narrow approach to social reform that had been taken in the past. This more comprehensive approach would involve exposing the students to the traditions of the past as well as giving them an idealized vision of the society of tomorrow.

Although Berkson did not attempt to frighten his readers into believing that the social crisis was so great that survival depended upon embracing the educationist's program of social action, he nevertheless committed the old reconstructionist error of trying to predetermine the course of future social change. His society of tomorrow, like that of his visionary colleagues, was weighted heavily on the side of a socialized economy and world government. Berkson claimed that the teacher needed a sound liberal education, yet this laudable view was undermined by his claim that the teacher should be a "representative of the moral aims of the community." This inconsistency had plagued the reconstructionists from the outset; it had also been a perennial contradiction in the role of the missionary. Although the educator—and the missionary—claims the right and competence to think his own thoughts and to make his own commitments, he wants to deny this right to those whom he is supposedly helping to reach maturity. The missionary has traditionally taken the same attitude toward those he hopes to save. With characteristic altruism, Berkson wanted the teacher to "see himself in the perspective of history as a carrier of enduring values—more, as an active co-worker with the religious leader and with the statesman in the age-long endeavor to bring about an ever more satisfactory realization of the ideal in the life of the individual, of the nation, and of the world community." [34] Unfortunately, Berkson did not recognize that as long as the teacher claims to possess the only truth, the student's powers of self-direction cannot be fully and honestly developed.

Movements that are in danger of disappearing are not left in the care of revisionists who appear to be increasingly susceptible to conservative ideas. Berkson thus remains today only an advocate, and a retired one at that, and not a leading spokesman for the reconstructionist position. Theodore Brameld alone has been able to sustain the revolutionary fervor of the earlier years. Furthermore, he has not been afflicted with the seductive appeal of nationalism or the "reactionary" views of those individuals who advocate that specific subjects should be taught. In short, he alone has possessed the necessary discipline to keep his vision fixed securely on the collectivist ideal. As his reward, if that is the proper term, he has become the chief steward today of the reconstructionist philosophy of education.

Until the PEA finally disappeared in 1955, the few remaining devotees of reconstructionism considered themselves to be true progressivists and loyal followers of Dewey, even though Dewey himself would have had difficulty recognizing the new form into which his ideas had been cast. The final collapse of the association and the attacks on progressivism made it seem that the remaining vestiges of reconstructionism had at last followed the tenets of the child-centered faction into oblivion. Despite the hostile atmosphere, Brameld was determined to do more than ensure the survival of the reconstructionist interpretation of progressive education; he wanted to dissociate it entirely from progressivism and to establish it as an entirely separate philosophy of education.

In *Patterns of Educational Philosophy,* published in 1950, Brameld had criticized progressivism for its "piecemeal methods of experimental change." Although he considered it a transitional philosophy, a "rationale" of a culture that was itself in a transitional stage between *"two great cultural configurations,"* he warned at that time against wholly repudiating the progressive principles. For the time being they needed only to be supplemented and strengthened. Brameld believed that the emphasis progressivism placed on the individual required special attention. The individualistic orientation was, in his opinion, part of the liberal tradition that was being everywhere challenged by collectivism. Consequently, as liberalism was replaced by the new social philosophy, its educational counterpart would also have to be retired to the status of a historical fact. Only then would the public believe that reconstructionism's greater concentration on "social reality—particularly *group* experience" was in harmony with the demands of the emerging society. Brameld's remarks about Counts' contributions to educational theory also indicated his new interpretation of reconstructionism. Brameld found the fighting tone of Counts' *Dare the School Build a New Social Order?* far more valuable to the cause of education than Counts' later attacks on communism and the Soviet Union. Of Counts' numerous works, Brameld regarded only the earlier polemical writings as important, for they had given an early and significant impetus to social reconstructionism. In spite of this contribution Counts would have to be placed, in Brameld's judgment, in the progressivist camp because of his considerable backsliding in later years.

A discussion of the new philosophy with which Brameld intended to replace progressivism appeared in 1955. However, as the title, *Toward a Reconstructed Philosophy of Education,* suggested, it did not represent the final statement. Brameld baptized the new philosophy "reconstructionism" to indicate that it should not be confused with progressivism, but its lineage was clearly visible. Brameld had drawn heavily upon the work that Raup, Axtelle, Benne, and Smith had done earlier with the idea of social consensus. Brameld made social consensus (his term was "group mind") the basis of the ideal social order and the goal of education. "Public education becomes," to use his own words, "a process of creating a kind of 'group mind,' a means of thinking and feeling the group's way toward achievement of unified ends that are desired by its individual members and that bind the curriculum into a unified whole. In this context social consensus becomes a methodological key to the remodeled school-community in all its dimensions." To deny the individual any justification for refusing to yield to the demands of the group, Brameld, borrowing the relativism of pragmatism but not its criterion for testing ideas, made truth synonymous with social consensus. Similarly, knowledge was no longer to be considered the pursuit or even the possession of the individual: "It is," Brameld says flatly, "equivalent to 'group mind.' " [35]

Brameld was very resourceful in seeing the educational value of techniques that, although used successfully in the past by politicians and churches, had so far escaped the attention of socially minded educationists. And he was quick to integrate them into his philosophy of reconstructionism. The use of myth-making was one of these. It would be too hasty, he wrote, "to conclude that the myth has always been, or need always be, a device used merely to distort reality, conceal truth, or pervert values." Without bothering to face the question of how the myth, a basically irrational force, could enable one to have a greater understanding of reality, Brameld pointed out its "culturally therapeutic" value. He praised its power to "lessen the tensions and the bewilderments from which too many of us suffer" and to "supply the quality of emotional and esthetic involvement without which commitment to a great cultural purpose and design cannot hope to inspire or even to occur at all." [36] Brameld promptly assured the reader that the reconstructionist would guard against any influence of an unscientific or dogmatic nature that might creep into the myth. But how the educational theorist could control the emotional forces that myths unleash when others have found them almost immune to rationality was left unexplained. Presumably, we are supposed to allow educationists to create and encourage myths because they will be using them to commit students to a "great cultural purpose and design."

The new philosophy also undermined the much older "reactionary" idea that education is supposed to help the individual to act more rationally, for its methodology also included the use of propaganda. Brameld took great pains to distinguish between propaganda and indoctrination; he rejected the latter as an improper educational technique. He decided, however, that propaganda was admirably suited for impressing "a fact, rule, or value upon students much more effectively than would a neutrally analytical approach." Brameld continued his praise of the educational value of propaganda: "There is no reason why learning for worthwhile ends should not be warmed with the persuasive qualities that advertisers so often exploit for their own ends. Reconstructionism, more forthrightly than other philosophies, with the possible exception of perennialism, believes that if education is to be a cultural force—if it is to shape attitudes and inspire action—it should make use of the colorful and dramatic qualities possessed by propaganda." [37] Indeed, Brameld had succeeded in making the methodology of reconstructionism a new and radical departure in American education, but it was not new to the world. Many dictators have been consummate practitioners of the techniques that Brameld advocated, as have lesser individuals who have subordinated education to political or religious ends.

In 1961, Brameld was finally ready to outline in *Education for the Emerging Age* what the new era, which would replace the one that lasted from the fifteenth to the late nineteenth century, would be like. He visualized its technology as highly automated and dependent on atomic power; the world population would be self-stabilizing; the economy would be publicly planned and resources distributed on the basis of need; and an international government under democratic but decentralized control would exist. Yet to bring the new era into existence required the dedicated efforts of men who were no longer satisfied with the vacillating characteristics of orthodox liberalism and experimentalism, both of which emphasized "openmindedness" and the experimental method as to the key to progress.[38] Those who aspired to aid in the birth of the new era would not be content to allow the schools to be diverted from their true mission of creating a "world civilization" by limiting them to the unpolitical goal of developing the rational powers of the human mind. Brameld severely criticized the Educational Policies Commission for its 1961 attempt to make this the central purpose of education. He casti-gated the commission for being "illogical" and for perform-ing a disservice to American education. To him it was as though an old friend suddenly had been discovered to have deserted the cause, leaving him to fight on alone.

Brameld has been unable to attract a following for his "new" philosophy of education; nevertheless, he remains today un-daunted in his efforts to rally the classroom teacher to engage in the art of political statesmanship. It is unlikely that he will experience greater success in the future because few teachers will be able to accept his justification of the use of propaganda or to see myth-building as a proper activity of the school. His chances for success have been further limited by the fact that many leading supporters of social reconstructionism in the forties have, in recent years, openly challenged the basic prin-ciples of his philosophy as both anti-individual and irrational.

As early as 1950, John L. Childs criticized the followers of reconstructionism for abandoning the principle of compromise as being too undemocratic. And in 1954 he was moved to state that because of the confusion which surrounded the idea of the "uncoerced community of persuasion," the reconstruc-tionists "have a moral obligation to review what they have said against the principle of compromise." [39] In his 1957 Bode Memorial Lecture, he warned that an educational program based on pupil planning and pupil problem-solving was in danger of ignoring the very thing that enables the young to become members of society—an understanding of what has been achieved by the generations that preceded them.

William O. Stanley noted that Brameld's philosophy repre-sented the first reformulation of Dewey's educational ideas, but Stanley found it necessary to admit that all existing the-ories, "including some which I have advocated in the past," are inadequate.[40] An investigation of the creative imagination that led to an interest in Zen Buddhism occupied the last years of Harold Rugg, who died in 1960. If he retained any of his earlier zeal for reforming society, it was not apparent in his last book, *Imagination,* which appeared posthumously. Similarly, Kenneth Benne has forsaken the problems of building a new society and has turned his attention to such existential concerns as the problem of self-identity. It is also worth noting that George Counts' most recent book is called *Education and the Foundations of Human Freedom* (1963), which suggests the same shift away from the collectivist model that still dominates Brameld's thinking.

The idea that the schools should be used to overcome the problems of racial integration, a high divorce rate, and chronic poverty, as well as to help America beat the Russians to the moon indicates that at least part of the social reconstructionist philosophy of education has become accepted as the "conventional wisdom" of our society. It is easier to bus children across town to previously segregated schools than it is to get employers to adopt nondiscriminatory hiring practices or to transform the real estate agent into a fair, honest, and humane individual who does not see the potential home buyer in the simple terms of black and white. Upgrading the science program and offering status and monetary rewards to cadres of eager but often culturally illiterate young scientists can also be accomplished without any great wrench to the social structure. Unfortunately, all these shortcuts, which are adaptations of Dewey's instrumentalist approach to education, pose a fundamental threat to a society that depends upon a citizenry that understands its past traditions and yet is free from prejudice and popular misconceptions. Freeing the individual intellectually so that he is no longer swayed unconsciously by his society still remains an alternative to social reconstructionism. Yet, for all the dangers that surround making the goals of education contingent upon a current social crisis, there is an even greater danger in having educational theorists abandon education for the sake of politics. Instead of being a countervailing force, one in which the educational theorist defends the individual's right to acquire the intellectual tools essential for the free life, the tradition of which Brameld is the main defender places the educator in the role of competing with the other factions in the community for the student's allegiance. Other influential interpreters of the social reform tradition of progressive education have begun to have second thoughts about making education a form of political action, and there is now hope that this epoch in American education may shortly come to a close.

NOTES

1. *Report of the Board of Directors of the Progressive Education Association* (February 1943), pp. 1, 2.
2. *Minutes of the Meeting of the Board of Directors of the Progressive Education Association* (October 15–17, 1943), pp. 5, 9–11.
3. R. Bruce Raup, George E. Axtelle, Kenneth Benne, and B. Othanel Smith, *The Improvement of Practical Intelligence* (New York: Harper, 1943), p. 40.
4. *Ibid.,* pp. 49, 101, 99, 58, 267.
5. Kenneth D. Benne, *A Conception of Authority* (New York: Bureau of Publications, Teachers College, Columbia University, 1943), p. 184.
6. United States Office of Education, *Life Adjustment Education for Every Youth* (Washington, D.C.: U.S. Government Printing Office, 1947), pp. 4, 65.
7. Charles Prosser, *Secondary Education and Life* (Cambridge, Mass.: Harvard University Press, 1939).
8. Raup, *et al., op. cit.,* p. 225.
9. Wilford M. Aikin, "Report of the Committee on College Entrance and Secondary Schools," *Progressive Education,* VIII, 4 (April 1931), 319.
10. Progressive Education Association, *Progressive Education Advances* (New York: Appleton-Century-Crofts, 1938), pp. 20, 21, 39.

11. Walter H. Gaummitz, "Developments in Secondary Education: 1890–1945," in Franklin R. Zeran (ed.), *Life Adjustment Education in Action* (New York: Chartwell, 1953), p. 24.
12. Educational Policies Commission, *Education for All American Youth* (Washington, D.C., 1944), pp. 142, 140, 252, 16.
13. United States Office of Education, *Life Adjustment Education for Every Youth*, p. 15.
14. *Minutes of the Executive Committee Meeting of the A.E.F.* (April 3–4, 1944), p. 2.
15. *Meeting of the New York Board Members of the A.E.F.* (October 4, 1946), p. 2.
16. John J. DeBoer, "Forward Progressives!" *Progressive Education,* XXV, 1 (October 1947), 225.
17. Theodore Brameld, "A New Policy for the A.E.F.," *Progressive Education,* XXV, 2 (November 1947), 259.
18. "A New Policy for a New Times," *Progressive Education,* XXV, 4 (February 1948), 46.
19. *Ibid.,* p. 58.
20. William H. Kilpatrick, *Philosophy of Education* (New York: Macmillan, 1951), pp. 221, 317.
21. George S. Counts, *Education and the Promise of America* (New York: Macmillan, 1945), p. 6.
22. John L. Childs, *Education and Morals* (New York: Appleton-Century-Crofts, 1950), pp. 270–71.
23. Kenneth D. Benne and Bozidar Muntyan, *Human Relations in Curriculum Change* (New York: Dryden, 1951), p. 67.
24. Hubert M. Evans, "The Social Character of Problem Solving," *Progressive Education,* XXVI, 6 (April 1949), 163–64.
25. Milosh Muntyan, "Discipline: Child-Centered, Teacher-Centered, or Group-Centered," *Progressive Education,* XXVI, 6 (April 1949), 173.
26. William O. Stanley, "What We Learn from Problem Solving," *Progressive Education,* XXVI, 6 (April 1949), 178.
27. Kenneth Benne, "Democratic Ethics in Social Engineering," *Progressive Education,* XXVI, 7 (May 1949), 207.
28. Benne and Muntyan, *op. cit.,* p. 142.
29. Willard B. Spalding, "The Stereotype of Progressive Education in the Profession and in the Public," *Progressive Education,* XXIX, 2 (November 1951), 43, 47.
30. Mortimer Smith, *The Diminished Mind* (Chicago: Regnery, 1954), pp. 65, 74–75.
31. Robert M. Hutchins, *The Conflict in Education* (New York: Harper, 1953), pp. 52–53.

32. Theodore Brameld, *Patterns of Educational Philosophy* (New York: World Book, 1950), p. 456.
33. Frederic Lilge, "Reason and Ideology in Education," *Harvard Educational Review* (Fall 1952), pp. 251, 256.
34. Isaac B. Berkson, *The Ideal and the Community* (New York: Harper, 1958), p. 293.
35. Brameld, *Toward a Reconstructed Philosophy of Education* (New York: Dryden, 1956), pp. 107, 194.
36. *Ibid.*, pp. 141, 143.
37. *Ibid.*, p. 205.
38. Theodore Brameld, *Education for the Emerging Age* (New York: Harper, 1961), p. 32.
39. John L. Childs, "Education and the Crisis in American Democracy," *Progressive Education,* XXXI, 3 (January 1954), 94.
40. William O. Stanley, "Current Tasks of Educational Philosophy," *Phi Delta Kappa,* XXXX, 1 (October 1958), 13.

SELECTIVE
BIBLIOGRAPHY

GENERAL WORKS

Among the more important books that contained the social reconstructionist educators' analysis of the depression, as well as their recommendations of the role that the school should play in effecting social reform, are George S. Counts, *Dare the School Build a New Social Order?* (New York: John Day, 1932) and *The Social Foundations of Education* (New York: Scribner's, 1934). A less extreme statement can be found in William H. Kilpatrick, *Education and the Social Crisis* (New York, Liveright, 1932) and *The Educational Frontier* (New York: Appleton-Century-Crofts, 1933), which he edited; in *The Great Technology*, Harold Rugg provides useful insights into the educator's analysis of social and economic change. Both the Progressive Education Association and National Education Association had commissions that published reports outlining the school's responsibilities for overcoming the depression and changing outmoded social values. For the most radical statement of this period, see the PEA's Committee on Social and Economic Problems, *A Call to the Teachers of the Nation* (New York: John Day, 1933); also see the NEA's Department of Superintendence, *Social Change and Education* (1935), *The Social Studies Curriculum* (1936), *The Improvement of Education* (1937), and the Educational Policies Commission, *The Purposes of Education in American Democracy* (1938).

For the development of the social reconstructionist position after 1940, see R. Bruce Raup, George E. Axtelle, Kenneth Benne, and B. Othanel Smith, *The Improvement of Practical Intelligence* (New York: Harper, 1943); Kenneth Benne, *A Conception of*

Authority (New York: Bureau of Publications, Teachers College, 1943); Kenneth Benne and Bozidar Muntyan, *Human Relations in Curriculum Change* (New York: Dryden, 1951). Life adjustment education, a variant form of the social reconstructionist position, is outlined in the NEA's Educational Policies Commission, *Learning the Ways of Democracy* (1940) and *Education for All American Youth* (1944). Also see Charles Prosser, *Secondary Education and Life* (Cambridge: Harvard University Press, 1939); and the United States Office of Education, Division of Secondary Education and the Division of Vocational Education, *Life Adjustment Education for Every Youth* (Washington, D.C.: U.S. Government Printing Office, 1947).

Among the books that helped to shape the thinking of the social reconstructionist educators, the following were the most significant: American Historical Association's Commission on the Social Studies in the Schools, *Conclusions and Recommendations* (New York: Scribner's, 1934); Charles Beard, *An Economic Interpretation of the Constitution of the United States* (New York: Macmillan, 1913); *The Economic Basis of Politics* (New York: Knopf, 1923), and *A Charter for the Social Sciences* (New York: Scribner's, 1932); John Dewey, *School and Society* (Chicago: The University of Chicago Press, 1902), *Democracy and Education* (New York, Macmillan, 1916), *Reconstruction in Philosophy* (New York: Holt, 1920), *Individualism Old and New* (New York: Minton, Balch, 1930), *Liberalism and Social Action* (New York: Putnam's, 1935); Thorstein Veblen, *The Theory of the Leisure Class* (New York: Macmillan, 1899), *The Engineers and the Price System* (New York: Huebsch, 1921). Also see President's Research Committee on Social Trends, *Recent Social Trends in the United States* (New York: McGraw-Hill, 1933).

The views of the radical educators can be put into perspective by comparing them with the attitudes of the intellectuals during the nineteen-twenties and thirties. For a picture of the intellectuals' disillusionment with the twenties, see Frederick Lewis Allen, *Only Yesterday* (New York: Bantam, 1946). Malcolm Cowley, *Exile's Return* (New York: Norton, 1934) also serves as a useful barometer of the intellectual community's attitude toward middle-class America during these critical years. As an example of the intellectual's disenchantment with capitalism, see Lincoln Steffens,

Autobiography (New York: Harcourt, 1931). Granville Hicks, *Where We Came Out* (New York: Viking, 1954); I. D. Talmadge (ed.), *Whose Revolution?* (New York: Howell-Soskins, 1941); and League of Professional Groups for Foster and Ford, *Culture and the Crisis* (New York, 1932) represents but a small part of the literature dealing with the intellectuals' interest and subsequent disillusionment with communism.

Progressive educators were often their own best critics; Boyd Bode, *Education at the Crossroads* (New York: Newson, 1938) and John Dewey, *Experience and Education* (New York: Macmillan, 1938) represent the best examples. The politicizing of educational theory has served to alarm extremists who bitterly charged that their social values were being subverted by progressive educators. As an example of the extremist critic, see Verne Kaub, *Communist-Socialist Propaganda in American Schools* (Boston: Meador, 1953); and Kitty Jones and Robert Olivier, *Progressive Education is REDucation* (Boston: Meador, 1956). More responsible critics of progressive education include Arthur Bestor, *Educational Wastelands* (Urbana: University of Illinois Press, 1953); Robert M. Hutchins, *The Conflict of Education* (New York: Harper, 1953); Mortimer Smith, *The Diminished Mind* (Chicago: Regnery, 1954).

A retrospective treatment of this period by individuals who were active participants can be found in John Childs' *American Pragmatism and Education* (New York: Holt, 1956); and Harold Rugg, *Foundations of American Education* (New York: World, 1947), *That Men May Understand* (New York: Doubleday, 1941).

Secondary sources that deal with different aspects of American social, intellectual, and educational life during this period include Daniel Aaron, *Writers on the Left* (New York: Harcourt, 1961), a critical study of the American writers' response to communism between 1912 and the early 1940s. For an examination of social and political liberalism in American Protestant churches between 1920 and 1940, see Paul A. Carter, *The Decline and Revival of the Social Gospel* (Ithaca: Cornell University Press, 1954). The most important history of the progressive education movement, particularly in its early phases, is Lawrence A. Cremin, *The Transformation of the School: Progressivism in American Education,*

1876–1957 (New York: Knopf, 1961). Other books that relate educational thought to social and intellectual developments include Merle Curti, *The Social Ideas of American Educators* (Paterson, N.J.: Littlefield, Adams, 1959); Richard Hofstadter, *Anti-Intellectualism in American Life* (New York: Knopf, 1963); Rush Welter, *Popular Education and Democratic Thought in America* (New York: Harper, 1957). For a comprehensive examination of socialism in American life from the seventeenth century to the present, see Donald Drew Egbert and Stow Persons (eds.), *Socialism and American Life,* 2 vols. (Princeton, N.J.: Princeton University Press, 1952); the influence that the Communists were able to exert on the American schools is dealt with in Robert Iversen, *The Communists and the Schools* (New York: Harcourt, 1959). Excellent treatments of progressivism and Roosevelt's New Deal can be found in Eric Goldman, *Rendezvous With Destiny* (New York: Knopf, 1952); Richard Hofstadter, *The Age of Reform* (New York: Knopf, 1961); William E. Leuchtenburg, *The Perils of Prosperity: 1914–32* (Chicago: The University of Chicago Press, 1958); Arthur M. Schlesinger, Jr., *The Crisis of the Old Order: 1919–1933* (Boston: Houghton, Mifflin, 1957), *The Coming of the New Deal* (Boston: Houghton, Mifflin, 1959), *The Politics of Upheaval* (Boston: Houghton, Mifflin, 1960). There are numerous books dealing with the intellectual history of this period, but the most relevant are Richard Hofstadter, *Social Darwinism in American Thought* (Boston: Beacon, 1955); Christopher Lasch, *The New Radicalism in America (1889–1963): The Intellectual as a Social Type* (New York: Knopf, 1965); Morton White, *Social Thought in America: The Revolt Against Formalism* (Boston: Beacon, 1957).

PERIODICALS

The official organ of the social reconstructionist educators, *The Social Frontier,* contains the most valuable source of their writings during the depression period. Of special importance are the editorial statements of George S. Counts, Norman Woelfel, and Mordecai Grossman; in particular see "Orientation," vol. I, no. 1

(October 1934); "Collectivism and Collectivism," vol. I, no. 2 (November 1934); "Teachers and Labor," vol. II, no. 1 (October 1935); "Teachers and the Class Struggle," vol. II, no. 2 (November 1935); "Towards a United Front," vol. II, no. 4 (January 1936); "Class and Social Purpose," vol. II, no. 5 (February 1936). In "Karl Marx and the American Teacher," vol. II, no. 2 (November 1935), Theodore Brameld challenged the social reconstructionist educators to consider the educational implications of a class struggle. For the debate that broke out between the radical and moderate members of the social reconstruction group, see R. Bruce Raup, "Shall We Use the Class Dynamic?" vol. II, no. 4 (January 1936); John L. Childs, "Can Teachers Stay Out of the Class Struggle?" vol. II, no. 7 (April 1936); John Dewey, "Class Struggle and the Democratic Way," vol. II, no. 8 (May 1936); William H. Kilpatrick, "High Marxism Defined and Rejected," vol. II, no. 9 (June 1936). For an example of the contribution that dissident liberals made to the discussion of educational and social issues in the journal, see John Dewey, "Can Education Share in Social Reconstruction?" vol. I, no. 1 (October 1934); Broadus Mitchell, "The Choice Before Us," vol. I, no. 2 (November 1934); Harold Laski, "A New Education Needs a New World," vol. II, no. 5; Charles A. Beard, "Property and Democracy," vol. I, no. 1 (October 1934). After the journal was incorporated into the PEA in 1939, it was called *Frontiers of Democracy.* Especially significant articles dealing with the role of the educator during wartime include "This War and America," vol. VIII, no. 63 (October 1941); John L. Childs, "This War and American Education," vol. VIII, no. 66 (January 1942); William H. Kilpatrick, "Our Schools and the War," vol. VIII, no. 68 (March 1942).

Between 1931 and 1933, *Progressive Education* included in its pages a number of articles advocating that teachers play a militant role in reforming society; after 1933, however, the journal is useful mostly as a source of contrast with the social radicalism of *The Social Frontier.*

For the mood of the liberals during the social crisis see, among others, *The Nation, The New Republic* and *Common Sense. The New Leader,* the organ of the Socialist party, and *The Modern Quarterly* should be consulted for an understanding of the intellectual ferment that was taking place among the Socialists. The polemics of the intellectual Marxists can be found in *Science and Society* and the *New Masses*.

PUBLISHED AND UNPUBLISHED RECORDS

The unpublished official minutes of the Executive Board and the Board of Directors of the Progressive Education Association provide a valuable source of information about the factionalism and the difficulties that surrounded shaping of official policy and eventually caused the association's demise. For the official records of the National Education Association, see the relevant sections in the *Proceedings of the National Education Association,* which were published annually.

Index